Ethically Sp

CW00591484

Scottish Cultural Review
of Language and Literature

Volume 6

Series Editors
John Corbett
University of Glasgow

Sarah Dunnigan
University of Edinburgh

James McGonigal
University of Glasgow

Production Editor
Rhona Brown
University of Glasgow

SCROLL

The Scottish Cultural Review of Language and Literature publishes new work in Scottish Studies, with a focus on analysis and reinterpretation of the literature and languages of Scotland, and the cultural contexts that have shaped them.

Further information on our editorial and production procedures can be found at www.rodopi.nl

Ethically Speaking

Voice and Values
in Modern Scottish Writing

Edited by
James McGonigal and Kirsten Stirling

Amsterdam - New York, NY 2006

Cover image:
©Jack Stevenson. Licensor www.scran.ac.uk

Cover design: Gavin Miller and Pier Post

The paper on which this book is printed meets the requirements of "ISO
9706: 1994, Information and documentation - Paper for documents -
Requirements for permanence".

ISBN-10: 90-420-2084-9
ISBN-13: 978-90-420-2084-9
©Editions Rodopi B.V., Amsterdam - New York, NY 2006
Printed in The Netherlands

Contents

Contributors

Ingibjörg Ágústsdóttir studied English at the University of Iceland from 1990 to 1995 and finished her Ph.D. in Scottish Literature at the University of Glasgow in 2001. She has published both academic articles and poetry in journals and anthologies. She currently teaches English at Akureyri Junior College, Iceland.

Anne-Kathrin Braun-Hansen studied English and German at Saarbrücken, Edinburgh and Freiburg, and received her Ph.D from Zurich University, published as *Dramatic Laboratories: Figurations of Subjectivity in Liz Lochhead's Writing* (Galda and Wilch, 2004). From 2000–5, she lectured in Comparative and English Literature at Zurich, before a postdoctoral research project at Stanford University on the meaning of noses in literary texts. She has two children and is currently on maternity leave.

Scott Brewster is Lecturer in Twentieth Century Literature and Culture at the University of Salford. He co-edited *Ireland in Proximity: History, Gender, Space* (Routledge, 1999) and *Inhuman Reflections: Thinking the Limits of the Human* (Manchester University Press, 2000). He has written essays on Irish poetry and fiction, the Gothic, deconstruction and psychoanalysis and is currently completing *Lyric* for the Routledge Critical Idiom series.

Jordana Brown writes for and edits magazines in Los Angeles. A showing in Paris of the film of Irvine Welsh's *Trainspotting* (where the subtitles greatly aided her comprehension of the dialogue) sparked an obsession with Scotland and its recent literature – and an M.Phil in Scottish literature from the University of Strathclyde.

Gerard Carruthers is Senior Lecturer in the Department of Scottish Literature at the University of Glasgow. He is co-editor of *English Romanticism and the Celtic World* (Cambridge University Press, 2003) and of *Beyond Scotland: New Contexts for Twentieth-Century Scottish Literature* (Rodopi, 2004), and has written critical essays on Munro, Carswell, Jenkins, Spark and Kelman. He is currently editing a critical edition of selected plays by James Bridie.

John Corbett is Senior Lecturer in English Language at the University of Glasgow, with interests in intercultural and translation studies, corpus linguistics, and the teaching and status of Scots language. Recent publications include *An Intercultural Approach to English Language Teaching* (Multilingual Matters, 2003), and, as co-editor, *The Edinburgh Companion to Scots* (Edinburgh University Press, 2003) and *Serving Twa Maisters: An Anthology of Plays Translated into Scots* (ASLS, 2005).

Beth Dickson taught English in schools before joining the Department of Curriculum Studies in the University of Glasgow where she pursues joint interests in literature and education. She has published on Scottish fiction, including the work of Naomi Mitchison, Willa Muir, William McIlvanney and A.L. Kennedy, and is currently researching Scottish cultural policy in relation to schools.

James McGonigal is Professor of English in Education in the University of Glasgow. He has combined work on literacy, language development, and special educational needs with critical writing on British modernist poetry (*The Star You Steer By: Basil Bunting and British Modernism,* Rodopi, 2000) and on cultural relations between Scotland and Ireland. His tri-lingual poem *Passage / An Pasaíste* (Mariscat, 2004) won awards in both countries.

Edwin Morgan has written from the 1960s onwards a distinctively inventive poetry, internationalist in outlook but with a strong focus on Scottish life. He is also a distinguished translator of Russian, Hungarian, and Italian poets. His *Collected Poems* and *Collected Translations* (both 1996) are published by Carcanet. He was created Scotland's first National Poet in 2004.

Suhayl Saadi is a novelist and stage and radio dramatist based in Glasgow. His short story collection, *The Burning Mirror* (Polygon, 2001) was short-listed for the Saltire First Book Prize and his latest novel *Psychoraag* (Black and White Publications, 2004) was short-listed for the James Tait Black Memorial Prize. He has edited several anthologies and read his work on several continents, details being available on www.suhaylsaadi.com

Kirsten Stirling teaches in the English Department of the University of Lausanne, Switzerland. She has published on gendered representations of Scotland in literature and on a range of Scottish authors including Hugh MacDiarmid, Alasdair Gray, Naomi Mitchison and James Hogg.

Kirsty Williams works for the BBC as a radio producer. Her doctoral studies at Glasgow University looked at the relationship between language and the body in contemporary Irish poetry. She has published on Seamus Heaney and on the role of art in urban regeneration.

Introduction

James McGonigal and Kirsten Stirling

In *Scottish Literature: Character and Influence* (1919), Gregory Smith described a central antithesis in Scottish literature. On the surface, he wrote, Scottish literature gives the impression of cohesion in form and in subject matter, but closer consideration reveals how varied the literature is, subject to the "stress of foreign influence and native reaction, almost a zigzag of contradictions" (Smith: 4). The phrase Smith playfully coined to describe this, the "Caledonian antisyzygy", was rather overused and oversimplified in Scottish studies throughout the twentieth century. The "zigzag of contradictions", however, is perhaps a more enabling term, since it implies not a static duality but a constant movement of contradiction and debate beneath the surface.

Contradiction and debate rose to the surface with the re-establishment of a Scottish parliament in 1999, challenging the Scots' sense of themselves in ways they had not foreseen. With substantial powers devolved from the UK government in Westminster, the parliament resumed after centuries of absence the sorts of political decision-making on complex social issues that necessarily involve debate over means and ends. Since proceedings were televised for news and current affairs programmes, Scots watching their elected representatives debate such issues were now pitched into a visibly ethical world.

Scottish writers, whose words had helped sustain the pressure for devolved power in the final decades of the twentieth century, might now wonder that its reality has often seemed as fantastic as their fictions. The contradictions involved in taking up such responsibility were brought home very early by public and media reaction to the new Parliament's attempt to repeal a clause in an earlier UK Education Act that had banned the "promotion" in schools of a homosexual lifestyle as an acceptable family form. And moral issues have continued to cause political problems in subsequent years. There have been resignations of two party leaders because of inappropriate use of

political expenses, intense public debate about the continuing presence
of sectarianism in Scottish society, and a lengthy public enquiry into
delays, evasions and massive overspending on the new Parliament
building in Edinburgh. Such coming to terms with responsibilities
may of itself be a significant phase of Scotland's growth to political
maturity. Having no-one else to blame may be a salutary if not a
comfortable experience for Scotland, as rights and wrongs are
discovered to be more complex than they seem, as narratives unfold,
half-truths unravel and underlying motives are disclosed.

Awareness of such a contradictory tension of aspiration and
reality has been in some ways typical of the country's literature, as
Gregory Smith suggested. Can the writing of the novelists, poets and
translators contemporaneous with the emergence of a newly
empowered Scotland help us to read the country and its people in a
new way? Perhaps most usefully, they remind us of a small nation's
sheer diversity. Whereas this volume's title signposts "modern
Scottish writing" as if it were a unity, the various contributors show
that there is no simple way to talk about Scottish literature as if it were
one thing. This is not a new point to make, of course, as Gregory
Smith's remarks make clear. His celebration of oxymoron and
incongruity reads like Bakhtinian dialogism *avant la lettre*, and
anticipates in many ways what has become the standard way of
reading Scotland in the early twenty-first century – as plural. As La
Corbie says in the prologue to Liz Lochhead's *Mary Queen of Scots
Got Her Head Chopped Off*, "Ah don't know whit your Scotland's
like. Here's mine" (Lochhead 1989: 11).

If a consensus view of Scotland's moral landscape emerges from
its writers in the chapters that follow, it is perhaps a central concern
with truth, and with the complex relations of the individual to the
community. The community that is imagined, however, need not
necessarily be the nation, and indeed in most of these chapters it is
not. "Community" in this volume covers the colliding language
worlds of contemporary dramatic translation in Scots, the small town
settings of novels by Robin Jenkins and William McIlvanney, the
virtual community to whom A.L. Kennedy's Jennifer broadcasts her
radio show, the ethnic minority experience of Scotland that informs
the work of Suhayl Saadi, or the Scottish gay community as

experienced by Edwin Morgan, feminist and masculine identities in Lochhead, Banks and Burnside, the troubling classrooms and schooling disclosed when we review how writers use education in their fiction or else explore the enduring half-life of the religious codes in which they were raised as children. Standing partly outside but partly within such communities is the more nebulous community of readers with whom every writer of fiction engages. In all of this diversity, however, we are interested in the relationship of the individual to his or her community, how the individual imagines the community, and also engages in some sort of interaction with it. Even isolated or local Scottish worlds are locked into large issues – of violence and guilt, sexuality and suffering, truth and lies, the negative and the numinous.

In the opening chapter, John Corbett discusses voice and nation through recent Scottish theatre, showing how translations of classical drama into Scots language have been used to explore issues of identity in contemporary Scotland. Edwin Morgan's and Liz Lochhead's translations of these classical texts into Scots asserts its status as a living and literary language. This is not unproblematic in the new Scotland: Corbett also charts various current controversies over what kind of Scots is judged suitable for such literary purposes. Of course, interpreting the works of other cultures has an ethical dimension, and representing the other also helps the "host" culture to take a new look at itself. As Corbett points out, such translation challenges preconceptions of margin and centre: in Lochhead's translation of *Medea*, the ruling Athenian classes "speak with a Scottish accent". This assertion of the validity of Scots reverses the statement of the newsreader in Tom Leonard's poem "The Six O'Clock News", itself an ironic reversal of the Standard English norm: "yooz doant no thi trooth yirsellz cawz yi canny talk right" (Leonard 1984: 88).

"Talking right" extends beyond how we speak to what we say, and what we intend. And this interest in truth applies beyond the moral world contained within the novels under consideration to the ethical responsibility of the writer to the reader. Kirsten Stirling traces A.L. Kennedy's reassessment of the notion of truth in her early fiction, and finds in her work an alternative morality: namely that truth may be found in a shared lie rather than in a bald statement of fact. A lie that is understood to be a lie shared between father and daughter or husband and wife may function as a "kind of truth". This logic extends in Kennedy's novels to the communal and even national level: communities may be founded on shared lies. This can include, for Kennedy, the community of writers and readers. Ultimately, in the words of her character Savinien de Cyrano de Bergerac, telling the truth is "what writers are for", but does the fiction writer also have a responsibility to lie in order to tell the truth?

This concern with what writers are for is echoed in Ingibjörg Ágústsdóttir's study of ethics in wartime in three novels by Robin Jenkins. Exploring the tension between private morality and public interest in times of war, Ágústsdóttir's chapter also applies the question of moral responsibility facing Jenkins' central characters to the moral responsibility of the writer to the reader. But Suhayl Saadi, writing from his own experience as an author of fiction, warns against over-emphasising the role of the writer in the community. While it should not be ignored, at the same time this role should not be taken as definitive. Through the description of three of his own stories, Saadi articulates an ethics of narration that moves subtly across and between cultures. The writer explores other voices, takes on other roles and explains the world to himself and to us from the perspective of others. As Saadi says, if we knew everything we wouldn't need stories.

Gerard Carruthers, in his reading of William McIlvanney's *The Kiln*, cites the central character Tom's apprehension that "each one of us remakes the world we live in", yet we see also how Tom is constructed by the expectations of his society. Carruthers traces the links between autobiographical "truth" and quasi-postmodernist fiction in McIlvanney's work. Beth Dickson also explores the boundary between the real and the fictional: her chapter situates the representation of education in Scottish fiction in the context of actual educational practice across time, and focuses on the problematic ethical relationships between teacher and pupil in Robin Jenkins' *The Changeling*, Muriel Spark's *The Prime of Miss Jean Brodie* and James Kelman's *A Disaffection,* novels where intimacy and trust are fostered or betrayed within school communities.

Among the many "other voices" gathered in this volume, three articles take a specifically gender-based approach to the question of voice and narration. Anne-Kathrin Braun-Hansen shows how Liz Lochhead, writing in the 1980s, provides a female voice that had been lacking in Scottish culture. She invokes the "canonical double-cross" of the Scottish woman writer: doubly othered, it has been argued, Scottish women writers are excluded from both the male and the English canons of literary excellence (Reizbaum 1992: 166). Lochhead's satirical reworkings of traditional fairy tales (like those of Angela Carter) "retell familiar stories from another angle", and this new angle allows a new perspective on questions of voice and identity in Scotland. Narrative perspective, in particular, becomes important in Kirsty Williams's analysis of Jackie Kay's *Trumpet* and Ali Smith's *Like*, where, in different ways, the description of "other" love is connected to the "other" narrative positions which combine to tell the story. Williams shows that both Kay and Smith, in their explorations of language and corporeality, also subvert the single authoritative narrative voice and thus open new dimensions on the subjects of their texts.

The stereotypically Scottish male identity with its heavy-industrial connotations of toughness, hard drinking and even harder attitudes has come under scrutiny by writers in a "post-industrial" age. Scott Brewster's chapter focuses on masculinity and violence in the work of Iain Banks and John Burnside, and he examines the barriers that protect and isolate the (male) individual from society in Banks's *The Wasp Factory* and in a series of Burnside's novels. He concludes by making an explicit link between Burnside's fiction and the philosophy of Emmanuel Levinas, reading in Burnside's writing a dramatisation of the necessity to abandon the self in order to approach the other.

Burnside's work is taken up in a very different way in James McGonigal's study of "negative theology" in the poetry of Burnside and Morgan. The Church of Scotland and the school system have historically been seen as powerful protectors of Scottish identity and difference within a greater Britain. Catholicism, once readmitted into Scottish culture, has also had an influential role in the education of descendants of the many hundreds of thousands of Irish economic migrants to Scotland through the nineteenth and into the twentieth centuries, sustaining identity and difference against the presbyterian grain. While religious observance has markedly diminished in the late twentieth century, the views of church leaders continue to be sought on moral issues and regularly reported in the Scottish media. Here McGonigal discusses how the two poets, writing from Protestant and Catholic backgrounds, find space for the numinous in a largely secular yet still worryingly sectarian Scottish society.

Jordana Brown too concentrates on the place of religion in a secular society. She removes Alan Warner's novel *Morvern Callar* from over-simplified associations that were made with Irvine Welsh and 1980s rave culture (in which it has often been located) and reads it as the central character Morvern's quest for salvation in a society lacking in spirituality. Brown's chapter also enters into the question of the author's ethical responsibility, since in *Morvern Callar* the male author-figure commits suicide at the very beginning of the novel. This virtual absence in the novel contributes to the spiritual emptiness of the world in which Morvern lives.

Is the moral world of Scotland changing? Recent statistical studies using the Scottish Social Attitudes Survey 2000 in comparison with the British Social Attitudes Survey of the same year (Curtice et al. 2002), reveal fascinating diversity in personal morality and in attitudes towards marriage, parenthood, sexuality and religion, across the generations and between geographical regions in Scotland. Younger Scots are much closer to British norms than their parents are. In terms of political values, however, Scottish centrist politics are markedly left of the English centre, and this can sometimes create problems for Scottish Labour politicians trying to balance Scottish and Westminster values in their policies.

That moral values are changing across generations does make the need for cooperation within and between communities an important issue in Scottish culture. This relates to both local and larger concerns. The chapters gathered in this volume focus on Scottish writers of the second half of the twentieth century, and the communities described are certainly Scottish, but the issues raised are universal. Questions are asked about the relationship of the individual to others, and therefore, on a larger scale, about the means through which a community is both constructed and sustained: linguistically, spiritually, ethically. If these multiple voices evoke a "zigzag of contradictions", it is at any rate a creative zigzag which discovers, or uncovers, many contradictory aspects of life in contemporary Scotland that need particularly to be brought to light in a re-emergent nation. Ethically speaking, Scottish writers point out the need to attend to many different narratives and retellings in order that Scots might live more honestly and clear-sightedly with themselves and with the wider world.

Bibliography

Curtice, John, David McCrone, Alison Park and Lindsay Paterson (eds). 2002. *New Scotland, New Society?* Edinburgh: Polygon.

Leonard, Tom. 1984. *Intimate Voices: Selected Work 1965–1983*. Newcastle: Galloping Dog.

Lochhead, Liz. 1989. *Mary Queen of Scots got her Head Chopped Off and Dracula*. Harmondsworth: Penguin.

Reizbaum, Marilyn. 1992. "Canonical Double-Cross: Scottish and Irish Women's Writing" in Lawrence, Karen K. (ed.) *Decolonizing Tradition: New Views of Twentieth Century "British" Literary Canons*. Urbana and Chicago: University of Illinois Press. 165–90.

Smith, G. Gregory. 1919. *Scottish Literature: Character and Influence*. London: Macmillan.

"Nae mair pussyfootin. Ah'm aff, Theramenes": Demotic Neoclassical Drama in Contemporary Scotland

John Corbett

Pre-devolutionary drama translations in Scotland forged links with peripheral and marginalised cultures, and literatures of resistance; for example, major theatrical productions were given to adaptations of Michel Tremblay's Québecois plays, and to Dario Fo's *Can't Pay? Won't Pay!* The immediate post-devolutionary period saw an immediate shift back to an exploration of "canonical" texts of Western culture, in particular Euripides and Racine; however, the medium of the new translations was still the urban Scots of the margins. This chapter discusses the cultural significance of the neoclassical turn in post-devolutionary Scottish drama.
Keywords: Liz Lochhead, Edwin Morgan, drama, Scots language, translation.

On 11 September 1997, the people of Scotland voted in a referendum for a devolved parliament, and in May 1999, the Scottish Executive came into being – for the first time since 1707, Edinburgh could call itself the capital of a nation validated by the apparatus of state, rather than sentimental yearning. A year later, in the summer of 2000, two of the major plays running in Edinburgh and Glasgow were translations with classical themes: Edinburgh's Royal Lyceum commissioned *Phaedra*, Edwin Morgan's Scots version of Racine, while in Glasgow, Theatre Babel produced Liz Lochhead's *Medea,* "after Euripides", also in Scots. These were not the only dramatic translations into Scots on stage that summer: in Edinburgh, down the road from the Lyceum, at the Traverse, at the same time as *Phaedra* was playing, audiences could catch Bill Findlay and Martin Bowman's version of *A Solemn Mass for a Full Moon in Summer,* by contemporary Québécois playwright, Michel Tremblay. Findlay and Bowman's translation continued a successful run of Scots language performances of Tremblay's plays that had started long before devolution (see Bowman and Findlay 2004; Kinloch 2000). However, the versions by Morgan and Lochhead signified something new in Scottish literature and drama: a return to neoclassicism that begs to be understood in response to a major political reconfiguration of the Scottish state.

Colonising the Classics

Neoclassicism runs like a golden thread through the labyrinth of literature in Scots. Gavin Douglas's translation of the *Aeneid* into Scots was completed in 1513, on the eve of the Battle of Flodden, which foreshadowed the eventual absorption of Scotland as the minor partner in the United Kingdom. The republication of Douglas' *Aeneid* in the early eighteenth century did much to inspire a revival of literature in Scots that saw its first shoots in the poetry of Ramsay and Fergusson, and then blossomed into the poems and songs of Burns. Ramsay and Fergusson both tried their hand at versions of Horace's *Odes,* and, indeed, Horace became the most translated poet into Scots during the eighteenth and nineteenth centuries. As I have argued elsewhere, there are some obvious reasons for this (cf. Corbett 1999). The literature of the classical era carried and still carries cultural authority, and one way of raising the self-confidence of a marginal culture on the cold, dark northern edge of Europe is, through translation, to appropriate the literature of classical Greece and Rome. Aeneas, in Douglas' translation, embodies the ideal qualities of the noble prince, and his example of nation-building at the expense of personal happiness serves as a role model for his aristocratic readers. Horace, as reworked by Ramsay, Fergusson and others, is the urbane critic of the metropolis – his classical example proves you can be as sophisticated as your fellow Britons at the heart of empire, whilst remaining apart from the centre, geographically and linguistically. Of course, not every Scot felt that way, as evidenced by James Boswell and others.

Douglas, Ramsay, Fergusson and those who followed them mined classical literature in order to lend their work authority, but also to give shape to different political visions of Scotland: Douglas sees Scotland as a peaceful nation under an Aeneas-like king, while Ramsay and Fergusson see Scotland as a nation of bourgeois sophisticates who inhabit a northern Athens while casting a critical eye southwards towards London's Rome. The neoclassical strain continued throughout the nineteenth and twentieth centuries. Horace continued to be translated into different varieties of Scots, as did other Roman writers such as Catullus; William Neill's *Tales owerset frae the Odyssey o Homer* offers a modern companion piece to Douglas' *Aeneid;* and in the late 1950s and early 1960s, Douglas Young translated two comedies by Aristophanes, *The Puddocks,* and *The Burdies.* The significance of the classicism of this period, however, continued to be transformed. The bourgeois sophistication of the early Horatian translations deteriorated into the Brigadoon-like sentimentalism of James Logie Robertson's *Horace in Homespun*, in which the Roman poet becomes a couthy, philosophical nineteenth-century shepherd, roaming the Ochils and complaining about the invention of such weapons of mass destruction as torpedoes. Neoclassicism in the Victorian and modern ages becomes complicit in different kinds of nostalgia: first the rejection of the modern world, with its terrors; then the rejection of the political settlements that yoked Scotland to England, and an attempted recovery of pre-Union nationhood through the composition of literature in Scots. As Hugh McDiarmid rallied his fellow Lallans poets with the cry, "Not Burns – Dunbar!", so the classical translators of the twentieth century tried to become latter-day versions of Gavin Douglas, translating a modern nation into existence.

Pre-devolutionary Classical Translations

Douglas Young's versions of Aristophanes are an interesting example of the modern variety of nostalgic translation. Less sentimental than kailyard translators such as Logie Robertson, Lallans translators like Young sought to raise national self-esteem by showing that the medium of Scots is fit to convey the works of classical authors. Young was a professor of Classics at St Andrews University, and in fact the translation of *The Puddocks* was suggested to him by one of his Honours students, Gordon Maxwell, who then went on to direct the amateur production given by a group of university students, "The Reid Gouns", in the Byre Theatre, St Andrews, in early 1958. The Foreword to the second edition of the play recalls early discussions with Maxwell, and also Young's anxiety that certain aspects of the play would not work well with a modern audience. The reviews (the most glowing of which are also quoted from in the second edition) suggest that Young's anxiety was ill-founded, although the professional production of his second translation of Aristophanes, *The Burdies,* suffered a much more mixed reception at the 1966 Edinburgh Festival (see McClure 2004 and the introduction to Corbett and Findlay eds, 2005).

Reading Young's *The Puddocks* today, one is struck by how Scottish it is. Its comedy is of the broad pantomime variety that continues to pack Glasgow and Edinburgh theatres around Christmas. In *The Puddocks* it is tempting to see the Scots Dionysius, Herakles, Aeschylus and Euripides as upmarket burlesques along the lines of *Snow White* or *The Babes in the Wood*. The structure of *The Puddocks* fits squarely within the Scots tradition of "flyting" – originally a public contest in which two rival poets engaged in exaggerated insult. *The Puddocks* is on one level largely an excuse for a flyting: Dionysius and Xanthius, bored by the feeble efforts of contemporary playwrights, descend to Hades to recover the late Euripides, and Dionysius ends up refereeing a lengthy dispute between Aeschylus and Euripides to decide which is fit to sit in the chair of honour at Pluto's side in Hades. There is a lot of slapstick and wordplay – but also a considerable amount of literary criticism along the way. Indeed the ghosts of Aeschylus and Euripides engage in a very early version of the "media effects" debate:

Aes:	A feck o warthie men hae learnt, like Lamachos the hero:
	frae Homer's impress my ingyne wrocht monie deeds o valour,
	like lyon-hertit Teukros or Patroklos, sae up-heezan
	oor citizens tae rival them whane'er they hear the trumpet.
	But, Fegs, I pit nae hures on stage, Phaidras or Stheneboias,
	a wife in luve that I have staged there's nane o ye can tell o.
Eur:	You'd fient a haet o sex-appeal.
Aes:	I wadna hae a haet o't.
	But Aphrodite sat on you and yours wi sic a wecht o't
	she fairly dung ye flat wi sex.
Di:	Crivvens! she gart your wife dae't.
	Ye're plagued wi cantrips like ye shawed wi wives o ither husbands.
Eu:	Puir sumphie, what hairm has the State taen frae my Stheneboias?
Aes:	When shamed by your Bellerophons ye brocht the noble spouses
	o noble men tae suicide, by drinkin hemlock puzhun.
Eur:	Was it no true, the story that I staged o Phaidra's passion?
Aes:	Owre true, by Jove. But makars maun aye hide awa what's vicious,
	no stage it or produce it here. Schuilmaisters teach the bairnies,
	we makars hae til educate the adolescent birkies.

Sae we maun mak whit's braw and uisfu.
(Young 1958: 34–35; ll. 1039–56)

It is lines such as these that led the young poet and critic Edwin Morgan to write of Young's translation in the *Saltire Review*:

Aristophanes' *Frogs* exploits a historical literary situation, the dearth of serious dramatists when Aeschylus, Euripides and Sophocles had all died; but its main interest is a permanent one. The author opens up the whole question of the value of art, its relation to the ethics of the State, and its influence on men. The question is tossed about on the horns of every sort of bull. The range of the humour is enormous. Douglas Young has obviously relished the situation, and his Scots version is lively and racy. It is at its best in the rapid give and take of dialogue. The translation becomes more comic than the original. (quoted in Young 1958: 51)

Possibly also the character of Euripides' allusion to "the story that I staged o Phaidra's passion" stuck in Morgan's mind too, as did the potential of Scots to convey "lively and racy" dialogue. As a Lallans poet, Douglas Young has often been criticised for moving away from the "naturalistic" and towards the "artificial" end of the continuum of literary Scots. However, in his foreword to the second edition, Young claims that the medium of his drama adheres largely to Scots as it was spoken in his day:

A glossary has been asked for by many, not only English, Irish, Welsh and American friends, but by many semi-literate North Britons: and I have added a fairly comprehensive glossary, which has inevitably put up the cost of publication. In compiling it, I was struck by the relative rarity of archaisms, neologisms and unusual dialectal words in my version, which in these respects hardly seems to represent the range of Aristophanes's language. [...] there are horizontal social dialects in Scots as well as vertical local varieties of speech, though the social differentiation is less marked than in the English of the unhappily United Kingdom. But for the most part I have adhered to the central literary tradition of Scots, with no more than a permissible shading of Fife and the North-East, which bulk large in my natural background. (Young 1958: x–xi)

The poet who elsewhere champions a form of "plastic Scots" (Young 1946) here gives way to the popular dramatist, restricting his stage Scots largely to a "core" that is familiar from the popular literary tradition and current east-coast speech. However, Young's stage Scots retains a fondness for anachronism, even if he substitutes the occasional contemporary Anglo-American slang for archaic Scots, as in the puddocks' chorus:

> [...] fleean the storm Zeus sends, we dive
> whaur the lochan's benmaist shadaws winkle;
> we steer the glaur wi our *ramstam jive*
> while the bulleran watters plapper and prinkle.
> (Young 1958: 9; ll. 245–49, emphasis added)

The energetic conjunction of Scots and English colloquialisms such as "ramstam jive" was later to become a hallmark of the stage Scots of Edwin Morgan. In various ways, then, Young's translations anticipate the neoclassical turn taken post-devolution. However, in both language and ideology, the recent reworking of classical themes in Scots by Morgan and Lochhead depart from Young's translations, and even from more recent classical adaptations such as *Klytemnestra's Bairns,* by Bill Dunlop (1990).

Klytemnestra's Bairns adapts Aeschylus' *The Oresteia* into different varieties of Scots and English – Klytemnestra and the Chorus speak a kind of literary stage Scots not unlike that used in *The Puddocks*, the captured Cassandra speaks English, and Orestes himself speaks a marked north-eastern Scots (he has obviously been in exile near Aberdeen):

KLYTEMNESTRA:Ye gangrel budies! Whit is it at ye seek?
     Whit is't ye lack?
     Here sall ye fin the breid an saut at mairks an honest hoose.
     But gif ye are here oan a maitter o state,
     ye'd best tak yer burthen tae ma mate.
     I hae nocht tae dae wi sic maitters noo.
     But gif it be sae, tell me, an he sall attend ye.
ORESTES: I am nocht sauf a merchant cheil. Yin at cams fae Phocis,
     far I an ma friere wis askit bi thaim at hid him i their keeping
     tae tell the fowk o Orestes at their bairn hid deed.
     A guid urn o finest bronze wis bocht tae haud his ashes.
     The loon at we met wit bade me tae speir gif Orestes
     wis tae be berrit exile, in faur-awa Phocis, or be carrit hame
     an berrit wi his kin.   (Dunlop 1990: 32)

Klytemnestra's Bairns foreshadows *Phaedra* and *Medea* in risking a Scots translation of a classical tragedy, rather than a comedy. Scots has been largely associated with comedy on stage; it is part of the renewed cultural confidence of Scottish playwrights and producers that large-scale professional productions of classical plays in Scots can kick away the usual support of pantomime burlesque. Liz Lochhead's earlier stage translations had been a couple of rollicking adaptations of Molière, while Morgan had dipped his toe into dramatic translation with a successful version of the tragi-comedy *Cyrano de Bergerac*. *Klytemnestra's Bairns* was a smaller-scale production, for the Edinburgh Festival Fringe, and the language used in it ranged from a fairly accessible literary Scots to a closer approximation of the Scots of Aberdeenshire – both poles of this continuum having their roots in the countryside. As Bill Findlay has observed, though, Lochhead and Morgan's stage Scots differs in its overt adoption of urban varieties as its basis – varieties largely scorned as corrupt even by the Lallans poets of the post-war period.

From the Doric to The Attic: Classical Translations in Urban Scots

More so than other varieties of Scots, urban Scots is stigmatised and thought fit only for comedy: as Tom Leonard wrote in the 1960s (reprinted in Leonard 1984: 86):

awright fur
funny stuff
ur Stanley Baxter
ur but
luv n science
n thaht naw

The urban Scottish playwright's task, post-devolution (though Morgan actually completed his translation in the year of the successful devolution campaign, 1996–7), is to show that the urban variety of Scots *is* "awright fur luv n science" and that it *can* carry tragic themes.

Morgan is explicit about this in an interview with Serena Tarling in the programme notes to the Lyceum production:

> I was talking to Kenny Ireland [the Artistic Director of the Lyceum Company] one day, and we were discussing the range of potential that Scots has as a language. I remember saying to him that I thought it would be interesting to take on a wholly serious play, a real tragedy, using the same kind of language I used for *Cyrano de Bergerac.* (Tarling 2000: 21)

In comparison, Lochhead's *Medea* was the final play in Theatre Babel's "Greeks" project, instigated by Graham McLaren, the Artistic Director. Earlier productions were David Greig's *Oedipus* and Tom McGrath's *Electra. Medea* opened in Glasgow in March 2000, and was successfully revived at the Edinburgh Festival Fringe in August 2001. Lochhead's reason for taking on the project was more personal than Morgan's:

> When Graham McLaren of Theatre Babel approached me about doing a version of Medea for his ambitious "Greeks" project I was deep into the second draft of a comedy, absolutely contemporary and set locally in downtown Glasgow, about a woman desperate to give birth to a child. Therefore, there was a frisson of slightly perverse attraction in the notion of next working on a play that would be – in every way – exactly the opposite: a tragedy, absolutely timeless and ancient, about a woman driven by female desperation of a quite different sort, to killing her children.
>
> Which is not a very elevated reason for taking on a Great Classic Play, but it's the truth. (Lochhead 2001: i)

Lochhead is less interested in the technicalities of the language than Morgan. Writing of the Scots she uses in *Tartuffe*, she says:

> it's a totally invented and, I hope, theatrical Scots, full of anachronisms, demotic speech from various eras and areas; it's proverbial, slangy, couthy, clichéd, catch-phrasey and vulgar; it's based on Byron, Burns, Stanley Holloway, Ogden Nash and George Formby, as well as on the sharp tongue of my granny; it's deliberately varied in register. (Lochhead 1985: i)

Of the language of *Medea* she says in her stage directions:

> The people of this country all have Scots accents, their language varies from Scots to Scots-English – from time to time and from character to character – and particular emotional state of character. (Lochhead 2001: 3)

Lochhead's language is perhaps less self-consciously experimental and more intuitive than Morgan's but they both have a basis in demotic, urban Scots. Medea, played by Maureen Beattie in the Theatre Babel production, did not have a Scots accent, and again Lochhead comments:

It was only after seeing the play in performance in Glasgow this Spring it struck me the conventional way of doing Medea in Scotland until very recently would have been to have Medea's own language Scots and the, to her, alien Corinthians she lived under speaking, as powerful "civilised" Greeks, patrician English. That it did not occur to me to do other than give the dominant mainstream society a Scots tongue and Medea a foreigner-speaking-English-refugee voice must speak of a genuine in-the-bone increased cultural confidence here. (Lochhead 2001: ii)

In short, urban Scots is now automatically "awright fur mair than funny stuff" – although Lochhead's *Medea* makes much more use of dark comedy than Morgan's unremittingly tragic *Phaedra*. But what exactly does this neoclassical turn in translation into urban Scots suggest about the political state of Scotland today?

Out of the Margins

First of all, the periphery has again staked a claim to the centre stage. If the Horatian turn in eighteenth-century Scots translations was an attempt to acclimatise Scotland's literati to a place at on the margin, by arguing (with Horace) that the margin was a respectable place to be – then the devolution settlement has pushed Scotland back to the centre. Edinburgh is again the metropolis, home of a parliament with limited but real powers. Devolution may be a far cry from the independence sought by Douglas Young and the Lallans makars, but it goes some way towards redressing the balance of power in what he termed the "unhappily United Kingdom". There seems suddenly to be no irony in giving the Corinthian or Athenian ruling classes Scots accents. However, both Lochhead and Morgan go further than Bill Dunlop in this by giving them *urban* Scots accents and dialects. The socially marginalised are recovered by this act of translation – but while the *Scotland on Sunday* reviewer referred to an "outstanding script" that "overflowed with marvellous Scots vernacular" (Brown 2000), Morgan's adaptation of Racine was not to everyone's taste. Michael Fry, the historian and social commentator, finds particular fault with lines in Act 4, in which Phaedra learns of Hippolytus' love for Aricia:

In part, she responds. "Tout ce que j'ai souffert, mes craintes, mes transports, la fureur de mes feux, l'horreur de mes remords, et d'un refus cruel l'insupportable injure, n'etait qu'un faible essai du tourment que j'endure" – language so exquisitely restrained and elegant that the thought of its coming from a broken woman is itself enough to bring tears to the eyes.

Here is Morgan's version:

"Whitever pyned me, the skeers and swaws o love, the strinth a me [sic] desires, the grue, the guilt, the jolt, the jilt, the "Naw!" that jauped ma sowl: aw this wiz foreplay tae the rack Ah'm lashed tae."

It is not so much the ugliness of these lines that grieves me – though I do find them ugly. It is, instead, that Racine with the lightest touch evokes at every phrase another form of anguish for a stricken spirit, and in the seamless sweep of a single sentence makes her whole world horrible. Does Morgan do this? I find, rather, he strains for effect, in particular that he substitutes for the full sense of the French – where he leaves gaps – a crude exercise in alliteration. And that he fails. [...] Braving the censure of the politically correct, I refuse to call a text wonderful just because it is in Scots, especially a mongrel Scots which does not balk at such terms as scenario, payola, or (heaven help us) niminy piminy verbotens. This does not demonstrate the maturity or utility, let alone the expressive power, of the language. If anything it does the opposite. (Fry 2000)

For Fry, translation has to "convey not the whole – that is impossible – but some essence of the original." Morgan, writing on translation in general, puts it differently:

it seems clear that the translation of poetry [...] tends to begin when the translator comes across some foreign poetry which interests and excites him, and he wants to convey, to bring across, to translate that interest and excitement for people using his own language. (Morgan 1992: 43)

Morgan privileges "excitement" over the notion of "essence" – it is a significant difference. It is the difference between the metaphor of translator as curator, preserving in the translation the intangible soul of the source text, and the translator as renovator, taking the source text as a blueprint from which to construct something that speaks to the concerns of the present day. The latter metaphor delights in the comparison of the old and the new – a comparison that should excite and please, but can equally shock and dismay. Shock is a response that Morgan anticipates. In the preface to the published version of the translation, Morgan says:

> In this translation I have used a Glaswegian-based Scots (but using Scots words from other parts of the country on occasion), partly hoping that the non-classical shock of it will bring the characters back alive, and aiming also, since the translation is quite close (though it may seem strange to pure anglophones), to find out what there is in this most remarkable play that survives and transcends a jolt into an alien register. (Morgan 2000: 8)

In the terms of Lawrence Venuti, Fry prefers an "invisible translation", a smooth, elegant text that will not obscure his memory or understanding of the French original. Venuti argues against smooth translation, claiming that their "invisible" appropriation of the source text into the literary canon of the host language is a form of imperialism (Venuti 1995). However, he acknowledges that the tradition of anglophone literary translation has socialised us into expecting our translations to be self-effacing and "invisible". Morgan's translation must one of the most "visible" to be staged by a major theatre company – the "mongrel Scots" that Fry disparages is surely designed at times to grate. It is an urban Scots that is at once as "artificial" as the literary Scots used by Lallans poets such as Douglas Young, and also as "stigmatised" as the demotic championed by Tom Leonard. Morgan combines the most criticised features of different varieties of literary Scots, and uses them as a medium to convey high drama.

Lochhead's translation of *Medea* caused less critical consternation than Morgan's – partly because her Scots is less experimental – much less so even than Bill Dunlop's – and she relies more on accent than dialect to convey the Scottishness of her characters. It is more immediately accessible, and is probably easier to stage – but the dangerous shock that you find in *Phaedra*'s linguistic experimentation is missing. The idiosyncratic quality of Lochhead's dramatic Scots lies partly in her ability to re-energise the clichés, catchphrases and slangy colloquialisms that she mentions in her introduction to *Tartuffe*. This is evident in an early exchange between Jason and Medea, when Jason is reproaching Medea about her attitude to his father, Kreon (Lochhead 2001: 17):

JASON: I've always done my best
                to calm him down   persuade him you should stay
                I could have crept back to you in secret   would have
                but you can't keep it zipped   you will talk treason
                court your own banishment
MEDEA: I can't keep it zipped!
                who   what   could be worse than you?

Jason's idiom is Scottish English ("can't" instead of "cannae") while the serving classes have more of a mixture of traditional Scots and contemporary slang, along the lines of Douglas Young's American-Scots idiom (Lochhead 2001: 6):

NURSE: bairns do you hear what a faither you have?
                I wish he were   no I'll not say it
                I'll no wish my lord and master dead   but by Gods
                the horror of how he treats those he should love!
MANSERVANT: get real old woman   what's the world about?
                Jason can do so Jason does
                hello bride bye bye bairns

The socio-linguistic hierarchy of Lochhead's *Medea* is still recognisably conservative: by and large, the vocabulary and grammar of the working classes have not yet reached the debating chambers of the Athenian Executive. But, as she says, at least the ruling classes now speak with a Scottish accent.

Monstrous Women

Other themes, beyond the inevitable issue of language, link *Phaedra* and *Medea*. First of all, in comparison to the largely phallocentric world of *The Puddocks,* each has a central female character and each is concerned with extremes of sexual passion – even, in *Phaedra,* monstrous sexuality. Scratch post-devolution New Scotland, and an unreconstructed patriarchal Calvinism and its concern with "the monstrous regiment of women" keeks out. Liz Lochhead in her introduction to *Medea* explicitly associates the issues raised by the play with the first serious political debate in the twenty-first century, the repeal of a law – widely known as "Clause 28" – forbidding the promotion of homosexuality in schools.

The bigotry which has been exposed by the furore over the abolition of Clause 28 shows that we are a long way from a truly tolerant Scots society. The Athenian (male) society of his time which Euripides scourged for its smug and conventional attitudes of unthinking superiority to foreigners and women is unfortunately not totally unrecognisable, quaint or antique to me as I survey mine two and a half thousand years later. (Lochhead 2001: ii)

It is Medea's rejection and the jealousy that results that turn her into an "unnatural" monster. The Chorus who has earlier urged Medea to "punish him [Jason] for us" later attempts to dissuade her from her revenge (Lochhead, 2001: 29)

> a mother should die for her young   Medea
> not be her children's murderess
> hell itself will reject you
> there is no reparation
> you can never be purified of this crime   for humankind
> it is our horror of horrors

Lochhead explicitly plays down the classical portrayal of Medea as a witch – "My Medea is not supernatural, not an immortal, but is all too human" (Lochhead 2001: ii) – but if anything this makes her killing of her children, along with her rival, all the more terrible. Medea's thrilling escalation of the cycle of hurt and revenge excites our sympathy, until it reaches a point where we recoil in horror. After the murder of their children, Jason confronts Medea (Lochhead 2001: 45):

JASON: I must have been mad   was mad for you
                I did not know you
                I know you now!
MEDEA: tigress? fury?   harpy?   witch?   she wolf?
                monster? yes I am!
                for I have torn out your heart and devoured it.

JASON: your pain is just as bad as mine
MEDEA   wrong   for I have your pain to comfort me

Lochhead's Medea is victim turned monster. Lochhead has also adapted various plays by Molière (most recently, *Miseryguts* from *Le Misanthrope*) which fit in more easily than *Medea* does to the long tradition of slapstick and pantomime in Scots. Even so, the character of Medea in her Scots version retains some elements of the pantomime dame, with her extreme emotions and awe-inspiring vindictiveness. Medea is, however, a pantomime dame dignified, sexualised and made into the tragic centre of the play. In comparison, Morgan, a gay poet and playwright, does not link his translation overtly with the political controversy surrounding the repeal of "Clause 28"; nevertheless, he does foreground in his introduction to the play the "unnatural" character of Phaedra's passion for Hippolytus (Morgan 2000: 7):

Consider the monstrous underbelly of *Phèdre*. In a famous and ominous line in the play, we are carefully informed that Phaedra was the daughter of Minos and Pasiphae. Her mother – and let us be precise about it – developed an ungovernable passion for a bull and strapped on a contraption representing the hindquarters of a cow; the bull thrust with enthusiasm and left her pregnant with a bull-headed boy, the Minotaur. When her daughter developed an ungovernable incestuous passion for her stepson, would it be surprising if she regarded this as "monstrous"?

Phaedra, then, is afflicted with an extreme passion that she regards as unnatural – and her husband, the king, is a noted killer of unnatural creatures, including the Minotaur. You do not have to recode Phaedra as a gay male to realise that the intensity of her sexual feelings leads to her take action that confirms her marginal status in society – that brand her, like Medea, as "other", "monster". The theme of repression haunts the play – Oenoene says of Hippolytus "Oor haill sex scunners him", and his reaction to Phaedra's confession of love is revulsion and denial (Morgan 2000: 37; Act 2, Scene 6):

HIPPOLYTUS: Ah'm dumfoonert.
              If a luk at masel, Ah grue, Ah grue!
              Phaedra...Gode naw. Naw! Blot it oot,
              Steek it, loack it, the secret thing, fur ay!

After the performance I saw at the Lyceum, I overheard a group of Edinburgh women in the bar next door, discussing the play. When one was asked what she thought of it, she replied that she thought the word "radge" was overused. It was an observant comment; the word appears frequently in Morgan's translation:

PHAEDRA:	Radge! Wherr am Ah? Whit've Ah sayed?	(Act 1, Sc 3)
PHAEDRA:	Forgie ma feelins, they're owre radge tae dowse.	(Act 2, Sc 5)
PHAEDRA:	Ma radge imaginins have skailed the cloaset.	(Act 3, Sc 1)
PHAEDRA:	Forgie me, faither. Divine mairciless Venus Breks yir faimly: hur vengeance is a gless Fur yir radge dochter's face.	(Act 4, Sc 6)
THERAMENES:	The hoarses are radge; nae thocht o rein or bit;	(Act 5, Sc 6)

"Radge" is a term popularised in Irvine Welsh's *Trainspotting,* in which the sense is usually "crazy", "mental" or "high on drugs". The word originally derives from Romany slang, and is defined in the *Concise Scots Dictionary* as (1) "mad, violently excited" and (2) "sexually excited". If these translations are a mirror held up to contemporary Scotland, then the conjunction of overt female (or gay) sexuality and madness is still a problematical social issue. Jason and Theseus being male, heterosexual and powerful, are serial seducers whose promiscuity is socially sanctioned. However, when women assert their sexuality, they are regarded as insane. Scotland might be the first post-modern nation in twenty-first-century Europe, but it is still haunted by Calvinist, patriarchal attitudes to sexuality.

Ootsiders

Other characteristics link the characters of Medea and Phaedra: both are outsiders to the societies they find themselves in – in Lochhead's *Medea* this characteristic is always evident in Medea's accent, and it is made explicit early in the play when Medea addresses the Chorus (Lochhead 2001):

MEDEA:	no one loves a foreigner everyone despises anyone the least bit different "see how she ties her scarf" "that hair outlandish"

> you walked by my house with eyes averted
> turned your nose up at my household's cooking smells
> "why can't she be a bit more like us"
> say you Greeks   who bitch about other Greeks
> for not being Greeks from Corinth!

Medea's tense cross-cultural relations with her adoptive society climax in an orgy of revenge. Phaedra embodies her society's multicultural make-up – she is a Cretan, living in Troezen, with an Athenian husband and a half Amazonian stepson. Ethnic rivalries abound. In one of his characteristically jarring collocations, Morgan links monstrosity, sexuality and ethnicity when, in conversation with Theseus, Aricia (a fellow Athenian, albeit the daughter of a rival family) hints at the foreigner, Phaedra's, love for his son (Morgan 2000: 65)

ARICIA: Tak tent, sir. Ye've gote big hauns an erms;
                 Ivrywan knows yir ethnic cleansin o moansters.
                 But ye didny cleanse them aw, ye stull left
                 Wan.

Morgan makes less of Phaedra's ethnicity in his translation than Lochhead makes of Medea's in hers, but the cultural configurations explored are new in Scots translations. Previously the dominant Other was coded as English, but, as Lochhead observes in her preface, the central character in her translation is a victimised (and vengeful) Other in a dominant society that is markedly Scots. In Morgan's play, too, Greek/Scottish society is dominant, but riven with ethnic tensions. It is tempting to relate this issue to a more general post-devolutionary re-examination of Scotland's multicultural and multiracial composition – a civic anxiety in Glasgow in the early part of the twenty-first century is how it deals with asylum seekers; indeed, the Scottish legal system has in recent times been branded "institutionally racist" by a report into the conduct of the trials of the alleged murderers of a young man from the ethnic community.

Horace in Tollcross

The main argument of this chapter is simple and not particularly original: classical drama in Scots translation continues to be used to explore the new identities being forged in contemporary Scotland. If the translations that followed the Act of Union were rural in their character and language, positioning Scotland as a valuable minor partner in a larger political unit, then the translations that have followed the restitution of limited political powers re-imagine Scotland as an urban nation, still wracked by sexual repression, and divided by tension – ethnic, sectarian, homophobic. Not all current translations go down this route, of course – Lochhead's *Miseryguts* updated Molière to satirise Scotland's media community, and Bowman and Findlay's translations of contemporary playwrights continued to explore the resonances of familial and sexual politics in Scotland and Quebec. To paraphrase Lochhead, however, it marks a certain cultural confidence to be able to explore our darker side in major productions of translations of classic texts. This does not lessen the need to admit that the issues raised by *Medea* and *Phaedra* require to be recognised and addressed in our own society, not in that of ancient Greece.

Let us end on a lighter, more optimistic note. I mentioned above that Horace was the most translated poet of the eighteenth century in Scotland – his Odes suited perfectly the sophisticated, literate Scot's need to fashion an identity that was at a critical distance from the new centre of a rising imperial power. Horace is still being translated, most recently by historian and cultural commentator, Angus Calder (Calder 2000). Calder follows Robert Fergusson rather than James Logie Roberston in bringing Horace back into the metropolis, specifically Tollcross in Edinburgh. The translations are in English, with occasional light touches of Scots – more Liz Lochhead than Edwin Morgan – and the experiences recounted are more middle class (rugby, Mozart and the Edinburgh Filmhouse figure more prominently than, say, football, pop music and the weekend multiplex). Still, the interaction between the world of the translation and the world of the translator is still there, and Horace is still pleasurable, in his infinite variety. Furthermore, Calder's very lightly Scots translation offers perhaps a more comforting vision with which to begin a new millennium and a new political dispensation:

1.11 Tu ne quaesieris, scire nefas, quem mihi, quem tibi…
Not you, dear, nor me, can forecast even in
general what will befall us. We must thole
what tabloid soothsayers cannot predict.
We can't deflect gales which will batter Argyll
and shake Embro slates. Over our coffee, now,
nasty time hurdles fast. Life's short. Keep cool. Don't
expect chocolate fudgecake with cream every morning.
Carpe diem. Enjoy this delicious biscuit.

Calder's versions of Horace link contemporary anglicised and globalised Edinburgh with the Scots poets of the vernacular revival – brother translators of the classical muse. They remind us that, in a changing world, one of the best ways of seeing ourselves is to look carefully at how we reinterpret the works of other cultures and classical writers.

Bibliography

Brown, Mark. 2000. "Theatre to be proud of" in *Scotland on Sunday* (31 December 2000).

Bowman, Martin and Bill Findlay. 2004. "Translating Register in Michel Tremblay's Québécois Drama" in Findlay, B. (ed.) *Frae Ither Tongues: Essays on Modern Translations into Scots.* Clevedon: Multilingual Matters. 66–86.

Calder, Angus. 2000. *Horace in Tollcross, eftir some Odes of Q.H. Flaccus.* Kingskettle: Ketillonia Press.

Corbett, John. 1999. *Written in the Language of the Scottish Nation: A History of Literary Translation into Scots.* Clevedon: Multilingual Matters.

Corbett, John and Bill Findlay (eds). 2005. *Serving Twa Maisters: Five Classic Plays in Scots Translation.* Glasgow: Association for Scottish Literary Studies.

Dunlop, Bill. 1990. *Klytemnestra's Bairns.* Edinburgh: Diehard Press.

Findlay, Bill (ed.). 2004. *Frae Ither Tongues: Essays on Modern Translations into Scots.* Clevedon: Multilingual Matters.

Fry, Michael. 2000. "The kind of talk that fair gars me grue" in *The Herald* (9 May 2000).

Kinloch, David. 2000. "Le chant de la flûte en os. Traductions en écossais des pièces de Michel Tremblay" in Kinloch, David and Richard Price (eds). *La Nouvelle Alliance: Influences francophones sur la littérature écossais moderne.* Grenoble: Ellug, Université Stendhal. 211–40.

Leonard, Tom. 1984. "Unrelated Incidents (1)" in *Intimate Voices, Selected Works 1965–1983.* Newcastle upon Tyne: Galloping Dog Press.

Lochhead, Liz. 1985. *Tartuffe.* Glasgow/Edinburgh: Third Eye Centre & Polygon.

—. 2001. *Medea.* London: Nick Hern Books.

McClure, J. Derrick. 2004. "*The Puddocks* and *The Burdies* 'by Aristophanes and Douglas Young'" in Findlay, Bill (ed.). 215–30.

Morgan, Edwin. 1992. "The Third Tiger: The Translator as Creative Communicator" in Hobsbaum, P., P. Lyons and J. McGhee (eds). *Channels of Communication.* Glasgow: University of Glasgow Department of English Literature.

—. 2000. *Jean Racine's Phaedra: A Tragedy.* Manchester: Carcanet.

Tarling, Serena. 2000. "Interview with Edwin Morgan" in Programme Notes to The Royal Lyceum Company's production of *Phaedra* (18–29 April 2000).

Venuti, Lawrence. 1995. *The Translator's Invisibility: A History of Translation.* London: Routledge.

Young, Douglas. 1946. *"Plastic Scots" and the Scottish Literary Tradition.* Glasgow: McLellan.

—. 1958. *The Puddocks, frae the Greek o Aristophanes.* Tayport: Makarsbield Press.

"Lying is good like this": The Collaborative Lie in the Early Fiction of A.L. Kennedy

Kirsten Stirling

In her fiction A.L. Kennedy questions the status of lies. In both *Looking For The Possible Dance* and *So I Am Glad* she demonstrates situations in interpersonal relationships where lying need not necessarily be construed as negative or as a form of deception, but rather as a kind of collaboration. She then extends this reassessment of the moral status of lying from the private sphere to the public, and highlights the responsibility of the receiver or reader in believing the lies they are told.
Keywords: Cyrano de Bergerac, fiction, nationhood, truth.

Truth, as everyone knows, is stranger than fiction, and in both her fictional and non-fictional writing A.L. Kennedy constantly questions the status of both terms. More particularly, she is concerned with the status of truth within fiction, and games that the fiction writer must play with the idea of absolute truth. Muriel Spark succinctly summed up the essential paradox in an interview: "I don't claim that my novels are truth – I claim that they are fiction out of which a kind of truth emerges" (Massie 1979: 11). Kennedy returns again and again to the way in which the fictional lie may be alchemised into some "kind of truth". She examines the moral status of lies in relationships, and considers the role of lies in writing fiction and imagining history. In *So I Am Glad* (1995), she questions both the function and the status of lies while highlighting the fictional status of the narrative. She establishes lying as a potentially collaborative activity, which may mask but also reveal the truth. In the same way, she proposes that fiction is a kind of collaborative lie. As Kennedy writes in her article "Not changing the world", "If I'm writing about (for example) love, murder, being a Scot [...], I will redefine those things in my terms as I make my fiction. I will be telling whatever lies are necessary to give some appreciation of what my truth is" (Kennedy 1995b: 100).

Kennedy explores the status of lies in interpersonal relationships in her first novel, *Looking For The Possible Dance*, which opens with a description of Margaret's most cherished childhood memory of her father: the night he took her to a dance at a local church hall and she

watched him dancing. This dance functions as a Golden Age myth for
Margaret: every other dance, every other relationship in her life is
judged against this memory. This memory of her father, however, is
explicitly located in a context which questions the validity of
memories and of words. Margaret recalls her father on this night
pointing at the moon and telling her that "everything else is a waste of
time" (Kennedy 1993: 1). When she asks him later what he had meant
by this, he claims not to remember the occasion; he also tells her that
he has never liked dancing as it hurts his feet. Then, to change the
subject, he remarks that the lavender bushes by which they are
standing were planted by Margaret's mother when Margaret was
three. Margaret remembers her father planting the bushes himself the
previous summer, and thinks, "Such lies" (4). And yet it doesn't seem
to matter:

At school, if anyone told her lies, Margaret wouldn't speak to them, but Daddy was
different. He was always more convinced by his stories than anyone else. And
because she wanted to please her father, to oblige, Margaret tried to believe him as
much as she could. This seemed to make him happy, which meant she could be happy
too. (4)

The alternative morality that Margaret constructs is partly based on
the fact that her happiness is grounded on such lies, but also on the
fact that she recognises her father's lies for what they are. While his
refusal to admit that he likes dancing threatens to negate Margaret's
memory and the controlling image of the book, the more utilitarian lie
about the lavender bushes both helpfully changes the subject and
constructs an image of home and family for Margaret, whose mother
left when she was young. Margaret is aware of her father's effort to
construct a different past for her, and of the lie involved in it. The
moral difference she makes between her father lying and other people
lying acknowledges the common context which she and her father
share: the lie is effectively negated because she knows it is a lie and
she is not being deceived. Margaret accepts her father's lies because it
makes life easier to believe them but also because she recognises that
she is being protected by his lies.

"Such lies", thinks Margaret about her father, and the
affectionate, indulgent tone of this acknowledgement and acceptance

of the shared lie is echoed in the short story "Warming my hands and telling lies", where the same phrase reoccurs:

> Once, out driving beside my second husband, I ran my fingers up his thigh. He asked me what I was doing.
> "Just warming my hands."
> "Such lies."
> "Yes, I'm warming my hands and telling lies." (Kennedy 1994: 176)

Here the lie, and the affection, occurs in the context of a sexual relationship. And by the end of the story (indeed the end of the page) the phrase "warming my hands and telling lies" has been transferred from sex to fiction: "I sat and typed out fabrications, keeping my hands snug and supple on the little, black keys" (176). In *So I Am Glad* (1995), Kennedy develops the alternative morality of lying in the context of a couple rather than a family. In parallel with this (fictional) relationship, she also highlights the way in which lies and truth become ambiguous terms when related to the writing of fiction. The developing relationship between Jennifer and Savinien provides the shared knowledge for a lie to become both recognisable and positive:

> I know he knows I'm lying. [...] He knows I know he knows I'm lying. [...] I know he knows I know he knows I am. Lying is good like this, it becomes a truth that only the parties included can understand and nothing to do with deception. (Kennedy 1995a: 76)

Lying here, even more than in *Looking for the Possible Dance*, is no longer a question of deceit but of a shared and private knowledge of the truth, and becomes something cohesive, creating a community of knowledge between two or more people. At the same time, this reciprocal understanding (I know he knows I know he knows) functions as a blueprint for how the narrative of *So I Am Glad* works, and for the relationship between reader and narrative voice. Narration is frequently paralleled with lying in the novel, as in the opening of the third section: "I hate secrets. No, that's a lie, and here I was hoping to tell you the truth. Start again" (Kennedy 1995a: 22). But this admirable narratorial desire to provide the reader with the truth is undermined when we discover that the entire structure of the novel depends, superficially at least, on a narrative lie. Jennifer informs us at the outset that she has no emotions (7); the book ends: "You'll have read, I suppose, the opening of this book, about all of that calmness I no longer have. Sometimes the best beginning is a lie. But I hope you'll accept my apology for it now" (280).

The narrative ellipses and interventions which characterise the style of *So I Am Glad* highlight the controlling role of the narrator, as when she introduces her memories of childhood abuse with "Now this section, you needn't read or really bother with. It won't add to your understanding of the book, or of the story it's trying to tell" (Kennedy 1995a: 69). Or when she heightens the suspense as to the true identity of her mystery lodger: "I don't mean to keep you waiting – I would love to tell you who he is right now – but I can only seem to focus on this particular afternoon and conversation" (39). She diverts attention from background information in order to highlight "important" plot developments: "I will tell you how I earn a living later, for now we'll move on to Tuesday afternoon when something important happened" (28). Of course the way in which Jennifer makes a living turns out to be very important, given the central themes of the book. She is a "professional enunciator" – for the span of the novel, primarily a radio announcer – and therefore her voice disseminates information on a wide scale. "No matter what you intend them to know, they will know it, hear it as if you were speaking their thoughts", Savinien enthuses (139).

Yet the reader encounters Jennifer's voice as writer, rather than speaker, and we are seldom allowed to forget that this is written narrative, as Jennifer highlights the textual architecture of the novel, foregrounding its very structural units: "This chapter will roll its way forward..." (Kennedy 1995a: 68); "Do you see? The third little paragraph I say?" (101). Or when Savinien, on finding out what year it is, states "Then I am the loneliest man in the world" and Jennifer comments, "Which is the perfect place to end this section because it looks so conclusive on the page. Except that we didn't finish there, we kept on, two unfictional people speaking in the emptiness of a small room" (56). The chapters, sections and paragraphs clash with the story they relate. The narrative voice, while constantly reminding us of the mechanics of novel writing, insists on the non-fictionality of what is being related, as if the breaching of the artificial structural units of the novel was a guarantee of non-fictionality or truth. The narrative voice's concern with the fictionality or otherwise of events coincides with the first scene in the book which is supernatural, or, to use the novel's own terminology, "impossible" (76). The first hint of the impossible is that Savinien's tears, sweat and indeed all of his "more fluid parts" (16) shine or burn with a silver flame. This revelation is prefaced with the paragraph: "A little advice here. If you find what I tell you now rather difficult to believe, please treat it as fiction. I won't be offended" (12).

Jennifer's concern with truth in her narrative is thrown into relief by the "impossible" status of the other main character, Savinien de Cyrano de Bergerac, who is, as Jennifer remarks, with understandable exasperation, "not only three hundred and seventy-five years old, but also dead and luminous and French" (Kennedy 1995a: 82). His appearance in the upstairs bedroom of Jennifer's shared house in Partick is never explained, is definitely corporeal and causes practical rather than supernatural problems for the other inhabitants of the house – such as his unfamiliarity with modern bathrooms and his inability to pay the rent. Just as he is slowly integrated into the life of the late twentieth-century household, so Savinien, in all his impossibility, is integrated into the fabric of the narrative. The term "impossible" is Savinien's own, as he attempts to explain his situation to Jennifer:

"Tell me who you are, then. Really."
"Savinien de Cyrano, which is the truth. I promise you. I swear on everything I no longer have that my name is my only possession. I am neither mad nor mistaken, I am only impossible. Men who tell lies will always say impossible things, but all men who say impossible things need not be liars. I would maintain this rule remains unaltered when we consider *being* impossible." (Kennedy 1995a: 76)

Each time Savinien tells Jennifer his name he insists on its truth (see also page 59), and, revealingly, in this passage where he explores his own impossibility, that impossibility is juxtaposed with "men who tell lies". This passage is immediately followed by the one in which Jennifer states "He knows I know he knows I'm lying." Lying as a shared and private knowledge of the truth becomes associated with Savinien's impossibility. Savinien is, as Jennifer tells us, a secret, her "own private secret" (Kennedy 1995a: 24), and their relationship is, to some extent, founded on their shared and private knowledge of his impossibility. If the model "He knows I know he knows I'm lying" may be said to describe the narrative structure of the novel, Savinien in a sense gives physical form to this model. From the beginning of the novel, and Jennifer's claim that she is completely without emotions, the reader is invited into a complicity with the developing narrative voice, its patterns of revelation and concealment and its fascination with fiction and truth. The intimacy of lying, which occurs between father and daughter in *Looking for the Possible Dance* and between (soon to be) lovers in *So I Am Glad*, and which is also re-enacted between narrator and reader, is made visible in the person of Savinien. Into a novel which claims to be about "unfictional" people (56), the doubly fictional Cyrano de Bergerac irrupts like a shared lie, a shared joke. He is doubly fictional because he was written by Edmond Rostand a hundred years prior to appearing as a character in Kennedy's novel – Jennifer tells Savinien "You're a character in a play" and he retorts, "Do I look like a play?" (80). Yet at the same time he is an actual historical figure, and Kennedy acknowledges the responsibility of doing justice to the life of someone who actually lived (March 1999: 116). So Savinien's status is further complicated: while impossible and doubly fictional, he is in fact more "real" than any other character in the book.

In *So I Am Glad*, the increasingly metafictional fabric of the novel turns Jennifer's preoccupation with truth and lies towards a questioning of the status of fiction. Her insistent reminders that this is a written narrative function partly to distance the controlling narrative voice from the events she relates, but also serve eventually to blur the distinction between narrator and author, the fictional writer of auto-biographical memoir and the writer of fiction: "But at the moment, thought is unavoidable. I'm writing a book – I have to think about it from time to time" (Kennedy 1995a: 186). The relation between the fictional and the real, narrative and textual structure, lies and truth is summed up in the act of fiction writing itself:

At the end of a page, a chapter, a day of work, I have to stop. I have to come back. Just when I'm tired, when I've allowed myself a certain sensitivity to events, I have to come back and leave everything behind.

> Sometimes friends will ask me what I've been up to, where I've been. Whatever I think of to tell them is nonsense. I generally lie politely, shut down with a smile. The truth is I spend all the best of my days being nowhere with no-one. I sit alone in a room, surrounded by events which cannot happen now. (Kennedy 1995a: 187)

The act of writing occupies a different space from the world of friends, a space she is required to "come back" from. But all the sensitivity and events experienced by the writer can, in the end, only be summed up as "being nowhere with no-one [...] surrounded by events which cannot happen (now)." Suppressing the "now" at the end of that sentence allows it to describe Jennifer's impossible relationship with Savinien which epitomises the fictional. As Jennifer tells Savinien early in the novel, "This doesn't happen. This is a thing which does not take place" (13).

But in a world full of impossible statements and claims, Savinien's impossibility may be quite appropriate. His existence is certainly less offensive than many of the other lies Jennifer encounters in her everyday life, particularly through the news she is required to transmit in her job as radio newsreader. Individual stories, she tells us, "are not the kind of thing I am meant to speak about. People, individuals, are to be avoided in case they seem more important than the big lies I have to retell" (Kennedy 1995a: 85). Savinien, impressed from a seventeenth-century viewpoint by the medium of radio, tells Jennifer that she has a position of remarkable power (38). And while he does not understand, as she says, the limitations of her position, he is right: the power is not hers but that of the voice of authority she ventriloquises. The "big lies" diffused via the medium of radio are multiplied on television and film, and Jennifer identifies her childhood with "the dawning of the Age of Stupid Lies", where there seems to be no clear distinction between fact and fiction, and she watches the Vietnam War alongside the "The Man from UNCLE" (188).

Whereas individuals may collaborate in lying on an interpersonal level, on a public level the collaboration becomes a collective process. Thus, in "The role of notable silences in Scottish history", the narrator tells us, "the city knows about lies, too. It makes them and loves them and forgets they were never the truth" (Kennedy 1990: 70). The "big lies" that Jennifer has to retell function in a similar way: it is the collectivity which is responsible for participating in the formation and perpetuation of grand public lies.

As far as I can understand, my entire country spent generations immersed in more and more passionate versions of its own past, balancing its preoccupations with less and less organised activity or even interest in the here and now. Far more recently the whole island of which my country forms a part was swallowed wholesale by the promise of a ravenously brilliant future. (Kennedy 1995a: 187)

It is possible to divide the passage into two different kinds of public "lie", each illustrating the principle of collectively participating in a lie. The construction of nationhood based on the rewriting of "more and more passionate versions of [the] past" implies a shared dishonesty, a communal process of producing variations on a generally agreed theme. On the other hand "the promise of a [...] brilliant future", contains the implication of a false promise made by one party to another, but does not exclude the idea that the other party collaborates in the lie by believing it. The British public have "swallowed" a story of the future, ravenous for the riches that were promised, but the future has ended up by devouring them. The explicit criticism of the British government in the passage above is echoed in a short piece Kennedy wrote for a special edition of the *Edinburgh Review* marking the imminent devolved Scottish parliament, in which she argues that

It would be good – but absolutely miraculous – if the parliament paid serious attention to issues of language. Westminster and Brussels have managed to consistently undermine democracy and increase day-to-day cynicism about politics. It would be good if the Scottish Parliament made some kind of effort to do things differently. But that would mean that promises were clearly stated, that lies were easy to spot, that truth and belief might even enter into the equation ... not on the cards really. (Kennedy 1999: 73)

Kennedy insists on the importance of the language of politics, and her use of the terms "promise" and "lie" parallels public language with personal relationships. "Lies" should be "easy to spot". As in the private sphere, once a lie is easy to spot, it becomes "a truth that only the parties included can understand and nothing to do with deception". Otherwise, the "promises" and "lies" are deception, and the communal collaboration in the production of belief consists only in being deceived, and thus perpetuating falsehood. It is hard, however, to draw a distinct line between the two types of lie which Kennedy brings together, the communal participation in myth-making in the construction of nationhood, and the forced swallowing of political falsehoods. Both are called "lies" in "The role of notable silences in Scottish history".

The narrator of this story regards all written record as composed mainly of lies, if only because "nothing is less believable than the truth" (Kennedy 1990: 63). The story opens: "I find it very hard to tell the truth. [...] Worse than this, I have discovered that, beyond a certain point, nobody really cares much if you lie. And I do lie. I can be honest with you. I can tell you that I do not tell the truth. I can also say that no one notices" (62). Again, participation in the process of lying is emphasised, although here it is the apathy of the public that facilitates or indeed justifies the lie. The reasons for lying are various. Like the "more and more passionate versions of [the] past" of *So I Am Glad*, the "history" of Glen Flaspog provides a much more interesting version of the past of a Highland glen:

> The glen's most notable feature is a series of spectacular falls, descending from twelve hundred feet above the valley floor.
> All cascades, the Grand McIver, the Evil Red McIver and the Torrent of the Weeping Mothers have now been without water for several centuries; in memory, it is said, of the dreadful Massacre of the McIvers, perpetrated by the Evil Red McIver upon his own kinsmen. (Kennedy 1990: 63)

This story is untrue, "but far more interesting than a brown and green glen with rocky grey bits and a couple of sheep" (64). The "notable silences" of history are the silences surrounding the true stories of all the people whose lives are too small to record, and what is left is the construction of history and myth. There is a slight difference between the lie that is the history of Glen Flaspog and the lies that Jennifer retells on the radio, which, we assume, are political. Both, however, illustrate instances of "lies" disseminated with the voice of authority.

The narrator of "The role of notable silences" rounds off her Glen Flaspog discussion by saying "And there's no point being Scottish if you can't make up your past as you go along" (Kennedy

1990: 64), which places the story closer to the model of the collaborative lie shared between Jennifer and Savinien, but transposed to a larger scale. In this case, making up the past seems to be a communal act of Scottishness. Susanne Hagemann has described "The role of notable silences" as an "explicitly constructionist view of Scottishness" (1997: 325). And yet, despite its Scottish focus, there is nothing exclusively Scottish about the narrator's conclusions, which comment on the construction of identity in general rather than specifically Scottish identity. Her statement about "being Scottish" is immediately qualified: "there's no point being Scottish if you can't make up your past as you go along. Everyone else does." What is important, as so often with Kennedy, is the "everyone else", rather than the simply Scottish. As Kennedy herself has stated, "by sharing my intimate, individual humanity – Scottishness included – I hope to communicate a truth beyond poisonous nationalism or bigotry" (Kennedy 1995b: 102). This "fiction with a thread of Scottishness in its truth" provides a Scottish stage for the working out of more universal ethical concerns. Thus the lie constructed out of a communal Scottishness becomes a model for communal lies of many kinds.

In the same story the communal, or collaborative, lie acquires a more negative aspect in the narration of another Scottish, or more specifically Glasgow, lie. The narrator recounts the murder of a friend in a Glasgow bar:

He was stabbed by a stranger in a bar. Earlier there had been fighting and one of the stranger's friends had been slashed with a glass. Because the stranger believed in lies about blood loyalty and city violence, he came to the pub to make them true. He walked straight in, quite quickly, and stabbed my friend. My friend had chosen to stand in the wrong place. (Kennedy 1990: 71)

The "lies about blood loyalty and city violence" may also be communally constructed. The stranger in the bar collaborates in the lies by believing them, and by believing them he causes them to become true. But the collaborative aspect of the lie is slightly different here. This is not a mutually supportive lie ("He knows I know he knows I'm lying") or a communal construction of shared identity, but rather a process whereby fictional constructions provide excuses for actual behaviour. Kennedy expands upon the claim that events may in fact be caused by fiction in *So I Am Glad*:

> Apparently my country was in the grip of an extraordinary phenomenon. The public as a whole, and in particular the criminal classes, has lost all ability to discriminate between fact and fiction. No misdeed, however ghastly, could not be traced back to a horribly obtainable novel, film, popular song or comic book. This made far more exciting reading than the usual tedious bulletins on mass unemployment and hopelessness. (Kennedy 1995a: 133)

Through various topical references, it is clear that *So I Am Glad* takes place in 1993–94, and Jennifer's reference to "a horribly obtainable [...] film" may refer to the Jamie Bulger case, the headline-making story of 1993 in which two ten-year old boys abducted and murdered a two-year-old in a style that the media linked to the film *Child's Play 3*, and which provoked debate about the links between violence and the media. The purported fictional antecedents of this crime provided a reason which otherwise seemed to be lacking. This extends the relationship between fiction and truth, because here fiction, it is claimed, creates truth, not in the way that Muriel Spark and Kennedy herself claim, but in a particularly unpleasant kind of mimicry. This is a claim that is consistently used against explicit, particularly violent and pornographic, fiction. However, the relationship may be more complex than it appears, because, as Kennedy suggests above, establishing a link between crime and fiction provides a narrative in which to read the crime. This makes for "far more exciting reading" not only because it includes "a spicy variety of Hollywood scenarios and pin-up pictures of movie stars" (133) but also because it provides a causal sequence of events which turns the inexplicable into a logical narrative. We are relieved of the responsibility of asking more difficult questions regarding the truth about violent and senseless crimes. Instead, the crimes are turned into narrative, and re-fictionalised.

This, in a sense, brings us full circle. Fiction creates true events, and true events create fiction. Rather than illustrating the kind of truth that Muriel Spark claimed could emerge from fiction, this is almost a caricature of the idea of the collaborative lie. A.L. Kennedy's inquiry into the status of lies and fiction, however, covers a whole spectrum of possibilities, from the shared lie which becomes beautiful, to the communal lie which becomes horror. In her fiction the word "lie" opens up to include a wide range of definitions, positive and negative, private and public. What is consistent throughout is the idea that not only the "liar", but also the recipient of the lie, are equally responsible, both in determining what kind of lie it is and in determining the consequences of the lie. The alternative morality which removes the option of an easy judgment of lying as bad, at the same time enforces a much more rigorous system of individual responsibility.

This shared responsibility between the teller and the receiver extends to the writer and reader of fiction. The reader also, Kennedy suggests, collaborates with the writer's fiction in order to create a "kind of truth". The love story between Jennifer and Savinien illustrates the possibilities inherent in shared collaborative lies, and both characters, it is worth remarking, are writers, Savinien in the seventeenth-century and Jennifer in the present. Together they also incarnate the possibilities that the collaborative fiction may have for the writer. Savinien perhaps sums it up best in *So I Am Glad*, when Arthur tells him about having seen Dennis Potter's last televised interview, when Potter was dying of cancer in June 1994. Savinien asks: "'This man, he was a writer?' 'Yes.' 'And he told the truth?' 'Yes.' 'Then he was a good man. This is what writers are for'" (196).

Bibliography

Hagemann, Susanne. 1997. "Woman and Nation" in Gifford, Douglas and Dorothy McMillan (eds). *A History of Scottish Women's Writing*. Edinburgh: Edinburgh University Press. 316–28.

Kennedy, A.L. 1990. "The role of notable silences in Scottish history" in *Night Geometry and the Garscadden Trains*. Edinburgh: Polygon. 62–72.

—. 1993. *Looking for the Possible Dance*. London: Secker and Warburg.

—. 1994."Warming my hands and telling lies" in *Now That You're Back*. London: Jonathan Cape. 153–76.

—. 1995a. *So I Am Glad*. London: Jonathan Cape.

—. 1995b. "Not changing the world" in Bell, Ian A. (ed.) *Peripheral Visions: Images of Nationhood in Contemporary British Fiction*. Cardiff: University of Wales Press. 100–102.

—. 1999. In "Poets' Parliament: a selection of writers' views on the new Scottish parliament" in *Edinburgh Review* 100. 69–77.

March, Cristie Leigh. 1999. "Interview with A.L. Kennedy" in *Edinburgh Review* 101. 99–119.

Massie, Alan. 1979. *Muriel Spark*. Edinburgh: Ramsay Head Press.

The Relativity of Experience in William McIlvanney's *The Kiln*

Gerard Carruthers

In late twentieth-century Scotland, links between the individual and working-class community values were strained by the impact of social change, greater educational opportunity, the loss of political certainties, and the rise of consumerism. Against this background and its relativism, William McIlvanney, exploring connectedness and patterning in literature in an ironic and cinematographic style, reasserts something of the post-Enlightenment Scottish philosophical approach to truth, individual and community.
Keywords: William McIlvanney, Calvinism, post-modernity, Scottish philosophy.

William McIlvanney's *The Kiln* (1996) is a historical novel exploring rather nicely the supposed end of progressive history. Paradoxically related to this terrain, it is also a *bildungsroman* even as it engages with the exposure of fictional transparency, which it does both in terms of the revelation of the fictive artefact and the myth of classical realism as viewed by post-modernism. In these two overlapping areas, of history and fictional theory, McIlvanney investigates those large imponderables of the late twentieth century, value and reality, and interrogates both from the perspective of what it means to be part of a community as well as a creative artist. In short, in its contemplation of the difficulty of concretely defining social and imaginative relationships, *The Kiln* is a novel that could consider no bigger contemporary philosophic terrain.

The Kiln is one of a series of novels where William McIlvanney deals with the vexed interplay of individualism and community in the working-class life of the west of Scotland. *Docherty* (1975), to which *The Kiln* is a sequel of sorts, shows a mining family fragmenting even as it is imbued with profound decency. The calamity of the Great War leads to the rise of Communism in the family, something that collides with older, entrenched values (most prominently a work ethic that is deeply rooted in the family identity). The physically and morally impressive patriarch Tam Docherty remains uncompromised in these qualities amidst family and community squabbles but a pregnant question remains: are loyalty and decency enough in themselves in a marginalised social grouping?

Questions of how much working-class identity *per se* is something to be proud of, or the mark of the exploited, have preoccupied McIlvanney's fiction from his first novel, the bleak *Remedy is None* (1966), where the working class university student, Charlie, becomes a murderer in frustration at the inability of his background to accommodate either his existential aspirations or to proffer to him a satisfactory sense of community. *The Big Man* (1985) features unemployed Dan Scoular who turns to illegal bare-knuckle prize fighting to support his family and who is thus entrapped by the criminal underworld. *Laidlaw* (1978) and *The Papers of Tony Veitch* (1983) show an interesting type of empowerment for the west of Scotland working class male protagonist, specifically Detective Inspector Laidlaw, whose solving of crimes allows him to wage an individual war on those who exploit the weak, and whose profession allows him time to ruminate on the condition of Scotland and, indeed, of Britain. The latter two novels show McIlvanney in the vanguard of the new wave of a "whodunit" fiction that is highly literate and philosophical as well as peddling murder mysteries as inventively accomplished as any in the genre.

Other writers, such as Allan Massie, regard McIlvanney as Scotland's finest contemporary fiction writer because of his structural and stylistic brilliance; his linguistic brio, vividly contemplative and metaphoric, as part of his honed craftsmanship as a "traditional realist", is a facet, however, that has never quite won him the acclaim that he is arguably due. McIlvanney is often regarded as too "traditional" in his outlook when, in fact, it is "the traditional" that is constantly interrogated and critiqued in his fiction, even as he does not concede that the simple smashing of tradition represents any kind of panacea.

In *The Kiln* the collapse of the post-Enlightenment belief in ever-increasing social progress is registered by two iconic figures, Alexander Fleming and Margaret Thatcher. The novel spans the years 1955 to the mid 1990s, the first of these dates (we are told by the narrator) being marked by the death of the inventor of penicillin. Fleming is among the tea-towel litany of innovatory scientists through whom Scotland has been wont to regard itself as at the very cutting edge of ever-increasing human improvement. He is a point of both linkage and discontinuity in *The Kiln*. Educated in Kilmarnock (the locus of the novel renamed as Graithnock), Fleming is dead in the same year as that which represents watershed enlightenment for another Ayrshire "lad o' pairts", the main protagonist, Tom Docherty. In general cultural terms, as well as for Tom personally, things are vigorously changing in 1955. It is the birthing year of rock 'n' roll and youth culture generally, and amidst this historic time of adolescent liberation, Tom Docherty finds he has increased educational and sexual opportunities. Here, first of all in the novel, we find the noting of a historic shift in the attitude to temporal propriety and, appropriately enough, *The Kiln* constantly crosscuts between this year of youthful iconoclasm and the period of the 1980s–90s (and so mimics that other post-war youth mode of choice, the cinema) where a very different iconic figure to Fleming presides. We are told that:

One woman, with all the vision of a soldier ant, had managed to screw up the UK. Dehumanisation by statute. There is no such thing as society. A self-fulfilling idiocy. (McIlvanney 1996: 257)

The unnamed figure is, of course, Margaret Thatcher, the Conservative Prime Minister (1979–1990) whose political credo trumpeted free-market economics as the essential and appropriate mechanism governing human behaviour. Where Fleming, the medical benefactor of his species, is to be named, Thatcher is repaid with anonymous reference to match the "dehumanisation" (wrought through social dislocation) she has visited upon others.

The Kiln is no lament for the past. In fact, its tone throughout combines satirical laughter (sometimes stretching towards the sardonic) with affection, as it acknowledges invariable instability down through the human generations. Some critics have expressed unease with William McIlvanney's presentation in his fiction of the working-class male figure. *The Kiln*, however, shows a modulated sensitivity to this type that appropriately spans the range from respect to ridicule (a gamut that is, in fact, characteristic throughout McIlvanney's oeuvre). Keith Dixon has offered a useful critique of this debate and a perceptive identification of the fact that

McIlvanney's fiction deserves a more engaged criticism than it has so far been granted (Dixon 1996: 187–98).

Tom Docherty is the grandson of Tam Docherty, a miner with a reputation for being able to use his fists. Tom's own father, Conn, has demurred from working in the pits and instead occupies himself with a series of misfiring maverick money-making schemes. Tom, about to go to Glasgow University in 1955, represents even further degeneration of the "working" ideal, at least in the eyes of the "hardman", Cran Craig, with whom Tom finds himself working in the brick-making factory in the summer before the commencement of his studies. Cran's hatred of the Dochertys is somewhat obscure (perhaps connected, it is hinted, with the Irish origins of the family), but probably has most to do with a rather primal atavism. The folk-memory of Tam Docherty's indefatigability and the continued defiance of the "disreputable" Conn, it can be inferred, stoke the "working-class" male resentment of Cran who finds an opportunity to strike at the family in the person of the vulnerable, seemingly "bookish", youngster, Tom.

Cran is at once, as the symbolism of his name implies, the embodiment of brute industrial power (something that becomes very much superseded in the period the novel charts) and also, given that his name is so obviously *symbolic*, part of an age-old story of human strife (epically Freudian in its male cross-generational conflict). The clearly rebarbative figure of Cran Craig combines industry (crane, often pronounced "cran" in the west of Scotland) and nature (craig = cliff in Scots) and so conforms precisely to what McIlvanney sees as the physical essence of the "west of Scotland where nature and industry encounter along the seaboard" (McIlvanney 1970: 169). In much of his fiction, including *The Kiln*, this physical environment is conducive to exemplary humanity; in the figure of Cran Craig, then, we see McIlvanney introducing an uncomfortable ambiguity into even his own previous symbolic geography in a way that is very typical of the way this novel operates.

Tom, who excels appropriately enough in the classics, undergoes a strongly signalled and somewhat ridiculous "rite-of-passage" experience with the gigantic villain, Cran. With trepidation, Tom finds in his last week at the brickwork that he will have to work in a two-man team with Cran at the kiln-face: "It was a prospect so frightening, he wished he could go in without being who he was, find a neutral identity for the night" (McIlvanney 1996: 194). Tom is aware of both his own inflated family "identity" and the epic identity of Cran whose chair in the worker's rest area sits constantly empty (Cran even stands during his break periods), with the assumption being made by colleagues that this has to do with Cran's prodigious machismo. The whole situation is, in fact, deliberately overloaded with meaning, played out as it is against the background of the kiln where we are pointed toward the formation of a significant experience in the identity of Tom. Cran loses no time in sadistically goading the youth when they are thrown together, until the younger man turns on him using a half-brick for a weapon (the metonymic representation is comically deft). Cran falls over and is suddenly defeated as his co-workers alerted by the disturbance find him bloodied and demanding that Tom be kept away from him.

So far, then, we have the appearance of an urban workplace tale of the emergence of justified manhood under unfair pressure, but it transpires that there is something else going on. As though a classical quest-hero working through a puzzle and slaying a great beast, Tom has, in fact, been aided by Cran's secret Achilles-like weakness, which is that he suffers from piles that have now painfully burst during their encounter. We have a cross-grained scene of all too literal deflation, then, where out of farce the martial prowess of the Docherty name is amplified. This is typical of the often-sardonic view that *The Kiln* takes of the formation of and connections in identity, even as the novel worries somewhat about the deformation of family, community and society that it charts, most especially in the second half of the twentieth century.

A strong strand in the novel, as we see in the altercation between Tom and Cran, is the idea of "Ah kent his faither" (the dismissive saying "I knew his father", often taken by commentators to stand for a smug parochialism at work in the Scottish cultural mentality). *The Kiln* identifies this attitude quite closely with Calvinism, at the centre of which historically stands the doctrine of predestination; it is implied that, in Graithnock and other Scottish communities, people are locked by expectation into a pre-determined family mould. Ironically, we see this happening in the mock-heroic episode in the factory even though Tom, like his father before him, actually represents a significant change in his family-pattern. Tom is re-imagined into the Docherty space by the community, and this can be nearly as deceitful as less predictable, or more creative, imaginative acts.

In his maturity, Tom is aware of an alternative, more individualistic capacity:

EACH OF US REMAKES THE WORLD WE LIVE IN, he would think. (McIlvanney 1996: 265)

This is not entirely a liberating apprehension, however, and Tom is often uneasy about his imaginative propensity, never entirely sure whether it is a strength or a weakness:

HE SEES HER IN THE LOCAL LIBRARY in the Dick Institute. Can we create what we want to happen by imagining it intensely enough? Do we project events, precipitate them out of thoughts and wishes as well as having them simply occur to us? He has sometimes thought mistakenly that he has seen someone in the street only minutes before he sees that person in fact. Has he wished her into the library? (McIlvanney 1996: 115)

Lurking near this train of thought is the Calvinist mistrust of the imagination with its tendency to make false, human-centred pictures and to distract from the grim post-lapsarian nature of the world. There is in the novel, then, a nice equipoise between the author's mistrust of Calvinist community-patterning and the Calvinist mistrust of individual patterning, which Tom channels against himself.

In the young Tom's discussions with John Benchley, we encounter in the latter a very humane Church of Scotland minister whose gentle, non-authoritarian pastoralism reflects again a change in the cultural temperature of the 1950s. However, even Benchley is full of dourness toward the condition of life. In a witty moment, we see the minister, a man for whom Tom Docherty has genuine affection, through the youth's eyes: "He seems to Tom like someone who endures life as if it were influenza and hopes to get over it soon" (McIlvanney 1996: 61). There is here, yet again, a fine balance. Tom never regrets his early, very thoughtful decision to become agnostic but his mental condescension to Benchley is at this point gently ironicised (even though his apprehension is not entirely lacking in justice). Tom thinks on the world with a post-Fleming confidence where passion and optimism are the penicillin in life. Later, imbued with more experience, Tom knows that people have reason to be suspicious of, and disappointed in, life.

One aspect of Tom's increasing enlightenment happens generally as death becomes a greater, more immediate reality in the novel. Tom's beloved brother Michael all too prematurely succumbs to a brain haemorrhage and Maddie Fitzpatrick, who initiates him sexually and who stands for all the vigour and freedom the young Docherty wishes to associate with life, lies dead before she is fifty. The human plotting of life, especially in our human relationships with others, is as uncertain as anything (not any more certain perhaps even than a supposed relationship with God – Calvinist mistrust of the world is somewhat justified). In middle age Tom lies alone in bed in a flat beside Edinburgh's huge Warriston Cemetery, a failed marriage and many other disappointments behind him, and wonders, still somewhat tied to the idea of teleology, if he has been experiencing "progress or regress" (McIlvanney 1996: 265).

Even here, though, it is implied in the sometimes self-mocking melodramatic turns that his musings take, that Tom is aware of the infection of his mood by the menacing presence of the nearby graveyard. If he is to be sceptical of the optimism and innocence of his youth, he is also to be sceptical of the pessimism and maturity of his later years. In either state he is constructing stories and making connections that can never be entirely trusted. Here we find the keynote attitude of *The Kiln* which says that, if humans should be wary of being too confident about their stories, they should also forbear from the co-relative conclusion that utter despair and inarticulation are the only courses in the face of inaccessible truth and reality.

The Kiln sees William McIlvanney grappling with the idea of post-modernity and this is particularly interesting in that McIlvanney is well-known in his dislike of those attitudes in various strands of that thought which see all values as hopelessly relative and endlessly malleable.[1] In *The Kiln* McIlvanney wittily goes on the offensive, inhabiting such notions first of all in two prefatory quotations. One of these is supposedly by Tom Docherty, whom we see in the course of the novel becoming a fairly successful writer: "At the moment of writing the author is fictive. Only the story is real." Roland Barthes' proclamation of the "death of the author" is here entertained. Where Barthes has in mind the absolute cultural materialism of the fictional artefact, Docherty/McIlvanney asserts the basic honesty in the utterance of the story. With only a little tweaking, Barthes' idea is made to encompass a belief in the integrity of fiction where the author is *part of,* or is *relative to,* the story, not standing omnisciently outside it. What one might infer from this prefatory quotation is McIlvanney's scepticism that the insights of structuralist thinking about endlessly subjective connectedness are as radically new as they are sometimes taken to be.

The second epigraph offers yet more "intertextuality" as McIlvanney's most celebrated fictional character, the police detective, Jack Laidlaw (who also makes a youthful appearance in *The Kiln*), is cited: "You must find the way to let the heat of experience temper your naivety without reducing your idealism to ashes." Here again, a pointedly fictitious "author" offers a comment on the frequently incongruous nature of actuality and perception or belief. The difficulties over discerning the solid and the less solid should not lead to abject surrender of discernment. What humans, whether writers or not, must do is allow the imagination (or making sense of experience) to come into play, while remaining on guard against allowing bad experience to suggest, as so often it does, that there is no summation or learning to be extracted from our very mortal and variously weak or disempowered existence. In a further framing of the novel McIlvanney dedicates *The Kiln*, "For Joan and for my nephews and nieces and their families – theirs is the true story". Within this no doubt sincere tribute, McIlvanney is also being a little mischievous. He claims that there is a "truer story" standing behind the events of *The Kiln*

---

[1] There is ample evidence of this in William McIlvanney's column in the weekly *Scotland on Sunday* from 2001 to the present where he frequently attacks trendy, post-modern and politically correct tinged abrogation of responsibility because of the supposed unavailability of any absolute truths in human society.

(something added to by the pictures of William McIlvanney in the 1950s and 1970s that adorn the book's cover); with this contention he does not mean to imply that his novel is "untrue", but that it is only one formulation of the truth through one man's eyes, making a kind of sense of his own background. The author does not speak for *the* truth, but for *his* truth manifestly emerging from a real communal context even as this truth is explicitly acknowledged as sometimes uncertain.

Two important ideas emerge here. Firstly, the refusal to despair in the face of relativity, the imperfect approximation to the truth, which is what McIlvanney dares to suggest he is representing in dealing at least semi-autobiographically with both his own family and his west of Scotland cultural background. Secondly, and overlapping with this approximation to the truth, is McIlvanney's implicit belief that the human feeling which underwrites the creative urge is a testimony that will be available to an even wider human community of readership (that is, including the empathy of readers from completely different cultural backgrounds than that he is describing). These ideas might well lead us to reading *The Kiln* in a tradition of thought that in its concern for community can be traced back to the Scottish Enlightenment. McIlvanney is, of course, heir to many literary and intellectual impulses in the generally post-Enlightenment and post-Romantic world and so one ought not to insist too narrowly upon a national intellectual inheritance. It is true to say, though, that in his novel McIlvanney stands in considerable accord with twentieth century heirs to the tradition of philosophical worrying about the place of feeling in the world, which had preoccupied such different Scottish thinkers of the eighteenth century as David Hume and Thomas Reid.

McIlvanney's approach in *The Kiln* rests on a platform that has much in common with the insights of such twentieth century Scottish thinkers as John Bailie, John Macquarrie and perhaps most of all with John Macmurray. Craig Beveridge and Ronald Turnbull provide an excellent summary of one of the Macmurray's central epistemological strands:

Our thinking about the nature of the self is [...] in need of revision. The self is customarily conceived, in the Cartesian tradition, as an observer and as an individual. As against this, Macmurray wishes to see the self as an agent and a person. We ought, he thinks, to abandon the quest for pure and certain knowledge (which in any case is illusory) in order to assess our thinking in terms of its contribution to the extension of community and friendship. All thinking, he wrote, is for the sake of action, and all action for the sake of friendship. The second important idea here is that the self is not an individual but a person, and persons are constituted by their relations with other persons. (Beveridge and Turnbull 1989: 98–9)

Feeling, then, which is precisely subjective is the mechanism for activity (or activeness) in the spheres of friendship and community (or is, in other words, the cement of society in the way that David Hume saw it). Holism of perception is not really available to humans in the first place. So the radical subjectivism of post-modern thought is not so entirely new so far as William McIlvanney, heir to certain Scottish traditions of thought resting on the primacy of feeling, is concerned.

The latter half of the twentieth century is historically particularised in *The Kiln* as a time of fragmentation as the various effects of greater educational opportunity, the growth of youth culture, the rise of the mass media, the breaking up of class culture, the smashing of many of the old political certainties and the rise of consumerism take place. Against this social background, William McIlvanney is interested in connection, in overarching metaphor and in patterning in literature (surrounded as he is by a post-modern context which largely tells him that patterns are deceitfully interested, or quite literally, fiction). There is a great movement to and fro in the novel between the ideas of patterning and flux. *The Kiln* is a novel of lyricism and playfulness, and of contemplation, generally, of the aptness of fiction in making any sense of life and it rehearses and foregrounds a number of modes and forms. It has a certain overstated metaphorical signal in its title, it echoes the idea of the classical epic quest (albeit with farcical undertones) and it utilises a cross-cutting technique, which both seems in accord with the orthodoxy of the later twentieth century that patterning and chronology are bankrupt but also highlights the fact that, of course, the late twentieth century does indeed have its own particular (relative) form of (cinematic) patterning – which is manifest in a very readable book (ironically part of the modernity of *The Kiln* is this very readability sprung from a technique, which would, of course, have confused a pre-cinema or even early cinema audience).

The newfangled filmic mode of the novel shows McIlvanney's confidence in his readership (he has enjoyed both critical and popular acclamation to a much greater extent than most Scottish writers of the last forty years) to absorb expressive change; the late twentieth century might be post-modern, fragmented, non-linear in narrative predilection and cinematic, but sophisticated communication rather than absolute confusion pertains among humans.

The Kiln is an extended internal performance as it is largely focalised through the ruminative mind of its central agent, Tom Docherty. It is full of external engagement too, not only in the charting of historical movement, but also in the questing by Docherty's mind after typologies of cultural explanation for himself. At one point his mother calls his name and he responds with a kind of mental soliloquy (which is again quite consciously and self-mockingly literary):

> Who was it that the name was looking for? Which of his split personalities would answer? Dr Heckle or Mr Jibe? The endless internal argument with his own life, the self-appointed seeker after truth? Or the dark joker, prepared to settle for turning the moment into laughter? Or maybe someone else altogether. For in him the highly developed Scottish propensity for duality of nature divided like an amoeba into a small riot of confused identities. He probably *was* having a nervous breakdown, a part of him reflected calmly, like a doctor observing a patient through a spyhole. (McIlvanney 1996: 143)

Names yet again are important in *The Kiln*. We see his mother's calling of "Tom" as a label reaching out to him, but inadequate to describe his multitudes. The possibility here, of course, is that Tom at this point is being portrayed as a rather precious adolescent, the writer *manqué*. Equally, of course, his apprehension is in keeping with the "modern" theme that preoccupies the novel: of identity being something problematic that humans too facilely construct. We see him ironically appropriating to himself the most famous of literary split personalities but reductively acknowledging no difference in the "two" sides: "Dr Heckle and Mr Jibe." In so far as there is any "real" split, this is between himself and his life, whatever these things are; which, in one sense, is to say no more than that calibration of the human to his social and cultural environment is a constantly difficult and moving thing. Tom's response to this permanent difficulty is to become "the dark joker" (or to laugh in the dark) as a kind of defiance, or as a solid (neo-literary) identity-construct. That we humans respond to the uncertainty of identity by creating provisional identities is what is postulated here and throughout *The Kiln*. What else can we do, but remain *relatively* coherent in the face of incoherence the novel asks?

The passage continues the joke of facing fragmentation with a flippant "riot" (to use McIlvanney's word) of metaphor where the oft-trumpeted split self of the Scots (the result, allegedly, of contradictory national existence and a puritanically-inclined religion) is seen in comically biological terms as "amoeba"-like. At once forensic and reductive, this description is brilliantly conflicted between supposed natural identification and creative sneering. It is truly a moment, one of many in *The Kiln*, of *reductio ad absurdum* where the prognosis is that we can never pin down identity completely, and that the best means of proceeding is to place a self-ironising cordon around our own attempts at identification. We see this studied equanimity also in the oxymoronic sentence that follows where Tom reflects "calmly" on the idea that he may well be in a state of "nervous breakdown". Again, then, reflection and supposedly actual experience are in collision; Tom is doctor and patient, diagnoser and sufferer. The circularity of the situation is only broken by awareness of the human construction of its terms. This self-cynical perception, ultimately, is the provisional stance of healthy agnosticism in the novel that refuses to believe absolutely in its own formulations, but which refuses also to surrender the notion completely of the provisionally autonomous agent, which is registered in its propensity to self-critique.[2]

Toward the end of *The Kiln* we are offered a series of self-standing, or typographically separated, reflections by Tom Docherty, as though from a writer's journal (here again, perhaps, the novel mimics the notion of the deconstructed creative *work*, revealing its own materials of formation). Each of these is introduced with the

---

[2] For an excellent reading of McIlvanney's *Laidlaw* (1977) that chimes somewhat with my reading of the attitude to experience in *The Kiln* see Ryan 2002: 65–77. Ryan concludes that "Meaning exists for Laidlaw only insofar as it is produced and reproduced in the contingent contexts of social life [...]" (69); also see Ryan 2002: 38–90 for a very wide-ranging discussion of McIlvanney's Scottish social, political and intellectual context.

words "That was when ..." so as to reinsert the assertion of historical time even as this sits in tension with the cultural trope of fragmentation that the novel embraces. Tom contemplates the summer of 1955:

THAT WAS WHEN he had his first awareness of experiencing the kiln, an accidental place which became a mythic centre in the mind – action in which you discover you, the self learned in happening beyond the lies of the word and beyond prevarication of the thought, the repeated point where existence hardens into being or breaks down into flux. The kiln had been the shifting nucleus of his summer. The kiln was not only in Avondale Brickwork. It was between Maddie Fitzpatrick's legs. It was in his head. It was where you found who you were. It was where he divested Cran Craig of his fearsomeness through the intensity of his own fear, where, by seeing Maddie Fitzpatrick clear, he saw himself more clearly, where a partial truce with his family earned him a partial truce with himself, where he began to compact into who he was. (McIlvanney 1996: 273)

There is here an interesting insistence on "action" *à la* Macmurray. "Word" and "thought" are deceptive quantities (again we find ideas superficially in keeping with the insights of post-modernity) as instruments of post-rationalisation. Yet action also is not temporally fixed so as to accord easily with reality. It is fluid: we see this in the idea of the "shifting nucleus of the summer" (where yet again scientific metaphor is sardonically utilised); it is the individual who matters (as a bundle of perceptions, to paraphrase David Hume) as stories constantly form and are smashed. Tom sees himself and his own fragility by seeing others in their fragility, and the tension in which he exists with his family is a product of a necessary, chafing agency to be somewhat calmed (in "partial truth") by this apprehension of constant *relativity*. Even as the word is mistrusted to some extent, metaphor here, albeit in slippery and often ironically used form, is necessary if any sense is to be made of the world at all. Tom begins to "compact into who he was", a nicely double-edged metaphor with its alternate connotations of solidity and bargained compromise.

We find dry wit as Tom contemplates the mantra of the novel, so in keeping with the modern apprehension of the radically subjectivised universe:

He lay insomniac at Warriston as he had lain insomniac that night with Gill. The most significant difference he could see was that this time he lay alone. Was that progress or regress? It certainly didn't *feel* like progress. Separate insomnias, please. *Une nuit blanche*. He likes that French expression. A white night. The problem with insomnia was that you couldn't switch the light off in your head. There were too many things you'd rather not look at. But you couldn't avoid them. And at this time of the morning every mote in the mind's eye had pretensions to be a Zeppelin. You saw an Andes of molehills. In the glare he realised that old griefs were still with him. You didn't live beyond them, you just found out how to live round them. They were like bad lodgers you learned to accommodate. In that repeated scouring of himself, he had yet again been trying to rebuild the world around him, Wasn't that what everybody had to do in the light of changing experience? To live in the world was to remake it daily. (McIlvanney 1996: 265–6)

Tom here wryly acknowledges the amplitude of his own trajectory of development; moving supposedly to a more sophisticated sphere, where he has not, in fact, become any less "primitive" and has repeated the kind of mistakes that he has made earlier in life. Again, then, we see that there is no teleological development: the myth of progress is once more undermined. Even as this is acknowledged, the imaginative, story-telling capacity is a still centre that redeems with humour and the capacity to bring about some certainty, even if this is the awareness of the failure to be certain. The quest that a "white knight" might pursue turns out to be a "white night", the dispelling of dreams and heightened wakefulness that is both an index of failure and of the stupidity of believing in romantic stories in the first place. And yet the ambiguity once again pertains. The very debunking playfulness of the language in the passage reveals that the creative capacity is off the leash once more and that Tom Docherty will renew his daily attempt to comprehend the world. Cleverly, McIlvanney inserts the implication that if, as much modern epistemology tells us, reality is bankrupt, we cannot avoid the urge to reality, or imaginative patterning. We may explicitly signal the artifice of this patterning, as here with overblown metaphoric humour, but we have no other tool with which to engage with the world but our minds and their propensity, whether reliable or not, to create connection and relationship.

Appropriately enough for a novel that entertains the idea of "the end of history", *The Kiln* has a deeply anthropological tone in keeping with the "primitive" essentials that Docherty is left to contemplate. The customs, totems and rituals of his background are delineated with a particularity that is allowed by the sense of central, progressive historical narrative being bankrupted. Tom's insomniac musings, most especially about death, are in keeping with this new state of uncertainty.

Paradoxically, the dilution of the old patriarchal society leads to an increased family affection. We see this as Tom's own son, Gus, while at primary school goes through a phase of referring to his father by his first name and there is thereafter closeness such as he had not experienced between himself and his own father. We see this at the party Tom holds while his marriage to Gill is breaking down. Gus, at this point, can relate to his father's depressed mood and offer him consolation. The family is shown at the forced occasion of Christmas dinner at the house of Gill's brother. On returning home they have a spontaneous snowball fight that is a much happier family occasion. *The Kiln* is a novel that is uneasy about family conditioning, even as it cherishes family relationships and embraces the potential positivity of change. We see this as the Docherty line continues not only with Gus, but also with Megan who goes one academic step further than Tom himself by undertaking postgraduate research at Oxford University. We have, then, the "lass o' pairts", an advancement upon Tom's role in the novel as "lad o' pairts"; the human advancement of female emancipation that is a by-product of the "crisis" of values that becomes so accelerated in the second half of the twentieth century.

A book that is an explicit point of reference in *The Kiln* is Maxim Gorky's *Childhood* (1913–14). The first name of the author is given only as its initial on a copy that Tom's Uncle Josey lends to Tom's grandmother, so that she pronounces it as "McGorky." Amidst this moment of comedy, something else is actually going on. In a moment of feeling Tom's grandmother domesticates the Russian classic, or brings it close to home with an instinctive gift for universalisation. Left-leaning, the humanist Gorky came to dislike the violent excesses of the 1917 Russian revolution and became a dissident. His account of childhood full of wonder at the world even as it recognises the propensity to chaos makes for a kind of template for *The Kiln*. It, and Gorky's life generally, informs the kind of humanitarian (non-totalitarian) socialism espoused by Josey and many men like him in Ayrshire and working-class Scotland. *The Kiln* accepts historical unpredictability and is not wedded to the idea, as totalitarian systems such as Communism are, that teleological narratives of progress must be maintained.

This attitude casts a nice light upon the withering perspective of the novel on Margaret Thatcher. It is actually under the guise of historical maturity that Thatcher suggests that society or human connectedness is entirely an outmoded fabrication (in her own peculiar teleological conceit as a representative of the people, it is something we have *moved beyond*). *The Kiln* shares with Gorky's *Childhood* an affectionate respect for the human circumstances of personal formation without in any way being sentimental about human beings. The competing ideas that society must be regimented (the collapse of Communism in Eastern Europe in the early 1990s is another point of wonder in the novel), or, on the other hand, a *laissez faire* free-for-all are seen as equally unsatisfactory extremes, and savage disrespect for the community of feeling is to be found, the novel implies, in both.

Ultimately, *The Kiln* dissects both optimism and pessimism about human nature. The optimism that the young Tom inevitably feels in the summer of 1955 turns to more bitter human experience. Pessimism, however, does not take simple priority over hope, something that is registered in the ending of the novel which chooses to dwell on the moment of Tom's joyful first trip to university: "GERONIMO, his mind is shouting" (McIlvanney 1996: 277). There is a nice irony here as the name of the American Indian, standing as a war-cry of bravado, comes directly from the culture of cinema that helps to provide the dechronologised mode of the novel. Choosing to end in this way, McIlvanney leaves us on a courageous note; the implication being in this circular, non-teleological world that fierce feeling is as valid as any other overarching mood.

This is the core of flawed humanity that the novel touches: a feeling sentience that remains even as post-modernity assaults our confidence in rationality, and without which we would have nothing. The novel appropriately ends with the Tom in cinematic expostulation, not out of nostalgia for some lost feeling or sensibility, but because the age of the mass media betokens extended communicative reach, or universalism, as much as the dislocation of individualism or of community. Tom Docherty's experiences are as often bleak as they are rewarding or funny but "Geronimo" is the correct *cri de cœur* in rightful anticipation that his experiences are going to be intelligibly human: making sense, or communicating, to a wide range of people.

Bibliography

Beveridge, Craig and Ronald Turnbull. 1989. *The Eclipse of Scottish Culture*. Edinburgh: Polygon.

Dixon, Keith. 1996. "'No fairies. No monsters. Just people.' Resituating the Work of William McIlvanney" in Susanne Hagemann (ed.) *Studies in Scottish Fiction: 1945 to the Present*. Frankfurt am Main: Peter Lang. 187–98.

McIlvanney, William. 1970. "Growing up in the West" in Miller, Karl (ed.) *Memoirs of a Modern Scotland*. London: Faber & Faber. 168–78.

—. 1996. *The Kiln*. London: Sceptre.

Ryan, Ray. 2002. *Ireland and Scotland: Literature and Culture, State and Nation, 1966–2000*. Oxford: Clarendon Press.

Resignifying HiStories: The Subversive Potential of Revision in Liz Lochhead's Poetry

Anne-Kathrin Braun-Hansen

This chapter presents several poems by Liz Lochhead which aim to change the reader's perception of female roles and identities. It analyses the spectrum of techniques used and discusses their respective efficacy in view of the claims of feminist theory. Certain forms of audience-conscious poetry are found apt to disrupt the audience's habits of perception and thus to enhance the creation of alternative roles and identities.

Keywords: Liz Lochhead, female identity, feminist literature, feminist theory, performativity, resignification, revision.

Scottish history has shown the difficulties and dangers of any attempt to establish one's "own" identity, if this identity is – perhaps necessarily – seen in difference to another, dominant identity (see Trevor-Roper 1983; Crawford 1992; Craig 1996). For Liz Lochhead, one of the many authors who bear the "Canonical Double Cross" of being female *and* non-English (Reizbaum 1991), the problem of identity forms a driving force of her writing. Her work reflects the struggle with her – predominantly male – Scottish literary heritage and with the dominant English discourse. As she has stated:

For me the process of becoming a writer has been to stop pretending to be all these things [grown up, posh, male, English and dead], or at least to stop pretending to be all these things all the time [...]. (Lochhead 1997: 124)

At the same time, however, her work seeks its place in the area of conflict between feminism and other political-philosophical movements. When Lochhead describes her project as an attempt "to retell familiar stories from another angle", she invokes the early feminist project of revision (Somerville-Arjat and Wilson 1990: 9). But her sceptical attitude towards the efficacy of such revisions and towards the creation of an untroubled female Scottish identity already bears the sign of poststructuralist doubt. If, as poststructuralism claims, we cannot communicate without recourse to pre-existing images and language material, if every utterance is also an iteration, then nothing "new" can ever be said or created. According to this logic, the creation of identities inevitably needs to resort to existing images and stereotypes, so that a revision of these images can never be truly subversive. Lochhead's search for identities is marked by this limitation, and the texts often mirror the impossible task of becoming one's own creator, with her most explicit negotiation of self-creation being her drama *Blood and Ice*, an imaginary biography of Mary Wollstonecraft-Shelley (1985). Nevertheless, her repeated attempts to cast new light on clichés and perceived truths achieve something more than their mere repetition. If a genuine subversion of the system seems impossible, her writing still explores the possibilities *within* the given limitations. Read along the lines of the poststructuralist thinker Michel Foucault, Lochhead's modest claim to "retell familiar stories from another angle" appears itself in a new light: when Foucault describes interpretation as the radical appropriation of meaning, an act that forces a new meaning and thus a new set of values onto a given system (Foucault 1998: 378), feminist revision – telling old stories "from another angle" – can indeed disrupt the power of a dominant narrative and thus make a change. Since the search for voice and identity is a central theme of Lochhead's writing, and since revision is one of her privileged techniques, Lochhead's work can thus contribute significantly to an exploration of the limits and possibilities of revisionary literature. The following analysis of a few selected poems will serve to investigate the scope available to such renegotiations of female images and identities. The poems, ranging from mere repetition up to successful subversion, show that quotations and reinterpretations of texts, linguistic elements, clichés or cultural stereotypes are by no means *guaranteed*, but are always *potential* sites of recreation and new creation.

Rewriting as Negation: "The Alternative History of the World, Part I"

One of Lochhead's most widely-known and -read poems cites the feminist project of revision ironically in its title: "The Alternative

History of the World, Part I". Although published as late as 1991, it is an outstanding example of early feminist strategies to re-visit historical and cultural commonplaces. The historical intertext of the poem is the *Book of Genesis*. The poem is subdivided into two parts, the first of which re-tells and comments on the story of Adam and Eve:

There was this man alone
In a beautiful garden.
Stark bollock naked
(Scuse my French, beg your pardon)
[...]
But there was Something Lacking ...
He coudny put his finger on it,
He was in a right tizz.
But, the Lord our God being a Male God,
He knew exactly whit it wis...
A slave.
And soon she was worn to a frazzle
Waiting on His Nibs
Ironing his figleaves
Barbecueing his ribs
[...]
So they were both Ripe for Revolting
When that Slimy Serpent came
But – would you Adam and Eve it? –
She got the blame. (Lochhead 1991: 12ff.)

"The Alternative History" is a model example of parodic imitation; it highlights the dependence of the parody on the (distorted) intertext. The poem ridicules and criticises the clichés and creates a reflective distance by presenting them "from another angle", but it cannot do so without repeating or at least evoking the intertext. This first part of the poem is, in fact, a later addition; earlier poetry recitals only include the previously and separately published second part ("What-I'm-Not Song", Lochhead 1993: 55ff.), which can be seen as the zero degree of revision, namely rejection. The "What-I'm-Not Song" consists of a series of humorously aggressive rejections:

I'm not your Little Woman
I'm not your Better Half

I'm not your nudge, your snigger
Or your belly laugh. (Lochhead 1991: 13)

It derives its outstanding humorous effect from the hotchpotch of
stereotypes and clichés connected by Eve's "I'm not[s]" and
aggressively repudiates the roles and choices previously imposed. But
whereas the first part of the poem at least creates a different, and
ironically distanced, point of view, the second is a mere negation-by-
repetition. Both versions of feminist revision in "The Alternative
History of the World" attempt to disrupt and rewrite the biblical story,
but neither of them creates a true "*Alternative* History".

Rewriting as Alteration: *The Grimm Sisters*

The Grimm Sisters from 1981 is among the earliest of Lochhead's
poems entirely dedicated to the revision of cultural stereotypes. *The
Grimm Sisters* was published as part of *Dreaming Frankenstein and
Collected Poems* in 1984 and is Lochhead's third poetry collection
after *Memo for Spring* (1972) and *Islands* (1978). It marks a turn in
her poetic development away from more personal, autobiographical
writing towards the relatively typical *persona*-poetry. This move can
be traced in the change of personal pronouns: where in *Memo for
Spring*, "Daft Annie On Our Village Mainstreet" is addressed in the
second person – "Annie / with your euphemisms to clothe you / with
your not all there / your sixpence short in the shilling" (Lochhead
2000: 131) – the madwomen in *The Grimm Sisters* usually take the
first person, as in "Harridan": "Oh I am wild-eyed, unkempt, hellbent,
a harridan" (Lochhead 2000: 75).

The first poem of *The Grimm Sisters*, "I: Storyteller", begins
with a comment upon the activity of storytelling in general. It reads
like a critique of the apparently neutral narrative stance of fairy tales
like those of the brothers Johann and Jakob Grimm. One of those
unknown voices that may have served the cultural-historically
interested brothers as informants appears in person:

she sat down
at the scoured table

in the swept kitchen
beside the dresser with its cracked delft.
And every last crumb of daylight was salted away. (Lochhead 2000: 70)

Storytelling here appears as one of the daily toils; sweeping dust from the kitchen floor is rated similarly as "salt[ing] away" the "crumb[s] of daylight". The alignment between storytelling and material housework becomes even more explicit in the second stanza:

No one could say the stories were useless
for as the tongue clacked
five or forty fingers stitched
corn was grated from the husk
patchwork was pieced
or the darning done. (Lochhead 2000: 70)

The direct comparison "To tell the stories was her work. / It was like spinning, / gathering thin air to the singlest strongest / thread" in the third stanza (Lochhead 2000: 70) confirms the impression that "Storyteller" is typical for the tradition of feminist rewriting as an attempt to reevaluate both the daily toils of women and to excavate their unmentioned cultural achievements. The following poems then critically examine the fairy-tale ideal of a loving family, which is, of course, more than often undermined in the tales themselves.

A cursory comparison between Anne Sexton's poetry collection "Transformations", first published in 1971, and Lochhead's re-writing of the Grimm tales a decade later reveals two very distinct approaches. Sexton's poems adopt their titles unchanged from the collection of the brothers Grimm. All of them are subdivided into two parts: the first part reads like a present-day "comment" or a free association on the tale, often adopting an autobiographical tone. The second part narrates the tale from a modern, feminist and psychological perspective, but retains the fundamental elements of the plot. The conspicuous double structure and the combination of a personal, deeply concerned tone with a cynical, inverted summary of the tale illustrate Sexton's preoccupation with ruptures and psychological abysses in the apparently innocent family constellations in her poems. In "Briar Rose (Sleeping Beauty)", for example, she suggests an incestuous drama:

Little doll child,
come here to Papa.
Sit on my knee.
[...]
Come be my snooky
and I will give you a root.
That kind of voyage,
rank as honeysuckle. (Sexton 1982: 290ff)

Lochhead's poems are of an entirely different tone and quality; they are visibly less concerned with psychological depth, and suffused with irony and humour. Although she, too, invokes the exaggerated paternal love in her version of "Briar Rose", "II: The Father" – "Stirring, forgiven, full of love and terror, / her father hears her footstep on the stair", (Lochhead 2000: 71) – this love does not entail the same dimension of sexual/incestuous threat. Instead, it is countered by Briar Rose's own, slightly derogatory, presentation of "my daddy, the King, / he's absolutely a hundred years behind the times / but such a dear" (71). The poem "III: The Mother" takes a similarly critical, and similarly ironic stance towards parental love:

But she's always dying early
so often it begins to look deliberate,
abandoning you,
leaving you to the terrible mercy
of the Worst Mother, the one who married your father. (Lochhead 2000: 72)

This is perhaps the utmost amount of pathos one can find in the poems. For Lochhead, the inversion of point-of-view is never entirely serious. When she describes her feminist project as "retell[ing] familiar stories from another angle", she immediately adds: "And so there's irony there" – irony, because Lochhead is aware that adaptations can only upset prior texts, but never efface and replace them (Somerville-Arjat and Wilson 1990: 9). The new interpretation never offers a closed narrative, but always leaves new gaps, from which irony can arise. Adaptation in *The Grimm Sisters* is not so much a serious project of feminist corrective but a play, juggling with the material. In "Rapunzstiltskin", for example, Lochhead deliberately intertwines two Grimm tales, "Rapunzel" and "Rumpelstiltskin"

(Lochhead 2000: 78–79). Instead of probing psychological depths, she picks eclectically from the surface of tales, as in "The Mother": "Tell me/what kind of prudent parent/would send a little child on a foolish errand in the forest/with a basket jammed with goodies/and wolf-bait? Don't trust her an inch" (Lochhead 2000: 72). Lochhead uses the source text not as "original", but as a *source* of constellations, figures and figurations.

Rewriting as Resignification: "The Furies"

Two other poems from *The Grimm Sisters* reinforce the observation that Lochhead's earliest revisions of literary material already display many traces of later texts and literary strategies. On a figurative level, a significant part of the collection *Dreaming Frankenstein and Collected Poems* is exemplary for Lochhead's incessant fascination with monsters or the monstrous as that which never quite fits and is never quite in place. On a methodological level, the poems are perhaps the earliest instances of texts that achieve an effect similar to what Judith Butler calls *resignification.*

Butler's concept ultimately derives from Jacques Derrida's notion that all linguistic utterances repeat the system from which they quote:

Could a performative utterance succeed if its formulation did not repeat a "coded" or iterable utterance, or in other words, if the formula I pronounce in order to open a meeting, launch a ship or a marriage were not identifiable as conforming with an iterable model, if it were not then identifiable in some way as a "citation"? (Derrida cited in Butler 1993: 13)

In *Bodies That Matter* (1993), Butler replaces the earlier term "performativity" by "resignification". Although this new term no longer refers to speech act theory, it still foregrounds its indebtedness to linguistics. Resignification semantically suggests a slightly more active role for the subject than the abstract noun performativity: it is the speaking subject itself who (intentionally or inadvertently) resignifies elements of meaning through the Derridean act of repetition. Although Butler is predominantly concerned with gender, her description of subversive resignification can serve as a fruitful model for identity in general. Her claim that repetition is "bound to persist as the mechanism of the cultural reproduction of identities" and that as a consequence, "the crucial question emerges: what kind of subversive repetition might call into question the regulatory practice of identity itself?" (Butler 1999: 42) leads to the conclusion that radical change must take place *within* the given socio-political framework:

> If sexuality is culturally constructed within existing power relations, then the postulation of a normative sexuality that is "before," "outside," or "beyond" power is a cultural impossibility and a politically impracticable dream, one that postpones ties for sexuality and identity within the terms of power itself. This critical task presumes, of course, that to operate within the matrix of power is not the same as to replicate uncritically relations of domination. It offers the possibility of a repetition of the law which is not its consolidation, but its displacement. (Butler 1999: 40)

The notion of "efficacious" repetition is, apart from Butler's apparent negligence of the material body (see Levinson 1999), a point that has evoked the strongest reactions from other theorists.

The limitations of Butler's theoretico-political thrust are due to a general limitation of human communication and intentionality: any message risks being misunderstood, since there is no guarantee that speaker and listener use the same system in encoding and decoding the message. The effects of a reiterational practice can thus not be calculated in advance. The systems (of communication, of social rules) are, on the other hand, not entirely free-floating and heterogeneous either, but relatively stable at a certain point in time. Efficacy is therefore a question of probability, not of "pure" chance. In order to account for the effect of a message being understood, the emphasis of analysis needs to be moved away from the "performer" towards the audience/the witnesses of an act of resignification. Lochhead's audience-conscious poetry embeds disruptive effects in a communicative situation that enhances their reception *as* disruptive effects – as instances of resignification.

In the poem "The Grim Sisters" (with an intentionally deviant spelling from the title of the collection *The Grimm Sisters*), Lochhead presents women entrapped in a cultural "matrix of power" (Butler

1999: 40). The speaker remembers the two spinster "grown up girls next door" who would treat her to a nice hairdo and many well-meant pieces of advice. The poem ends laconically:

Wasp waist and cone breast, I see them yet.
I hope, I hope
There's been a change of more than silhouette. (Lochhead 2000: 74)

Whereas "The Grim Sisters" retains an emotional and temporal distance between the young speaker and the two older women, this distance steadily decreases in the two following poems, which show that elements of resignification can be traced in Lochhead's revisionary poetry – re-visionary both because they entail a critique of the intertext and because they envision a change. The poems are part of the subgroup "The Furies" and are called "I: Harridan" and "II: Spinster". In "Harridan", the speaker describes a project for a History of Art class. She has to write an essay comparing depictions of apparently mad women in paintings by Hieronymus Bosch and Pieter Brueghel [sic]:

I was scholarly, drew parallels [...]
Compared and contrasted
Symbolism and Realism in the Flemish School;
Discussed: Was Meg "mad" or more the Shakespearean Fool? (Lochhead 2000: 74)

The "scholarly" distanced study of the paintings nevertheless incites an increasing identification with the madwoman Meg – "These days I more than sympathise" (Lochhead 2000: 75) – and finally results in the recognition that the speaker herself could well be driven to the brink of madness:

Oh I am wild-eyed, unkempt, hellbent, a harridan
My sharp tongue will shrivel any man. (Lochhead 2000: 75)

As so often in Lochhead's poems, it is the *voice* through which woman, especially the woman in a liminal position, defends herself, but this same tool also turns her into a human monster – "My sharp tongue will shrivel any man". The over-identification with the madwoman causes the speaker to abandon her own role as a rational, detached observer-scholar, and to assume the role of the observed stereotype. There are, however, signs that the identification is not complete. The critical recognition "The fool I was!" (Lochhead 2000: 74) and the emotional "These days I more than sympathise" (75) *frame* the following exclamations of apparent madness; instead of fully identifying, the speaker wears Meg's madness like an armour. Since Mad Meg is characterised by single, external items – "she has one mailed glove, one battered breastplate on. / Oh that kitchen knife, that helmet, that silent shout" (Lochhead 2000: 74) – the speaker can mentally put these on in order to turn the "silent shout" into explicit language. The poem both demonstrates how characters are made up from external features, and how the change of role can invert the signs: "The roles are [...] simultaneously made and unmade, adopted and abandoned, to reveal various kinds of difficulty experienced by the single woman in securing her social place" (Varty 1997: 645). When the speaker stylises herself as Mad Meg, she turns the silent figure of contempt into a vociferous menace to the male population. Varty nevertheless insists that the "loud emotion of the speaker" is not necessarily perceived by society, that "[o]ne way in which society conspires to collective deafness is to make the aggrieved woman laughable, and Lochhead points to this with the incongruous collation of 'kitchen knife' with 'helmet', details lifted directly from Breughel's picture. This locates the battle field in the home, toys swiftly with the tendency to ridicule and at the same time highlights both the pathos and the nightmare of the situation" (Varty 1997: 646). The ambivalence of this gesture of threat and ridicule also allows another reading, namely that the appropriation and reinterpretation of the ruling signs in a Foucauldian sense – the resignification of their prior meaning – could result in an appropriation of power, even if a loss of control is always part of the game.

If "Harridan" describes the entire process of entanglement with another role, the two subsequent poems, "Spinster" and "Bawd", show, in a sense, the outcome. Both are instances of character studies in which the stubborn insistence on the validity of social clichés creates an involuntary distance between speaker and utterance. They are fine examples of Lochhead's art to create almost realistic, yet deeply ironic monologues, where the irony is often tragic. "Spinster", which will be analysed exemplarily for both, consists of a list of resolutions that, in the course of the poem, achieves a fairly precise description of what kind of woman – better: what cliché – is speaking:

This is no way to go on.
Get wise. Accept. Be
A spinster of this parish.
My life's in shards.
I will keep fit in leotards. (Lochhead 2000: 75)

The series then develops a momentum of its own: the language moves from health resolutions – "Go vegetarian. Accept. [...] Be frugal, circumspect" – to a witch-like invocation of obsessive self-control:

I'll cultivate my conversation.
I'll cultivate my friends.
I'll grow a herbaceous border.
By hook by crook I'll get my house in order. (Lochhead 2000: 75)

The linguistic twist of the parallelism consists in its deviant effect: the future aspect serves as a performative act in the linguistic sense – making what it says come true. The parallelism suddenly turns into satanic invocation and catches the moment where the "normal" unobtrusively enters a potential danger zone. This moment of collapse, where the mere insistence on a particular enunciation suddenly produces an entirely different meaning, a "slippage between discursive command and its appropriated effect" (Butler 1993: 122), demonstrates well what Butler describes in the context of subversion:

The law might not only be refused [as, for example, in "The Alternative History of the World, Part I", A.B.], but it might also be ruptured, forced into a rearticulation that calls into question the monotheistic force of its own unilateral operation. Where the uniformity of the subject is expected, where the behavioural conformity of the subject is commanded, there might be produced the refusal of the law in the form of the parodic inhabiting of conformity that subtly calls into question the legitimacy of the command, a repetition of the law into hyperbole, a re-articulation of the law against the authority of the one who delivers it. (Butler 1993: 122)

The "parodic" aspect of Butler's subversive performativity has incited similar bewilderment to the term performativity itself. In the context of "Spinster", it becomes clear that parody does *not* designate a psychic condition, which would more suitably be described by frustration or, according to the title of the group ("The Furies"), perhaps even stifled fury. The parodic effect rather derives from the gap between the law ("You need to accept your present and future state as the spinster of your local community") and the specific instance of "parodic inhabiting of conformity" ("Get wise. Accept. Be/A spinster of this parish"). Interestingly, the law is not represented by an external voice, but exists only in form of self-commands. The internalisation of the interpellator brilliantly demonstrates how the law and its subversion come into effect in the same place, the site of the subject's identity.

Returning the Look: "Almost Miss Scotland"

In Lochhead's poem "Almost Miss Scotland", part of the latest poetry collection *Bagpipe Muzak* from 1991, the female lyrical "I" enters a social field that is notorious for its clichés and sexist norms, namely a beauty contest. The rules of the game rely on external appearance and regulate the "right to watch" (namely that of male spectators looking at sexualised female bodies) as well as the language and values of the participants:

Then this familiar-lukkin felly
I'd seen a loat oan the telly
Interviewed me aboot my hobbies –
I says: Macrame, origami,
Being nice tae my mammy –
(Basically I tellt him a loat o jobbies).
I was givin it that
Aboot my ambition to chat
To handicapped and starvin children from other nations
– How I was certain I'd find
Travel wid broaden my mind
As I fulfilled my Miss Scotland obligations. (Lochhead 1991: 3ff.)

The mesh of social, ideological and gender-related determination could hardly be more closely knit than at this site of female commodification; however, the lyrical "I" manages to escape. The first and most important step is to break the monopoly of looking by redirecting it towards the male jury. What she perceives there – a "wee baldy comedian bloke/Whose jokes were a joke", a Highland singer who looks like "a pig in a tartan poke" – enables her to invert the roles, even if just in her fantasy:

How would *they* like their mums to say that their bums
Had always attracted the Ladies' Glances.   (Lochhead 1991: 5)

The inversion of the look and the seizure of the monopoly of so-called "objective" judgement is precisely what makes her realise her own position (see Kaplan 1997; Freedman 1991; Mulvey 1989):

In a blinding flash I saw the hale thing was trash
I just Saw Rid
And here's whit I did. (Lochhead 1991: 5)

What she does is not, as she first imagines it to be her duty, to stand up and criticise the chauvinist set-up of the contest. Instead, she simply leaves:

[...] I cannot tell a lie, the truth is that I
Just stuck on my headsquerr and snuck away oot o therr.
(Lochhead 1991: 5)

The lyrical "I" rejects the old set of appearance-based (or even market-based) identifications, and the casting-off of the old identity could be read as a symbolic death, which Slavoj Zizek, following Jacques Lacan, distinguishes from real death and defines as an ethical act (Zizek 1992). In a radically different approach, the philosopher Frithjof Bergman describes this kind of refusal also as an ethical turn: "Such a turn is within our power, and it can reverse the position of the self so abruptly that one has an acute experience as of a weight that suddenly is being lifted" (Bergman 1977: 88). This is more or less what happens in "Almost Miss Scotland": she does not change her "nature", but simply realises that certain parts of her identity must come to occupy a different position in terms of importance: "They and not the rest represent myself" (Bergman 1977: 89). More appropriately, one must consider this turn as only half the step towards a new identity, since she dismisses one part without yet affirming a new set of identifications. In Bergman's terms, one could say that the identification with beauty as surface appearance and its commodification within a chauvinist system no longer adequately represent the speaker and must therefore retreat to a marginal position within her system of identifications; "Miss Scotland", however, is more ironic about this serious proposition:

Because the theory of feminism's aw very well
But yiv got tae see it fur yirsel
Every individual hus tae realize
Her hale fortune isnae in men's eyes (Lochhead 1991: 6)

Her behaviour could be read as an ethical act, an act of self-determination or self-constitution. But reading "Almost Miss Scotland" exclusively as a moment of ethical decision would be at the cost of ignoring the alternative identification: if putting on her "headsquerr" – a (tartan?) headscarf – is an indication of what kind of identity she may choose instead of the commodified one as a beauty queen, one must conclude that it is a retreat into another, perhaps older, set of clichés. Such an ambiguous ending is common to most of Lochhead's texts – possibilities of change never remain unchallenged, the narrative or plot offers resistance to easy solutions. In "Almost Miss Scotland", the choice consists merely in choosing the lesser evil; the subversive moment of the returned look opens the speaker's eyes to the "real", to the power structures that determine her role in society, but it has, as it seems, only a limited liberating effect.

The above poems, from "Alternative History" to "Almost Miss Scotland", show four sectors of the range within which revision can operate. The instances of resignification seem the most radical in view of their attempt to subvert the dominant role system. But the other subversive gestures – the carnivalesque refusal of "Alternative History", the deeply ironic "Storyteller Poems" that deprive the fairy tales of their psychological depth and possibly of their power, and even the demonstration, in "Almost Miss Scotland", of a failed subversive gesture – perhaps all work towards the same end. The question has been raised, however, whether ridicule or irony can at all be subversive, or whether it even reinforces the dominant value system, and the same has been said about resignification and performativity – the subversive effect can indeed be guaranteed in none of the three strategies. "Almost Miss Scotland" reveals perhaps best what is at stake in negating, alternating and resignifying narratives: the effect is to some degree arbitrary and cannot be determined in advance; the role of "intention" is therefore limited, although not entirely negligible. The poem is in a sense symptomatic to Lochhead's depiction of processes of self-determination, since the female subjects in Lochhead's texts generally do not manage to break the vicious circle, but remain trapped in a mesh of determination.

Although the poems' individual strategies differ considerably, they all work towards a resignification of cultural narratives. Resignification in this sense becomes a tool not only to explain the subversion of gender roles, but also to explain the subversion of gendered intertexts. In a more general sense, examples like the above suggest that only flexible concepts of identity create an opportunity for a turn towards self-determination. The refusal to fulfil roles and norms imposed by a dominant culture or gender can be a performative act, it can result in a new, or different, subjective identity. Such reconstructions of selfhood are particularly vital for groups whose identity is not firmly established in history; a literary praxis from a doubly marginalised viewpoint like that of Liz Lochhead can therefore simultaneously add to a critique of poststructuralism's qualification of identity and ethical agency, and can create an imaginary environment where new forms of identity may be tried out. They are thus, in a sense, janus-faced just like the monsters and manifestations of the monstrous that appear throughout Lochhead's work.

Bibliography

Bal, Mieke. 1999. *Quoting Caravaggio: Contemporary Art, Preposterous History*. Chicago and London: University of Chicago Press.

Bergman, Frithjof. 1977. *On Being Free*. NotreDame, Indiana: University of Notre Dame Press.

Butler, Judith. 1993. *Bodies That Matter: On the Discursive Limits of "Sex"*. New York: Routledge.

—. 1999. "Gender is Burning: Questions of Appropriation and Subversion" in Thornham, Sue (ed.) *Feminist Film Theory: A Reader*. New York: New York University Press. 336–49.

Craig, Cairns. 1996. "From the Lost Ground: Liz Lochhead, Douglas Dunn, and Contemporary Scottish Poetry" in Acheson, James and Romana Huk (eds). *Contemporary British Poetry. Essays in Theory and Criticism*. Albany, NY: State University of New York Press. 343–72.

Crawford, Robert. 1992. *Devolving English Literature*. Oxford: Clarendon Press.

Foucault, Michel. 1998. *Aesthetics: Essential Works of Foucault 1954–1984, vol. 2*. (ed. James D. Faubion). London: Penguin Books.

Freedman, Barbara. 1991. *Staging the Gaze: Postmodernism, Psychoanalysis, and Shakespearean Comedy*. Ithaca and London: Cornell University Press.

Godzich, Wlad. 1994. "Emergent Literature and the Field of Comparative Literature" in *The Culture of Literacy*. Cambridge, Mass. and London: Harvard University Press. 274–92.

Hobsbawm, Eric. and Terence Ranger (eds). 1983. *The Invention of Tradition*. Cambridge: Cambridge University Press.

Kaplan, E. Ann. 1997. *Looking for the Other: Feminism, Film, and the Imperial Gaze*. New York and London: Routledge.

Levinson, Brett. 1999. "Sex without Sex, Queering the Market, the Collapse of the Political, the Death of Difference, and Aids: Hailing Judith Butler" in *diacritics*, 29(3): 81–101.

Lochhead, Liz. 1985. *Blood and Ice*. In *Plays by Women: Volume Four*. Selected and introduced by Michelene Wandor. London and New York: Routledge. 81–118.

—. 1991. *Bagpipe Muzak*. London: Penguin.

—. 1993. *True Confessions & New Clichés*. 4th ed. Edinburgh: Polgyon.

—. 1995. "Kidspoem/Bairnsang" in *Penguin Modern Poets, Vol. 4: Liz Lochhead, Roger McGough, Sharon Olds*. London: Penguin. 61–2.

—. 1997. "Writing as a Woman in a Small Country: Round-table Discussion" in Charnley, Joy et al. (eds). *25 Years of Emancipation? Women in Switzerland 1971–1996*. Bern: Peter Lang. 121–44.

—. 2000. *Dreaming Frankenstein & Collected Poems*. 6th ed. Edinburgh: Polygon.

Morrissy, Julie. 1994. *Materialist-Feminist Criticism and Selected Plays of Sarah Daniels, Liz Lochhead, and Claire Dowie*. Dissertation, University of Sheffield.

Mulvey, Laura. 1989. *Visual and Other Pleasures*. Basingstoke: Macmillan.

Reizbaum, Marilyn. 1991. "Canonical Double Cross: Scottish and Irish Women's Writing" in Lawrence, Karen R. (ed.) *Decolonising Tradition: New Views of 20th-century "British" Literary Canons*. Urbana: University of Illinois Press. 181–84.

Rothenberg, Molly Anne, and Joseph Valente. 1997. "Performative Chic: The Fantasy of a Performative Politics" in *College Literature* 24(1): 295–304.

Senelick, Laurence (ed.). 1992. *Gender in Performance: The Presentation of Difference in the Performing Arts*. Hanover and London: University Press of New England.

Sexton, Anne. 1982. "Transformations" in *The Complete Poems*. Boston, MA: Houghton Mifflin. 221–95.

Somerville-Arjat, Gillean, and Rebecca E. Wilson (eds). 1990. *Sleeping With Monsters: Conversations with Scottish and Irish Women Poets*. Edinburgh: Polygon.

Trevor-Roper, Hugh. 1983. "The Invention of Tradition: The Highland Tradition of Scotland" in Hobsbawm, Eric and Terence Ranger (eds). *The Invention of Tradition*. Cambridge: Cambridge University Press. 15–42.

Varty, Anne. 1997. "The Mirror and the Vamp: Liz Lochhead" in Gifford, Douglas and Dorothy McMillan (eds). *A History of Scottish Women's Writing*. Edinburgh: Edinburgh University Press. 641–58.

Zizek, Slavoj. 1992. *Enjoy Your Symptom!: Jacques Lacan in Hollywood and Out*. New York and London: Routledge.

Ethics of War in the Fiction of Robin Jenkins

Ingibjörg Ágústsdóttir

This chapter discusses the ethical significance of warfare, focusing on how this is reflected in the fiction of Robin Jenkins. It addresses the question of whether writers can contribute towards a public awareness of the moral implications of warfare. Several viewpoints on the morality of war are discussed, followed by an analysis and discussion of some of Jenkins's novels.
Keywords: Robin Jenkins, warfare, World War Two.

Despite the present state of international affairs, darkened by the cruelty of warfare and terrorism, many of us are fortunate enough to have escaped the horrors experienced by people where war and terrorism are part of everyday life. However, by standing by passively while watching our politicians make decisions which actually involve our countries in a war taking place elsewhere, we do in many ways become part of that war. While we can claim that we are innocent of killing other people because we are not directly acting as agents in that particular war, it is nevertheless difficult and practically impossible to refute the claim that we are in some ways implicated when our governments' interference results in the killing of innocent civilians. In this sense, public, or political, responsibility incorporates the more private aspects of our moral involvement. Nevertheless, we may ask ourselves the question when and how does private responsibility merge with public or political responsibility – is there any definite boundary between these two? Is it possible to distinguish between the public and private and thereby retain a fixed and private sense of morality which is not in danger of being compromised or disrupted by political agendas which rule that certain "immoral" or questionable actions are necessary in order to achieve the general Good – dilemmas within the sphere of politics referred to by C.A.J. Coady (1993: 373) as "the problem of dirty hands"? These questions are central to this chapter, which is concerned with the ethical significance of warfare, and especially how this is reflected in the fiction of Scottish novelist Robin Jenkins (b. 1912). Can the writing of Jenkins and his like contribute towards a public awareness of the various moral implications of international warfare?

Politics, Innocence and the Ethics of War

Peter Johnson examines the question of moral innocence and absolute virtue, and how these relate to political life, in some detail. Johnson argues that for the morally innocent "the importance of morality lies in its connection [...] with the idea of absolute virtue", and that from the standpoint of absolute virtue, "moral actions are not performed for the sake of advantage" (Johnson 1988: 6–7). On the other hand, political morality "signifies a public world [... where] effective action [...] seems to require that we put aside moral considerations which we would otherwise respect," whereas absolute virtue opposes this argument, since it believes that "nothing could override morality" (Johnson 1988: 7). Therefore assassinations and killings of other human beings conducted to "serve the public good" do not comply with notions of absolute virtue and moral innocence. When placing moral innocence in a political context, we are faced with many problems, one of them being that those who are morally innocent lack guile and cunning when these very characteristics are needed in the context of various political manoeuvres. Basing his argument partly on Plato's assertion that it is "impossible to act politically and retain virtue uncompromised", Johnson concedes that politics "excludes moral self-sufficiency" (Johnson 1988: 28; 45). Thus it seems that absolute virtue and moral innocence are inadequate concepts in moral philosophy concerning itself with political life and its policies, such as those concerning the state's involvement in warfare.

The more specific scope of the ethics of war presents various problems of interpretation. According to Jeff McMahan, most contemporary treatments of the ethics of war are developed within the framework of "the theory of the just war", which "provides a defence of the use of violence in war that parallels both the common-sense justifications for the use of violence by individuals and [...] common-sense justifications for the use of violence by the state for the domestic defence of rights" (McMahan 1993: 386). However, the theory of the just war and its components raise a number of considerations. The requirement of discrimination, for example, which stipulates that force "must be directed only against persons who are legitimate targets of attack", immediately raises the question of what determines "whether a person is a legitimate or illegitimate target of violence in a war" (McMahan 1993: 387). In any case, despite the best efforts of military authorities to ensure that no innocent civilians are targeted, does this not happen very frequently in warfare, even though it is often by accident? Within the ethics of war, moreover, there are other lines of thought, which argue in different ways from the just war theory. The realist view argues that war is justified when serving the national interest and this perspective could thus be compared to Johnson's definition of political morality in its putting aside of the moral considerations that are normally applied in everyday life. On the other hand, the absolutist belief (referred to as pacifism) argues "that there are certain acts which can never be justified, simply because of the kinds of acts they are" (McMahan 1993: 385), which would seem to place the pacifist view in line with Johnson's definition of absolute virtue and moral innocence. As is obvious from the above examples, therefore, when discussing the ethics of war we find ourselves in a minefield of contrasting, dichotomous, and paradoxical theories that seem to raise at least as many questions as they answer within their reasoning.

War and Morality in Robin Jenkins's Fiction

Robin Jenkins was a committed pacifist and was a conscientious objector during World War Two, working in the forestry in Argyll. Accordingly, Jenkins's view on war corresponds with the absolutist belief described by McMahan, which refuses such compromises as represented by the just war theory, arguing that "the challenge to provide a moral justification for war can never be met" (McMahan 1993: 386). This aspect of Jenkins's thinking is strongly echoed in his writing and the concept of war and its various moral implications become central issues within his examination of human fallibility and its impact on people's responses to various moral and social dilemmas. Jenkins's novels often demonstrate sharp criticism of what Jenkins clearly sees as the ethical wrongness of war. Within these concerns, the dual nature of society's responses to warfare as portrayed in these narratives thus becomes relevant not only to Scottish society but to the whole world as viewed through Jenkins's perspective. An early novel by Jenkins, *Guests of War* (1956), illustrates how the concept of war can be used as a metaphor for local everyday occurrences, while the novel simultaneously draws our attention to the moral ironies of actual war between nations. The novel has a historical basis and focuses on the evacuation of women and children from the slums of "Gowburgh" (Glasgow) to the "respectable," middle class Borders town of "Langrigg" (Moffat) during World War II, and charts the various problems caused by the clashes and conflicts that take place between the two social groups. The principle on which the plot is based is the safety of Gowburgh women and children from the enemy's bombs, and in his portrayal of the evacuees' arrival and subsequent stay in Langrigg, Jenkins makes clear the essential moral paradox of this principle when set against casualties on the enemy's side. The following passage emphasises the duality of wartime politics as the narrator sarcastically hints at the enormous injustice inflicted upon the innocent in the name of national safety during war:

Thus at last [...] Langrigg had opened its doors to every refugee. Although behind some of those doors the hospitality offered might fall short of cordial, nevertheless the gesture by the whole town was admirable, not to say miraculous; and all over the country similar gestures had been made. From the savagery of war women and children must be saved, not merely because their husbands and fathers might otherwise be reluctant to contribute to it, either by making shells or by firing them, but also because Authority, likewise protected from that savagery for other reasons, could not with equanimity anticipate the mutilation, blinding, maiming, and roasting of innocent children under its jurisdiction. Chivalry, compassion, and conscience haunted even chancelleries; and perhaps, when duty compelled that orders be issued encompassing the mutilation, blinding, maiming, and roasting of innocent children under the enemy's jurisdiction, those ghosts have not even then been wholly exorcised, they still linger and receive their tribute of solemn obeisances and heroic salutes. (Jenkins [1956] 1988a: 110–11)

Jenkins's approach to war is marked by this kind of sarcastic reference to the dark consequences of warfare, and his distaste for war is made explicit throughout. Another early novel, *Love is a Fervent Fire* (1959), links the brutality of war with religious responsibility in its suggestion that a country's involvement in war should call for some kind of repentance. The protagonist, Hugh Carstares, is burdened by moral guilt on returning home from the war, but realises that in Scotland "no penance [for the war] was considered necessary, and … none was being done at all, not even by those who professed belief in God" (Jenkins 1959: 19). The blindness of ordinary "stay-at-home" citizens to the suffering inflicted on innocent people during war is emphasised in a scene where Carstares visits his dead friend's parents: "He had found them not only reconciled to their son's death, but even proud of it. They had begotten a hero, reared him lovingly, and yielded him as a sacrifice. [...] Carstares [...] had been as discreet as he could; he had kept his hands steady" (Jenkins 1959: 19). The parents of Carstares' friend are unaware of their son's terribly painful death, nor do they recognise the suspect morality of his actual participation in the war. They perceive their sacrifice as honourable and heroic because they believe in the moral stance taken by their country's politicians, and this results in their "blindness" to suffering and death on the enemy's side.

A Would-Be Saint (1978) tells the story of Gavin Hamilton, who, like Jenkins himself, becomes a conscientious objector during World War II. Gavin's reasons are based on religion: "[...] if he became a soldier he would be denying Christ. Because Christ had been denied so many times this war, and many wars in the past, had come about. It was so much easier to kill one's enemy than to love him" (Jenkins [1978] 1994: 109). In trying to follow Christ's example, Gavin does in many ways display the kind of moral innocence that is classified by Johnson. Certainly, Gavin does not compromise his moral standards for the acceptance and liking of his fellow forestry workers, and his refusal to be beholden to anyone who approves of the war is his way of escaping moral involvement. The concept of "dirty hands", and of private morality as endangered by a specific political wartime agenda, is made clear through the perspective of Gavin, who believes that even children are not wholly innocent of the brutal deaths caused by war, because of the moral standards bred in them by their society:

One of the worst horrors of war was that children were put in a position where they must look on other children as enemies, whose deaths might be prayed for but did not have to be mourned.

They were not to blame, yet they were not innocent.

They were to be pitied. But who had a right to pity them? Not ministers or priests who told them that Christ's commands to love their enemies did not apply. Not politicians who promised them a guilt-free future when the slaughter was over. Not airmen who thought that the killing or maiming of children was a risk that could be honourably taken. Not soldiers who killed other soldiers who were the fathers of children. Not even their own parents who accepted as a legitimate consequence of war the deaths of other parents' children. (Jenkins [1978] 1994: 194)

Finally, in *Just Duffy* (1988), war is again a central theme, but Jenkins approaches the question of war even more specifically here in making it a determining factor in the actions of the protagonist, Duffy, and hence the concept of war is central to main plot developments. Set in the Scottish Lowland town of Lightburn, which is situated somewhere on the outskirts of Glasgow, the story revolves around a morally aware teenager who decides to wage a private war against the selfishness, hypocrisy, and immorality he sees in his community. Duffy is characterised by a curious blend of naivety and ingenuity, his apparent simple-mindedness and his uncompromising view of moral behaviour making him seem a moral innocent of sorts. Duffy has been described as "an ambiguous figure who could be either saint or fool" (Norquay 1993: 13), and as "the holy fool *manqué*, innocent but dangerously idealistic" (Dickson 1988: 11). These descriptions and the overall presentation of Duffy in the novel would seem to accord with my classification of Duffy as fitting Johnson's description of moral innocents in some ways. Duffy is seen by many of the other characters as a simpleton, but he is, in fact, more intelligent than most people realise, although the plot eventually reveals that his intelligence is quite misguided and dangerous. But Duffy also represents an intense questioning of the moral and religious justifications for war. Thus we are early introduced to his moral reasoning:

Duffy was well aware that though most human beings were capable of atrocities very few committed them and the great majority condemned them utterly: except of course if they were done to win a war. No one cared how many babies or cats were burned to death in Hiroshima or Dresden. (Jenkins [1988] 1995: 11)

Duffy asks his history teacher "what gave nations the right to declare war and thereafter claim that the killing of their enemies was permissible and legal", to which the teacher replies that most nations would argue that God gave them that right (Jenkins [1988] 1995: 2). Duffy's dislike for war, and for human atrocities in whatever form, is evident, but unlike Jenkins himself, or Gavin of *A Would-Be Saint*, he does not take the absolutist/pacifist stance and view warfare as completely and utterly unjustifiable. Rather, he transposes the religious justification used for wars in past history unto himself, thus deciding that if he should ever declare war himself, "he too would give God as his excuse, but with more right, for his purpose would be to save not to destroy" (Jenkins [1988] 1995: 2).

The above quotation clearly hints at the dangers inherent in Duffy's way of thinking. This is further established after Duffy declares his war by spraying a challenge on the wall of the Town Hall:

WAR IS DECLARED
ON DEFILERS OF TRUTH
AND ABUSERS OF AUTHORITY. (Jenkins [1988] 1995: 35)

By ensuring that there is a "declaration of war," that his intentions are "known" to the public, Duffy now sees his war methods as legitimate, and the means are thus to be justified by the end. Arguably, therefore, Duffy adheres to the realist view of warfare, seeing war as justified "when it serves the national interest, [and as] unjustified when it is against the national interest" (McMahan 1993: 385) – the "national interest" being, in this case, Duffy's intended gift of a new moral understanding to his society. At first, Duffy's war consists merely of breaking into the local library where he, along with his "army" of social misfits Helen Cooley, Mick Dykes, and Johnnie Crosbie, tears a page out of hundreds of books, a symbolical gesture meant to force people to face the truth about themselves, as Duffy believes that books are false representations of reality. The question of truth and its various representations in history and literature is thereby brought to the fore through Duffy's symbolic acts. Moreover, by putting human excrement on the hymn books in one of the local churches, Duffy believes he will remind the upper class owners of these books of their ordinary humanity, meaning that they should never regard themselves as superior to other people.

Strange as these acts of "war" may seem, they are "innocent" in that they do not involve hurting or killing a fellow human being. Yet it is soon implied that Duffy's war may eventually turn into something altogether more sinister. Setting himself up as a judge, as morally just, and *justified*, Duffy initially decides that his war makes deceit "necessary and permissible" (Jenkins [1988] 1995: 61). Moreover, he threatens his friend Cooley with a knife when she refuses to help him defile the hymn books because the smell disgusts her, and argues that "In war the penalty for refusing an order is death" (109). Duffy's moral ideals and his obsession with his war and its justification eventually leads to the novel's terrifying climax, when he bashes Crosbie's head in with a brick to prevent Crosbie from betraying him to the police. Even as he commits the foul crime, he imagines himself as "not an assassin or executioner but a deliverer" (155). This perspective can be interpreted in two ways. What the novel tells us straightforwardly is that Duffy sees himself as delivering Crosbie from the pain caused by a mortal tumour on his brain. Alternatively, however, Duffy may here view himself as the deliverer of his society: what harm is there in one death, of a mortally ill boy at that, when this one death will guard the general interests of the people in ensuring the success of Duffy's moral campaign? Although Duffy does not see his actions in specific political terms, but rather in a moral and religious light, his actions are comparable to various political or wartime strategies in which innocent lives are sacrificed in the name of the general Good. In a sense, therefore, Duffy's private sense of morality has been taken over by thoughts of public interest, although the action undertaken here does clearly originate in the fact that Duffy's initially well-intentioned idealism has become distorted into religious and social fanaticism.

Jenkins's use of a symbolism of war in *Just Duffy* obviously suggests the double morality of those who are involved in war. In this context, *Just Duffy* is highly relevant to discussions concerning the ethics of war, and thereby this novel by Jenkins is not merely a *Scottish* novel, but also has direct universal relevance in its intense questioning of the moral and/or political reasoning that is often used when nations declare war on other nations. Thus Duffy's war becomes an epitome for the supposedly "moral" killings committed in times of war, killings that are sanctioned and approved of by those who authorise them and by the populations of the nations involved. Duffy's little war therefore suggests a criticism of the moral inconsistencies of our world, where human relationships may seem decent and pleasant enough on the surface and within our local communities, but where wartime killings, injustice, and brutality are taking place all around us, and where we, the voters of governments, are inevitably implicated in actions carried out by the state. Moreover, Duffy's initial good intentions that ultimately lead to evil could reflect the more general issue of organisations that, in working for a cause they consider "good" and "just", would not hesitate to kill innocent people in order to achieve their mission. In this context, consequences of many organised activities of separatists are especially relevant. In this sense, *Just Duffy* carries a timeless moral message, and is as relevant to humanity today as it was when it was first published.

Author, Readership and Ethics of War

Just Duffy is certainly not only a story about the dangers of idealism, or a reminder of the moral inconsistencies of warfare, but also an *appeal* towards all humanity to reverse the process that characterises international relations and to prevent the disaster of a nuclear holocaust. Moreover, this appeal is meant to apply on both political and personal level in terms of readership. *Just Duffy* is one out of very few of Jenkins's novels set in Scotland where Scots dialogue is not used at all. The use of Standard English was, according to Jenkins, applied because he hoped that *Just Duffy* would have "universal appeal" (Jenkins 1997). Many aspects of the narrative, and the novel's publication date (1988), which means that it was written before the end of the Cold War and when the threat of nuclear war between the USA and the USSR was still present, reveal Jenkins concern over the production of nuclear weapons and the use of nuclear deterrence in international relations. Moreover, Jenkins's approach in *Just Duffy* to the question of armaments production and the nuclear threat carries the general message that we should not only question our politicians on the state's international and armaments policies, but that we are also largely responsible ourselves for allowing our governments to carry forward their various schemes for weapons production. Two quotations from the novel suffice to demonstrate how Jenkins, through the perspective of Duffy, lays the blame at the door of both private and public aspects of society:

the sunshine and pleasant air that morning caused the people in the main street to be cheerful and friendly. He [Duffy] received his share of neighbourly smiles. All the same, as he smiled back, he reflected that if nuclear war broke out and millions were killed it would not be governments and generals who were most to blame but ordinary, good-hearted, well-disposed people like these, who had let themselves be deceived by official lies and instinctive fears. It was as if deep down they did not really believe that the human race deserved to survive. Otherwise why did they look on with approval and complacency when scientists on their behalf made weapons more and more destructive and governments by their dishonesty and arrogance made the use of such weapons more and more likely? And why did they condemn as misguided fools or even traitors those who did protest? (Jenkins [1988] 1995: 41)

He had once heard someone declare on television that the greatest lie of the twentieth century was that it regarded human life as sacred. Politicians, ministers of religion, judges, everyone in authority, proclaimed that sanctity, and yet they knew that in their own lifetimes many millions of people had been killed in wars and many millions more had died of preventable disease and starvation. They knew also, and gave it their blessing, that new and more powerful weapons were being invented, able to lay waste the whole world. (Jenkins [1988] 1995: 149)

The narrative conveys a sense of impending disaster, stressing the need for a serious rethinking on the part of ordinary citizens and on the part of the state and the religious establishment.

Can the literature of writers like Jenkins raise our awareness of the moral consequences of international warfare, and, more specifically, can narratives like *Just Duffy* enlarge our understanding of the many ethical problems involved in both political and private responses to war? What kind of moral responsibility does the writer have towards his readership? For Jenkins, moral values and ethical issues are always central to his narratives, and this seems especially true of his consistent reference in his fiction to warfare and the pain, misery and casualties caused by war. On a general level, Jenkins approaches issues of war from a moral standpoint, clearly suggesting that the kind of morality that applies to normal, everyday, and private life should also be respected and adhered to on a political and public level. Or, as argued by Robert L. Holmes in his study of war and morality, "if one allows the relevance of morality to individual human conduct, it cannot consistently be denied to the conduct of states" (Holmes 1989: 22). War – as one aspect of state policy – should therefore not be swept under the carpet as irrelevant to moral and ethical discussion, even when war is "justified" as being necessary for defending the nation, or for helping other nations escape oppression. For Jenkins, the problem of war is first and foremost a moral and ethical one, rather than political – Jenkins claims that he is not a political writer, but rather motivated by the desire to regard his central issues on a moral level, and claims that "where some person would be regarding a thing politically, I wouldn't, I would regard it morally" (Jenkins 1997). In writing *Just Duffy* specifically as a "universal appeal", Jenkins has also conveyed to us his sense of moral responsibility as a writer, and has clearly written his appeal in the hope that he is a novelist who can make his audience listen to, acknowledge, and perhaps even make real, his desire for change.

Bibliography

Coady, C. A. J. 1993. "Politics and the problem of dirty hands" in Singer, Peter (ed.) *A Companion to Ethics*. Oxford: Blackwell. 373–83.

Dickson, Beth. 1988. "Recent Fiction: Familiar Themes of Good and Evil" in *Books in Scotland*, 28. 9–12.

Holmes, Robert L. 1989. *On War and Morality*. Princeton: Princeton University Press.

Jenkins, Robin. 1959. *Love is a Fervent Fire*. London: Macdonald.

—. [1956] 1988. *Guests of War*. Edinburgh: Scottish Academic Press.

—. [1978] 1994. *A Would-Be Saint*. Edinburgh: B&W Publishing.

—. [1988] 1995. *Just Duffy*. Edinburgh: Canongate.

—. 1997. Personal interview with Ingibjörg Ágústsdóttir, Fairhaven, Toward (21 March 1997).

Johnson, Peter. 1988. *Politics, Innocence, and the Limits of Goodness*. London and New York: Routledge.

McMahan, Jeff. 1993. "War and Peace" in Singer, Peter (ed.) *A Companion to Ethics*. Oxford: Blackwell. 384–95.

Norquay, Glenda. 1993. "Disruptions: The Later Fiction of Robin Jenkins" in Wallace, Gavin and Randall Stevenson (eds). *The Scottish Novel Since the Seventies: New Visions, Old Dreams*. Edinburgh: Edinburgh University Press. 11–24.

Finding Her Religion: The Search for Spiritual Satisfaction in Alan Warner's *Morvern Callar*

Jordana Brown

Nearly all of the critical attention that Alan Warner's novel *Morvern Callar* (1995) has received has painted its titular heroine as an amoral raver. This chapter seeks to remedy that misinterpretation, arguing instead that Morvern Callar is merely desperately in search of what contemporary Scotland cannot offer her: a spiritual identity.
Keywords: Alan Warner, rave culture, religion.

At the tail end of the twentieth century, an "extraordinary boom [took] place in Scottish literature" (Ritchie 1997: 2). New young writers, led by Irvine Welsh, whose *Trainspotting* was published by Secker and Warburg in 1993, produced a body of work that was surprising not only for its sudden appearance and its volume, but for its provenance. These were not Oxbridge educated Englishmen and -women producing familiar comedies of manners. These were voices from the outlying regions of the realm, writing, often from a rural setting, about some of British (and Western) society's most troubling issues. Drugs, crime, poverty, urbanisation, millennial angst: these were the themes of this new literature, along with some more familiar topics such as class and relationships. Not surprisingly, the media immediately sought to qualify this new literary phenomenon by both capitalising on and labelling it.

　　Coincidentally, at the same time "a new underground culture of music, drugs and lifestyle [...] became mainstream as corporate 'clubculture'" (Redhead 2000: xvi). Raves emerged out of the subculture and became widely popular "warehouse parties" marked by "drugs, sex, dancefloors, dealers, police and DJs", where young people took new drugs like ecstasy and, bathed in strobe lights, danced all night long to the repetitive beats of electronic music (Champion 1997: xiii). The emergence of this "rave generation" made the media's job much easier, and such disparate Scottish authors as Welsh, A.L. Kennedy and Duncan McLean were referred to variously as members of "the chemical generation", "the repetitive beat generation", or the "Scottish Beats", as no one in the media was able to "see beyond an identification with rave music" to what were in fact scathing exposés of the state of modern Scottish culture (Dale 2000: 131). Anthologies were quickly created that attempted to demonstrate how "this new fiction emerged and how it was influenced by – and in turn influenced – the fast changing club and popular culture of the late twentieth century" (Redhead 2000: xxv). Even some of the authors themselves seemed to lean into the rubric – Welsh came the closest to actually fitting it, with his book *Ecstasy* being "sure to cement Welsh's image as a poster boy for the rave scene" (Gold 1996: 22). (To be fair, it wasn't only Scottish authors who were grouped in this fashion. English writers like Nicholas Blincoe, Alex Garland and Jeff Noon and even Irish authors like Roddy Doyle were thrown into the mix in books such as *Repetitive Beat Generation* and *Disco Biscuits*.)

Not all authors were receptive, however, and arguably none rejected the label as vehemently as Alan Warner. He was hesitant to be interviewed for Steve Redhead's book, *Repetitive Beat Generation*, "feeling that he had little in common with many of the other writers" (Redhead 2000: 127), and he has criticised literary critics for having "all these cool buzzwords they think they need to constantly apply, but the intellectual level of response is relentlessly depressing" (Small 2000: 46). About his writing being classified as "representative of youth and/or rave culture [...] he is both scathing and despairing" (Dale 2000: 121), and he considers this grouping by the press to have the "implication by the way it was reported that none of these individual writers' work [...] could stand on its own. [...] My books are being reified into things called 'Alan Warner's post-Irvine Welsh books'" (Small 2000: 46). But perhaps most damningly, Warner has said "It always seemed to me that my treatment of that so-called 'rave culture' [...] was pretty cynical. I think there is a clear mocking of the ephemerality of it. [...] All the fashion and style mags that interviewed me [...] didn't consider for a second that I was actually attacking aspects of that culture" (Redhead 2000: 131–2). The categorisation of his debut novel, *Morvern Callar* (1995), as part of this body of "rave fiction" is not only wrong, it reflects a disastrous misreading of the book.

This mislabelling is but one symptom of a wider failure by critics to understand the subtle intricacies of *Morvern Callar*. Indeed, the quality of insight that critics offered in their reviews is shockingly bad and so pervasive that it forces the question, Did anyone even read the book? Responses range from the confused: "*Morvern Callar* [is] a funny exploration of groping adolescent relationships in rave culture which is set far from the city in rural Argyllshire (and has no swear words)" ("Scots Writers" 1997: 83) to the misguided, as in one that describes Morvern's conscience as "rudimentary" (Fiennes 1998: 34), and another that has Morvern "[r]efusing to mourn her boyfriend's not unexpected suicide" (Biswell 1995: 22). Sadly, the resulting film version, adapted from the novel and directed by Lynne Ramsay (and produced by Company Pictures in 2002), has brought little illumination to the minds of critics. One describes the related texts as a "book, and now a film, in which things happen apparently without effect" (Leigh 2002: 26). Another has the cinematic Morvern "[w]andering around dazed and confused through wild times and horrific events, her glazed eyes, inscrutable features and calm control suggest[ing] a Stepford Wife who has deliberately detached herself from the cares of an indifferent World" (Hunter 2002: 7). Even Ramsay herself seems mistaken when it comes to her source material, writing that the book "reads as one long existential monologue in which [Morvern] never attempts to explain her motivation" (Ramsay 2002: 9). But by far the most catastrophic misreading of the novel is the following:

Not even the discovery that her live-in lover has killed himself in a particularly gruesome way can penetrate Morvern's emotional anesthesia. [...] While Morvern's opacity is obviously meant to convey hip disaffection, the novel's matter-of-fact amorality quickly grows tiresome. Mr. Warner's true forte is his deadpan rendering of the idiosyncratic trappings of Morvern's morbid world. Unfortunately, these appalling but convincing details never add up to anything in particular; ultimately, understanding their significance is as impossible for us as it is for Morvern herself. (Kornreich 1997: 7.21)

Now, Warner's book is not wholly indecipherable; indeed, there are many reasons why Morvern is opaque, why she reacts the way she does to her boyfriend's suicide, why she appropriates his novel, why she leaves Scotland for the raves of Spain. The reasons include such heavy emotional concepts as grief, betrayal and hopelessness, but not one of them involves Morvern being a raver "who lives only for music and the next rave" ("Morvern Callar" 1997: 52). *Morvern Callar* is a much more serious, subtle and symbolic book than critics have portrayed, and within its pages Warner displays a deep ambivalence about many things, including the "wholesomeness" of rural Scottish towns and, as mentioned, rave culture. Seeing Morvern as a depraved club kid lacking in moral fibre is a superficial judgement based on her behaviour following the suicide of her boyfriend. A closer reading reveals that Morvern, far from being an empty opportunist or a shallow hedonist, is deeply unfulfilled by her life in Scotland, and that, rather than being wretched, she is desperately seeking salvation. *Morvern Callar* is not a bit of rave propaganda; it is a book that, in part, charts a young woman's quest for religion.

It is doubtful that Morvern has simply lost her faith and is looking to regain it, however. Her environment, which Warner only ever refers to as "the port" but is "clearly identified via railways, islands, hotels and folly as Oban", is a typically modern place in which nature is often concealed by capitalism and commotion (Gifford 1995: 14). There is no intimation that the port town has ever had a strong spiritual identity, a sign that modern life has bankrupted the spiritual. Rather than gathering in church, the port's inhabitants gather in The Mantrap, the local pub. In fact, in the few descriptions of the town that Warner provides (all filtered through Morvern's consciousness), a place of worship is only mentioned once, in passing: "Across the bay between the walls of St John's and Video Rental you saw snow on the mountains" (Warner 1995: 6). When St John's Episcopal Cathedral has become something the town's inhabitants look past, not to; when the church is nothing more than a means of establishing position in space, it is clear that religion is not a prevalent force.

The only other mention of a specifically Scottish religious building in the novel is the Tree Church. It is described by Morvern as a church grown out of trees: an "[e]vergreen hedge for the walls with arch-shaped holes cut in for windows. The gardeners have trimmed a big roof-shape and in the summertimes the door has a rose bower around" (36). Like much of Warner's fictional "port", it really exists (though Warner also patently intends its name to be a play on True Church). Located on the Glencruitten Estate, two miles southeast of Oban is a church

not built of stone, but rather of wood – living wood [...] constructed out of trees, shrubs and plants, carefully grown. It has hedge pews, tree walls, a shrubbery church doorway and a chancel area complete with raised garden altar. (Kilmore 2002)

But for Morvern, this place might as well be imaginary. She only knows of it because it is a part of her boyfriend's prize possession, the "model railway-set of his childhood village" that he constructed in the loft of their flat (Warner 1995: 37). Later, when Morvern winches her boyfriend's body up to the loft, the set becomes utilitarian, ironically serving as his temporary resting place. The railway layout sets the boyfriend apart because he has the time and money to invest in it – Morvern says "He's spent hundreds till it seems exactly like the real thing", though she can't understand why (37). The implication is that something so fanciful and frivolous as a church made of foliage can exist only in a town that fathers rich men and never in Morvern's working-class realist sphere, a sphere that is so narrow that Morvern has never even travelled the short distance to her boyfriend's home village, as if the psychological journey were too great.

Furthermore, even if Morvern had access to the church, it would not offer her succour, as it is a borrowed place, part of her boyfriend's experiences and memories. Therefore, though it would seem to be the perfect combination of the natural and the spiritual, at the beginning of the novel the Tree Church does not serve as a holy site, but, like St John's, as a landmark, in this case so Morvern can explain where her boyfriend came from.

Yet, conversely, spiritual hints abound in the narrative. Initially, the fact that Morvern's boss at the superstore is called Creeping Jesus offers hope that there is some sort of religious influence present. However, this hope is dashed with the revelation that the port's inhabitants use nicknames to show familiarity and to create a sense of intimacy. Warner has said that "[s]ome reviewers find this pretentious, but everyone has a nickname in my community" (Alvarez 1998: 18), and that he considers them "the manifestations of a very strong confident culture", tied up with the tradition of oral storytelling in the

Highlands (Dale 2000: 129). Thus, in addition to Creeping Jesus, The Golden Binman, Overdose, Shadow, Tit, Pongo, Melon, Sulee and The Shroud, among others, populate the town (Warner 1995: 15). One of the things that binds Morvern to her community is the fact that she recognises these people by their nicknames and likely also knows their provenance. But the source of Creeping Jesus's name is never revealed, and though he does "[look] down on [Morvern] through the mirrors" of his office, he is not a holy man, rather staring at her "over his beard in that perv way" (11–12).

Names again play a role when Morvern and her best friend Lanna seduce two boys the night after Morvern's boyfriend's suicide. They have "the names John and Paul, like disciples" (23). But their inclusion cannot be read as indicative of the presence of spirituality in the port. For one thing, they are not natives – their "Central Belt accents" give them away (17). For another, they are certainly not portrayed as religious men: instead of spiritual enlightenment, they bring Morvern and Lanna sexual excitement. Still, it is difficult to take the names of these two boys as accidental, especially since none of Morvern's other sexual partners, particularly her beloved boyfriend, is named at all. Of course, the fact that John and Paul were also Beatles is significant in its own way, in light of Morvern's dedication to music. Ultimately perhaps, these dead ends are symbolic not of religion itself, but of Morvern's desperate search for it: she feels its absence so deeply that she cannot help but see signs everywhere, just beyond reach. That these signs are empty of meaning demonstrates how aspiritual Morvern's existence truly is and highlights Scotland's religious bankruptcy and loss of a strong religious tradition.

There is another reason why the port is aspiritual, however, and that is because although he once existed there, God, in the form of Morvern's boyfriend, commits suicide on the first page of the book, and therefore the entire narrative takes place in his absence. There is much textual evidence that implies that Morvern's boyfriend was indeed God. The first and simplest indication of this connection is the way in which Morvern refers to him. While Lanna calls "Him by name", Morvern never does, only ever using the pronouns Him or His when she mentions him, but always with the "H" capitalised (7). Furthermore, Morvern does seem almost to have worshipped her boyfriend. However, in a book rife with unusual grammatical inventions and creative punctuation, this is not enough to create a definitive link between the dead boyfriend and God.

Fortunately, there is more to go on, and the key is to understand that Alan Warner has written himself into his novel as Morvern's boyfriend. This is important because if Warner, like every author, is the god of his own book – in that he creates the world within it, populates it and watches over it – and Warner is also the boyfriend, then, with a bit of syllogistic logic, the boyfriend is therefore also God.

Creating a link between Warner and the boyfriend is easy. They possess many superficial similarities (including the fact that they are both writers), and cumulatively, these similarities prove that it is no accident that Warner made the boyfriend in his own image. Morvern tells Lanna's grandmother, Couris Jean, that her boyfriend "grew up in the village at the far end of the pass, just beyond the power station. His father owned that hotel at the top of the stairs above the railway there" (36). In the press notes that were written to accompany the release of the film of *Morvern Callar* in the United States, Warner states, "I was born in the rural town of Oban on the West Coast of Scotland [...] My parents were hoteliers and I grew up in a 44 bedroom hotel" (Warner 2002). Despite being born in Oban, however, Warner grew up in "the village of Connel", which more closely matches the geography of the book (Thomson 1997). But more importantly, when asked why he killed the novel's main male character on the first page, Warner says: "I wanted to kill the male! Right away, I'm dead. Me. The big guy who usually says, 'Here's this girl Morvern and she does this and she does that.' I zap myself in the first sentence and that's me out of the book" (Donald 1995: 10). Clearly, Warner sees himself as the boyfriend, because when he was asked in an interview if there were a real-life model for Morvern, he said, "Of course [...] she was a girlfriend" (Thomson 1997). Following this logic, if Warner is the god/author of the novel, and the boyfriend within the novel is Warner, then we can read the boyfriend as God.

Therefore, by having Morvern's boyfriend commit suicide, Warner has, in one stroke, killed off three ideological figures: the male protagonist, the author himself and God. This is why later, when

Morvern takes the boyfriend's book and puts her name on it, she has done more than appropriate a book. By making her boyfriend's novel her own, Morvern casts off the controlling influence of the boyfriend/God and takes the reins and starts dictating the path of her own life.

There are two ways of looking at the fallout of the boyfriend's death and its impact on Morvern's spirituality. One is that the boyfriend/God has sinned in slitting his throat. Therefore it is not surprising that Morvern denies him a "Christian burial", as Warner calls it, choosing instead to dispose of his body in the Highland wilds (Donald 1995: 10). Nor is it strange that, in the absence of God, Morvern is having trouble finding religion in her life.

The more likely interpretation of the boyfriend's suicide is that he is a Christ figure who sacrifices himself for Morvern's sake. This theory gains strength when we consider that there is very little reason for his suicide. From all accounts, the relationship "He" and Morvern had was a happy and decent one. They had been together for five years, and when asked what her foster parents think of her boyfriend, Morvern says, "they know he's good to me" (Warner 1995: 38). Her foster-father's response to the news that the boyfriend is gone is also telling: "Ah Morvern. All the love in the world rising up leaving just hate" (44). And in his tender suicide note, the boyfriend writes, "I love you Morvern; feel my love in the evenings in the corners of all the rooms you will be in" (82). In that same note, he also displays a shocking degree of resistance to the idea of death: "I don't want to leave this life which I love so much. I love this world so much I have to hold onto this chair with both hands" (82). He seems reasonably happy with his life and his relationship, he has enough money so he doesn't have to work, and he has the gift of creative expression, as represented by his novel.

Critics have presented various theories as to why the boyfriend kills himself, but because it happens on the first page of the novel, and the reader is never given any concrete background information about "Him", it is difficult – if not impossible – to pick one. Could it be that his guilt at having betrayed Morvern by sleeping with her best friend Lanna pushed him over the edge? Hardly likely, as the note intimates that he knows his suicide is just another, bigger betrayal of Morvern's trust. Is it that the death of his father, also referred to in the suicide note, and the subsequent inheritance was too much responsibility? Possibly. But in the end, the only reason given for the suicide is the amorphous one provided by the boyfriend himself, in the note he leaves behind: "I have decided to play this prank on myself. Keep me on my toes [...] things became too cushy for this oldest of chancers" (82). In the absence of a concrete reason, however, it is equally possible to see his suicide as a sacrifice for Morvern's redemption.

It is clear early in the novel that Morvern's existence does not hold much hope. Though she's only 21, she has worked at the town's superstore for eight years: "Cause of tallness I had started part-time with the superstore when thirteen", which in turn ruined her "chances at school doing every evening and weekend", "so when fifteen or sixteen you go full-time at the start of that summer and never go back to school" (10). Without an education or any means of increasing her income, Morvern has no hope of ever escaping her job at the superstore. She herself acknowledges that she is "stuck in that job for ever" (9).

Depressingly, Morvern receives a slew of signals from her community that serve to highlight that she is trapped. Red Hanna, her foster-father, is four months away from the retirement and freedom he spent his life working overtime to earn, but only feels "empty"; "I'm fifty-five: a wasted life", he says (44, 45). In his foster-daughter he sees nothing but the same bleak future: "heres you, twenty-one, a forty-hour week on slave wages for the rest of your life; even with the fortnight in a resort theres no much room for poetry" (44). In a similar vein, one night in The Mantrap a local tells Morvern that the glitter embedded in her "special knee" from a childhood accident (which is the single thing that makes her different from all the other high school dropouts working dead-end jobs and represents her hope of someday escaping their shared fate) "would sink deeper and go invisible the older" she gets (17, 19). A worried Morvern responds, "I don't want the glitter to go away" (19). Here is the ultimate indication that staying where she is and growing old will rob Morvern of her uniqueness.

Furthermore, it certainly seems as though the boyfriend believes he is sacrificing himself for Morvern's sake, though he couldn't have predicted to what degree she would take advantage of all he left behind. His suicide note offers ample evidence: "I was always looking for peace but here, you take it instead", he exhorts (82). The irony is not only that the boyfriend clearly thinks he is helping Morvern by killing himself and thereby thrusting her into grief and despair, but that despite the fact that God-the-boyfriend is dead, he continues to control Morvern's life. At his death, the boyfriend left her not only a slew of unopened Christmas presents and his unpublished novel (which she appropriates by replacing his name with hers), but a balance of £6,839 in his bank account. Though Morvern chooses what to do with this money, the shadow of the boyfriend/God follows and, to some degree, influences her every action. It may be his money that allows her to flee her bleak future, his death that allows her rebirth in finding both her spiritual home and her self, but she is compelled to honour "His" memory and "His" death by escaping her home in the first place. Andrew Biswell writes that the boyfriend's "shade hangs over the novel as if to remind us that the death of the author is not necessarily accomplished by mere physical decease" (Biswell 1995: 22). No matter how far she runs, she cannot escape her boyfriend's influence, and there is no intimation that she wants to.

Upon coming across the money in the boyfriend's bank account, Morvern considers what she could do with it:

> With that kind of money there were cassettes you could get from the mail list and you could send away for bobby-dazzler clothes out the catalogue and get extra driving lessons on top the ones He'd already paid for. (Warner 1995: 55)

However, without seriously pursuing any of those other options, she chooses escape: "I walked straight to the travel agent" (55). Jenny Turner writes, "Morvern will be able to buy herself just as many Silk Cuts and Southern Comforts, clothes, CDs, beauty products and holidays as a girl could ever want. And she certainly does so. But what is really important about the money is that it gives her the wherewithal to escape" (Turner 1995: 23). It was the right choice – almost immediately after leaving the port, Morvern is rewarded spiritually for deciding to get out. Though her first stop in Spain is the hotbed of iniquity and noise that is a Youth Med holiday, once she flees to the countryside, she quickly comes into contact with a much warmer and more elaborate strain of religion than could ever exist in the port town. In that "resort so much smaller than where I'd been", a look around assures Morvern that she is no longer home:

Where you would expect a jumble of hills and a circular folly above a port: none. Where you would expect piers with a seawall between and an esplanade of hotels beyond: none. Where you would expect stone houses hunched round a horseshoe of bay with The Complex tucked away round a back: none. The resort I was looking at was really another place. (Warner 1995: 151)

One of the first things Morvern does after finding solitude is one of her own personal rituals, a typically Morvern-esque rebirth: using a "peel-off-mask-with-cucumber", she peels "the thin film back away from [her] forehead and down" and then throws "the mask of [her] face shape into the toilet and [jerks] the flush" (152). Having cleansed herself and shed her old skin, Morvern is prepared to experience Spanish culture and religion.

Later, it becomes apparent that she has arrived just in time for some unnamed Catholic ceremony. Silently, and without any hindrance from the locals, Morvern joins "the procession of people on the inland road across the dry places towards the villages of Poor Jesus and St Michael In Excelsis" (153). Though there is humour in their verbatim translation into English, the names of the Spanish towns carry obvious religious significance and serve to highlight the differences in spirituality between Spain and Morvern's utilitarian, commercial "port town". The experience is deeply foreign as well as being profound and spiritually affecting to Morvern; the "burning torches", "little girls in black lace" and "white chapel" at the top of a hill covered with olive trees could never exist in the port town, and therein lies their appeal (153). The anonymity of the town, the namelessness of the ritual and the calm acceptance of the villagers underscore the ubiquity of religion in Spain. This could be any town, any fiesta; it is an oft-repeated and all-inclusive routine of religious observance.

The most significant icon for Morvern, however, is the "pale model of the virgin saint girl" that is carried on a throne from the top of the hill to the harbour, with the whole town following behind (154). After being blessed in a seaside church, the model is launched out to sea against a background of fireworks and set on fire by remote control. The next day, Morvern swims out and finds "her burned face looking up at us from the seabed below" (156). Obviously, Morvern sees herself in the saint statue. When the model first passes her by, Morvern notices that "[s]he was as tall as me", and later, in the church, which is made out of blue glass and the hull of a ship, Morvern thinks that "[w]ith the light filtering in you were already drowned and on the bottom of the deep sea with the living people above" (154, 155). Having been set adrift by situations beyond her control, she is undergoing a rebirth, and as indicated above, has already ironically predicted the ritual by ceremonially flushing the mask of her own face down the toilet.

Invigorated and spiritually refreshed, Morvern, having spent all her money, is forced to return home, stopping in London where – during a debauched night with the publisher of "her" book – she has her next religious experience, evidence that she is attempting to bring her newfound spirituality back home with her. In the early dawn hours, Morvern, editor Tom and book designer Susan come upon a Catholic church, and Morvern leads them in. Not only does she no longer see past churches, she even feels comfortable enough to go inside. While Tom and Susan are more interested in snogging, Morvern shows that she is still a neophyte when it comes to religion. She sees a parishioner (though, tellingly, not one from London: when the woman admonishes Tom and Susan for kissing in a church, "it was in a foreign language", yet another clue that Britain and its native-born are wholly without religion) cross herself with holy water and copies the gesture, then watches "the old woman [to] see what knee you genuflect on" before she has a "little prayer" (165). She is earnest in her desire for spirituality, but remains unschooled in its practices.

Later, back in her flat in the port, Morvern keeps trying. Having put a bit of religious music on the CD player, she "got down on the polished floorboards and tried hard with a wee prayer", but she is farther from the influence of Spain's Catholicism, and it does not go smoothly: "I suddenly jumped up and paraded about all agitated" (174). After she changes the music, "the praying went an awful lot better" (174). Obviously, at this point, religion is still not something that comes easily to Morvern, and clearly, the farther north she travels, the more hostile to religion the environment becomes. Shortly afterwards, she heads to The Mantrap to find Red Hanna. Despite the fact that The Mantrap is not a church, there are "a couple ministers in shiny sou'westers and shepherds' coats" standing outside, admonishing folk to "Abandon hope all you who enter" (179). Morvern calls back "I always do", but at least now it seems as though she actually does have hope, a testament to how fruitful her short sojourn in Spain truly was (179).

The sudden appearance of two holy men in the port points to two things. One is that because Morvern is feeling more comfortable spiritually, she is now seeing religious signs everywhere, including in her own heathen hometown, and this time, the signs are real, not just empty promises. This raises the possibility that there have always been ministers in the town but that Morvern, lacking spiritual fibre, has simply not been able to see them. The other implication raised by the ministers' appearance is the superficially hopeful sign that there is indeed someone looking out for the spiritual health of the community. However, by trying to stop people from going for a drink in the pub, the ministers reveal themselves to be preaching a forbidding and restrictive religion, nothing like what Morvern experienced in Spain. Her flippant reply demonstrates that she has no respect for their brand of religion – they are going about it the wrong way, as she already knows from her fledgling understanding of Catholicism.

As it turns out, however, religion for Morvern is more than Catholic traditions and ceremonies. When her boyfriend's second planned windfall (£44,771.79, the inheritance from "His" father's death) arrives and she can leave the port to take up more permanent residence in Spain, she is immediately able to see the spiritual in her environment. She considers the path from her hired apartment to the beach front to be "like out the Bible under the fierceness of such sun", and she sees "a burning bush blazing away" one morning (190, 211). Despite the fact that she goes into churches and sees ministers in her home country, it is only when Morvern is in Spain that she makes these kinds of references, yet more evidence that Spain overflows with spirituality and that Morvern bathes in it, absorbing it and – in the ultimate expression of her newfound comfort with her own spiritual identity – makes it her own, creating her own rituals that she practices with more dedication than the most devout believer. Living an extremely ordered and, in its own way, ascetic life, she shaves her legs every morning before doing her nails and sunbathing on her balcony. She eats all meals at the same restaurant before heading to the beach to swim, and the waitress knows her well enough to bring her "the usual breakfast" (191). She talks to nearly no one. And finally, she dances. Indeed, it is the infamous Balearic raves – the same raves that the media latched onto as a means of categorising this novel and others – that are the religious and healing experience for Morvern, and all of the ceremonial ablutions she enacts every day really only serve to prepare her for her evening entertainment: "You have an all-over tan so's you can wear the real shorter stuff at the raves" (190).

Once inside the "rave catacombs", Morvern takes refuge with the other true believers, abandoning herself to the "huge journey in that darkness" (202, 203). Like the persecuted early Christians who secretly practised their religion from the safety of catacombs, Morvern has found in the raves not only a safe place, but a ritualistic spirituality of her own. Baptised with the mineral water she continually tips over her head, Morvern dances to "DJ Sacaea['s] swirly bass patterns", losing herself in the music, the lasers, the anonymous bodies, and the sweat and heat they produce (202). Clearly, however, Morvern is not at the raves for the same reasons others are. She shuns attention, male or otherwise, as at the restaurant she frequents: when "two young men [manoeuvre] from a further away table to beside" her, she quickly gets up and leaves, knowing that "a plagueing was coming from those two" (201). She goes alone to the rave, not with a group ready to party, and inside, the music makes it impossible to talk to anyone. This is not to say that she has no physical contact. Rather, she willingly joins the bodies sliding against each other on the dance floor, but only because it is "part of our dance. If the movement wasnt in rhythm it would have changed the meaning" (203). Morvern will even cuddle or share kisses with anyone, but the moment a "male hand [slides] up and [starts] to go a bit dirtyish", she pulls away (204). Plainly, Morvern takes the raves very seriously and, with all the rituals she undergoes to prepare for them, they are a very sombre (though not sober) experience for her.

It is within the rave too that Morvern commits the ultimate act of religious confirmation and sacrifices her body to her faith: "You didn't really have your body as your own, it was part of the dance, the music, the rave", she says (203). At this point the conversion is finished, and Morvern herself has become Godlike. The pick-'n'-mix symbolism is all there: like Moses, she sees a burning bush; like the Virgin Mary, she surrenders her body. By removing her boyfriend's/God's name from his novel and thereby gaining authorship of her own life, she has substituted herself for God, and it's a nice fit. Later, as proof that Morvern has attained spiritual supremacy, Warner mimics the saintly procession that was Morvern's first experience of Spanish religion. Awaking in an orchard the morning after her ultimate corporeal sacrifice in the rave, she sees "a scarlet speck moving over the dry earth by the irrigation sluice: it was one of my broken nails being carried away by ants" (213). Now Morvern is the saintly figure, and a relic of her body is carried in an ironically reduced procession.

The final spiritual experience in Morvern's conversion takes her full-circle back to the Tree Church that was so long a symbol of her dead boyfriend's hometown through the model he made. Poor again and back from years spent in Spain, Morvern takes shelter from the snow, "does a genuflection" immediately upon entering the church, then prays briefly and dozes a little, showing not only that she is able to enter a church near the port town but that she is comfortable enough with herself, her spirituality and her memories to seek out and spend part of a night in her boyfriend's church (228). She has found a way to merge with "Him"/God, and she has been reborn, has found religion and is able to bring it back with her to the pagan port town.

In one last piece of religious contrivance, Morvern returns to the port pregnant with "the child of the raves", as she phrases it, which is a significant detail when we take into account that the raves were for her a redemptive force (229). Considering both her new godlike status and her strange reversal in sexual licentiousness (Morvern's aforementioned refusal to engage in anything remotely sexual in Spain comes after a burst of nearly non-stop sexual activity in the first half of the book), it is easy to make the leap that this was a virgin birth. Furthermore, since Morvern did have a long-term relationship with

God (in the guise of the boyfriend), it is not so hard to believe that he would choose her to mother his child. This idea is taken to its natural conclusion in *These Demented Lands*, Warner's semi-sequel to *Morvern Callar*. The book is positively awash with religious symbolism – from *Psalm 23*, the name of a doomed ferry, to the Christ-like figure of the Aircrash Investigator, crucified on a propeller – as though it magnifies and explodes the earlier book's subtle religious subtext. So it's not a surprise when, against the backdrop of an apocalyptic rave full of smoke and flame, Morvern's millennial baby is born in "the rear of a Volvo hatchback that's been filled with hay", attended by the "three wise kings" (The Argonaut, the [Devil's] Advocate and the Aircrash Investigator), who "followed the light in the eastern sky" to be there (Warner 1997: 210, 212). The baby is even referred to as "the Messiah" (212). The only marked difference between this neo-Nativity and the original one that occurred 2,000 years earlier is that Morvern's child is a girl. The message is that as a result of the death of the male God as guiding force, and following Morvern's Iberian conversion and sacrifice, it is now females who are equipped and empowered to save humanity.

In the end, there is overwhelming evidence that Warner meant his novel to contain a rich religious subtext and that it is Morvern's "transubstantiation" that has fooled the critics. Though on the outside she may look like a raver, a morally vacant pleasure-seeker, in fact, throughout the book's narrative, she is miraculously transformed into a spiritually whole individual, devout in her own way. Rather than being either a reprehensible and amoralistic novel or a tract that captured the spirit of the mid-1990s rave scene, *Morvern Callar* is an ultimately hopeful fable about a girl who, with the help of luck or fate or some divine intervention, found religion. With her holy child at her side, Morvern seems destined to be a new St Columba, bringing sacred healing to a country that is spiritually adrift.

Bibliography

Alvarez, Maria. 1998. "An Ear for the Girls" in *Telegraph Magazine* (16 May 1998). 18.

Biswell, Andrew. 1995. "Mortal Remains" in *Times Literary Supplement* (31 March 1995). 22.

Champion, Sarah. 1997. "Introduction" in Champion, Sarah (ed.) *Disco Biscuits: New Fiction from the Chemical Generation*. London: Hodder and Stoughton. xiii–xvi.

Dale, Sophy. 2000. "An Interview With Alan Warner" in *Edinburgh Review* 103. 121–32.

Donald, Ann. 1995. "The Death of the Author" in *The List* (10–23 February 1995). 10.

Fiennes, William. 1998. "Mortal on Hooch" in *London Review of Books* (30 July 1998). 34.

Gifford, Douglas. 1995. "Genres of Defiance and Despair" in *Books in Scotland* 54. 14–17.

Gold, Kerry. 1996. "The Tartan Hordes" in *LA Weekly* (18 October 1996). 22.

Hunter, Allan. 2002. "Second Coming Is Poetry in Motion" in *Scotland on Sunday* (4 August 2002). 7.

Kilmore & Oban Church of Scotland. [Online]. Available from: <http://www.oban-church.com/sisters/htm> [4 November 2002].

Kornreich, Jennifer. 1997. "Morvern Callar" in *The New York Times* (18 May 1997). 7–21

Leigh, Danny. 2002. "About a Girl" in *The Guardian* (5 October 2002). 26.

MacIntyre, Lorn. 1995. "Death Explodes the Rural Myth" in *The Herald* (18 February 1995). 4.

"Morvern Callar" in *Kirkus Reviews* (1 January 1997). 52.

Ramsay, Lynne. 2002. "From Oban to Cannes" in *The Observer* (6 October 2002). 9.

Redhead, Steve. 2000. *Repetitive Beat Generation*. Edinburgh: Rebel Inc.

Ritchie, Harry. [1996] 1997. "Introduction" in Ritchie, Harry (ed.) *Acid Plaid: New Scottish Writing*. New York: Arcade Publishing. 1–4.

"Scots Writers Spurn Their Neighbours" in *The Economist* (26 April 1997). 83.

Small, Chris. 2000. "The Great Escape" in *Product* (December/January 2000). 46–47.

Thomson, David. 2002. *Deeply Aroused*. [Online]. Available from: <http://www.salon.com/sex/turn_on/2002/09/12/morvern/> [16 October 2002].

Thomson, Graham. 1997. "Interview with Alan Warner" in *The Barcelona Review*. <http://www.barcelonareview.com/arc/r2/eng/warnerint.htm>. (4 November 2002)

Turner, Jenny. 1995. "Fairy Lights" in *London Review of Books* (2 November 1995). 23.

Warner, Alan. 1995. *Morvern Callar*. London: Jonathan Cape.

—. 1997. *These Demented Lands*. London: Jonathan Cape.

—. 2002. "Notes From the Author", Preliminary Press Notes for the American release of the film version of *Morvern Callar*.

Songs of the Village Idiot: Ethnicity, Writing and Identity

Suhayl Saadi

Self-definition through the act of writing fiction is complicated for an ethnic minority writer in Scotland by issues of language, voice and cultural identity. Employing narrative structures that deliberately express that complexity through multiple time-frames and voices can undercut still-powerful colonial mythologies, and present an alternative paradigm of the inner life of social minorities, by means of an allusive, transcendental or musical approach to the poetics and politics of fiction in a multi-ethnic society.
Keywords: Ethnic minority writing, literature, music, narration, voice, Sufism.

In some ways, whenever I write, I am posing questions of self-definition. I do not mean this simply in the narrow "identity politics" sense, but rather in the sense that literature represents an exploration of the spatial and temporal place of humans in the order of things, an aspect of which nexus might be called "society".

Much of this dynamic of self-definition concerns the interaction between the interior and the exterior, a process of quest for underlying realities through a kind of antinomian pantheism. Some of this entails a reaching downwards to the substrate and outwards across wavering social barriers – artificial constructs which too often have been confused with petrified, geographical features – in order to explore and evince the inherent interconnectedness of culture. Faith, that need to construct a raison d'être for being and to connect with a greater whole, involves an attempted slippage of consciousness, an elision from the individual to the whole that at root is not dissimilar to certain processes which occur in literature, in the fictional architecture that is being (re-)constructed by each reader, and in the partly-internalised compositional techniques that are the stock-in-trade of the writer. The transfiguration of literature into logos.

In a sense, both reader and writer begin from the outside, from something akin to Muriel Spark's sense of permanent, indefinable exile, what she has called "a constitutional exile", or "restlessness". In this context, I wish to discuss three of my stories, in an attempt to evoke the processes that were/are at work within and between each, particularly in relation to the interaction between the literature that a writer produces and the society in which a writer lives and of which his or her works form a miniscule, yet singular, part.

Taking the third party narrative voice (the voice against which James Kelman has so effectively inveighed) and using it in ways which beguile and subvert the structures that dominate the societal mind, which expose these as pliable, malleable, deceptive, and as just one constructed set of voices among many, just one scale of notes in an infinitely musical universe, can surely be as powerful a tool as writing in any demotic. I know, because I've worked within both literary styles. It is probably no accident that one of the strengths of my writing is sometimes thought to reside in the manifold voices through which it "speaks" (Abdel-Moneim Aly 2001). In itself, this represents an ongoing refusal to allow the generic group of white, middle-class English writers to monopolise referential thought. I am Wandering Jew rather than imperial adventurer. I appropriate, dissect, dissimulate and re-invent voices, some of which might be imagined as belonging exclusively to one particular social class or ethnic group. It is a syncretic, and at times ecstatic, process, which through thematic coefficients, tends somehow to turn the constituent voices back to the physical, and therefore potentially democratic, moot of song.

The three stories all derive from the same period in my life, i.e. 2000–2002. This is important, not merely in the obvious chronological sense of the writer being at a certain age and in specific circumstances with regard to other individuals in his life and the broader society around him, but also in the sense in which fiction initiates what A.L. Kennedy has called "conversations in the mind". It might be said that such interactions are based on previous conversations between a particular mind and an elliptical vision of society, and possibly also onthe initially subconscious anticipation of "conversations" yet to come.

These stories differ in some respects from the high-octane, hallucinogenic, urbanised fiction of, for example, *The Burning Mirror* (2001), through which I have attempted to delineate some aspects of possible "Asian Scots" thought-experience. There is a slowing of the pace, due in part to their length: *The Saelig Tales* and *The Spanish*

House are novellas, while *The Aerodrome,* at around fifteen thousand words, is a long short story. But the change of pace also resides in the fact that they are situated on a different plane, both literally in their largely rural settings, and figuratively in their possible origin. They arose partly as the result of a desire on my part to explore other voices (although, to be accurate, this is hardly a new feature: conversations over the silver wall with the "daughters of the city", as in the ancient tale, have always formed the discourse from which much of my art springs), and they are also part of an ongoing attempt to (re)-construct the world using varying, sometimes quantal, sensibilities. In addition, there was the practical reason that they were written at a time when I was limbering up to begin another novel, in consequence of which the pace and timbre of the stories is much more akin to the novel than to short (especially urban) fiction.

Nonetheless, the three stories differ hugely from one another in theme, characters, setting and length. Partly they represent the playing out of an obsession with fictional assonance and etymology. Firstly, this process occurs in the literal sense of following the possible names of mountains, rivers, songs and cities (some of the loci where societies are formed and exist, and through which ultimately literature comes to be written), many of which can be traced back to ancient, and sometimes surprising, sources. However, there is also a less linear dynamic that might be likened to weaving a carpet, using symbols and processes ingrained in the hands of the weaver, techniques which have become internalised and hence, to some extent, forgotten. The threads converge at points, sometimes anticipated, sometimes not, which are scattered through various layers of the carpet. As I weave, I learn. Every word I write is an act of re-discovery. And there lies the joy.

By definition, these processes are never exclusive; at the risk of reiterating the banal, it should be stated that all writers do it differently, drawing on complex underlying agendas stemming from their various life experiences, belief systems or moral framework(s), the need to feed and clothe themselves etc., all of which are inherently fluid. So Zadie Smith's London melting-pot narratives will differ from Jim "Kalashnikov" Kelman's white working-class Glasgow, which will differ again from, say, the visionary, trans-national work of Patricia Duncker (which is expressionist and, at times, mystical and illuminative) or from the emotionally intense and deeply poetic writings of Aamer Hussein, or from the heightened, perceptive realism of Jackie Kay.

In Scotland, while there is a now venerable tradition of writing stemming from white working-class experience, work by those from black and minority ethnic groups, partly because of the demographics of migration and socio-economic class, remains at an early stage. From the evidence of various anthologies and the recent output of certain writers, I believe that this situation is gradually changing. Until such processes reach some kind of fruition, however, literary culture cannot be said truly to approximate to Scottish society, any more than does the currently all-white Scottish Parliament or most of the other power structures of the state.

The Saelig Tales

The Saelig Tales, a novella, opens on a summer's evening in the walled back garden of a vicarage in southern England. The vicar is sitting at the table there when another man, who appears to be a gardener, enters through the garden gate and joins him. It transpires that this gardener is John Rotherfield, the vicar's old friend (both men are in their seventies). This becomes the framing narrative for three textually-separate internal narratives.

The Saelig Tales is partly an exploration of the nature of story-telling and the elusiveness of objective "truth" as expressed through narration. Language is of this planet, it consists of a set of symbols which themselves cannot approximate to anything beyond human perception. Yet somehow, as the Scottish writer/intellectual, Alastair Reid, elucidated in his Edinburgh Festival lecture in 2003, these symbols are able to signify regions beyond themselves, regions that stretch toward the cold, blue light of infinity. Much of my prose tends at times to strive for the poetic, not simply in the acoustic, sibilant sense, but in the figurative manner of song and storytelling being a form of two-way communal transfiguration. Behind every writer, there is a composer; within every reader there is a musician.

I spent part of my childhood living in a Lincolnshire village, so to some extent the geography of rural England is the geography of my mind. This aspect of Britain, the rural, the "old", the essentially pre-industrial, has in the last twenty years become subsumed into commuter land for millions of (mainly white) bourgeoisie and petty-bourgeoisie, the sources of whose wealth lie in the multi-ethnic cities. In some senses, rural England, rich or poor, is perceived by many as a white enclave. Within this model, there has occurred the transformation from a reduced-but-active farming community to a mixture of impersonal agribusiness and bucolic pastiche. Sometimes, it is portrayed as a mythic never-never-land of tolling bells and bicycling vicars, a pristine England that "existed" before mass emigration from the New Commonwealth changed forever the demographic complexion of this country.

I love the countryside, not just in the sentimental manner of the jaded town-dwelling escapee, but because some of my happiest memories, moments of play, day-dream and story-making, lie within its frame. Those amber vistas that are no more! The mindset of childhood, a five mile-radius of infinite possibilities, an awareness of the ubiquity of magic in the diurnal, is very much akin to what is aimed at by the writer; a particularising of the general, an intense, almost musical close-up of the universe. When I use the image of childhood here, I am thinking of the individual experience, an awareness of the immanence of magic, which in spite of everything remains the great strength of our consciousnesses. Those things in our individual consciousness which we consider to be somehow objective, rational, unaffected, actually derive from transmutational nodes of whose existence we are pretty much unaware. It is partly to elucidate such nodes that I write. (Of course, I do not believe that such an analogy can be extrapolated to whole cultures or groups of peoples, as in discredited Western Romantic theories of cultures or nations having "childhoods" or "adolescences".)

And so, through the interleaving fiction of *The Saelig Tales*, I lay claim to rural England. It is mine, because I have written it. Performed out of love, this is an intensely political act, the significance of which I well recognise. I am no class-impressed South Asian scribbler arriving in this country to dwell as a supercilious, yet eternally craven, visitor. I am not the wandering subject with a colonised hindbrain. Indeed, in this aspect, I am not wandering at all. In the dream-a-rama sense, rural England – its landscape, its people – is mine.

The first internal narrative in *The Saelig Tales* documents the words of an Anglo-Saxon monk, Aelfrith of Wurth, who in the face of impending Viking invasion decides to secrete, in the structure of the unusual church which he has built, a mass of parchment relating to his lifelong itinerant quest of compiling the songs and customs of his own land. This section switches between first-person and third-person narrative and builds to the ecstatic appearance of the "golden woman" and her sensual dance in the bell-tower with the monk's assistant, the novice Aethelfrith, and to the illuminatory, pantheistic vision which this unification renders to the monk (the scribe) as he looks on.

The very English Home Counties setting of the frame-story, that kind of anaesthetised, church bell ringing, de-bestialised version of D.H. Lawrence which has become so prevalent in so-called "popular" fiction as well as through the potted aspidistra crime genre of Agatha Christie and others (John Bull in a Barbour jacket), begins to be undermined and its complacency to be eroded by the seeding of complementary histories, of other possible truths. This sense of unease seeps into the summer vicarage garden as we learn of the vicar's betrayal of his best friend, many years earlier.

Yet the undermining of the complacency of the construct occurs also through opening the doors to the mythical-esoteric and by the sudden unheralded changes in voice which maqam the piece.[1] The effect of all this is to begin to open up a fresh dialectic, where not only the roots of those qualities which are traditionally considered as being "English" are exposed and brought into question, but also the very nature and dynamic of logical-analytical narrative itself is deconstructed, perhaps not so much in the Barthian sense as through a mediaeval or Sufi-like sensibility. This is pursued further, in the frame-story, through the interaction between John Rotherfield and

---

[1] The word *maqam* means "place" or "situation". In the context of music it refers to the specific Oriental tone scales, of which there is an enormous variety in Arabic music due to the vast range of different microtones, or else to a special kind of musical suite, consisting of improvisations based on certain standard rules of performance and aesthetics.

Sufi mystics during the collapse of the Ottoman Empire in the closing days of the First World War, and the process by which this interleaves with his quest for aesthetic perfection as personified by his lover, Caroline.

The second narrative is an Elizabethan period story of the bewitching of an effete aristocrat by a miller's daughter and the gradual transformation of this mutually exploitative relationship to genuine human love, and it is told partly in Elizabethan-style verse. And this is a feature of *The Saelig Tales*; the style of the language changes in response to shifts in the context. When we return to the framing narrative, the voice of a gardener has altered from its southern English peasant burr to an educated but gone-to-seed middle-class accent, and this raises the suggestion of dissimulation, of fakery, on his part and on that of the overall narrator. We move from a late 1960s time-frame that is still, in 2005 CE, broadly recognisable as contemporary, to a tenth-century one, then back again to the 1960s, but with allusions to the First World War and to the capture of John Rotherfield by Turkish forces, then to the late sixteenth-century story, then back to Rotherfield's physical and spiritual journey through eastern Anatolia as the Great War ends in chaos, with White Russians, Armenians, Young Turks, prisoners-of-war and others all forming part of the narrative.

Then, for the third internal narrative, we're in a nineteenth-century village on the south coast of England, with the story of a curate who, deep in a summer's night, encounters smugglers looking to secrete a strange cargo in his church. As the frame narrative evolves, a story set during the protagonists' youth among the oxbows of the old river also unfolds, a story that involves the conflicting trajectories of their various loves. The vicar and Rotherfield loved the same woman, Caroline, and the story is one of betrayal and redemption (or the lack of it). A nexus is revealed between Caroline and the mythical woman who appears in various guises in each of the internal stories, tales which are being read, during the night in the vicarage garden, by Vicar Synnot to John Rotherfield from a book that he had purchased a short time before, in a house sale. The theme is that of spiritual progression towards a kind of enlightenment, or at least towards a state of greater awareness. Ideas of secretion, of hermeneusis, recur throughout the narrative. The story builds to a confrontation between the gardener and the vicar, and to a final resolution of sorts.

This is not a linear, conventionally logical story. The concept is to allow the reader to conceive a series of underlying structures, quite different from, and yet complementary to, that of the literal narrative. This represents a sub-textual approach based on a Sufi aesthetic. The original meaning of Anglo-Saxon *saelig* is "holy" and so the historical term *Saelig Sussex* would mean "The Holy Land of the South Saxons" and "The Saelig Tales" would be "The Holy Tales". To concatenate various and deeply English incarnations of Sussex – ecstatically-holy Saxons and unseen yet feared Norsemen; the dances of dissimulation between proto-capitalist and aristocratic Elizabethans; and the cloak-and-dagger night games of Victorian curates and smugglers – with Sufi ideas cloaked in those of John Ruskin and his magic architectural lamps, is itself unusual and might be seen as an example of the use of the tactic of paradox as a key to structural-symbolic meaning. At the mythopoeic level, it is a reinvention of England. But this is no England we have ever known. The story is a meta-geography where every thing holds signification; it is a place, a society, of multiple interlocking levels, played out in a gently hallucinogenic folk-song of swaying steeple bells.

Recently, long after the completion of *The Saelig Tales*, I learned that the seminal text *The Journey of the Soul: The Story of Hai bin Yaqzan* by the eleventh-century Andalusian writer, Ibn Tufayl (from which Daniel Defoe may have derived his novel, *Robinson Crusoe*) at one point was translated into English by an academic vicar from the Home Counties who, as it happens, had planted a Syrian fig-tree in his garden. In *The Saelig Tales*, Vicar Synnot too cultivates a fig-tree in the outer part of his manse garden.

Fig-trees, and figs, are heavily symbolic in various cultures. In Christian symbolism, the fig-tree, which bears fruit with no visible blossom and before even leaves appear on its branches, has represented at various times a knowledge of worldly good works, impulsiveness, a lack of intelligence, a type of the church or of each person's heart, a sign of the Lord's Second Coming, and the Virgin Birth. In symbolic terms, it has been contrasted with the olive and vine trees. Part of my project is to allow the reader to awaken to the perpetual and core nature of the influences of cultures which usually are considered Other in so-called Western thought, and the manner in which such profound concepts underpin our society and literature.

This is a living process, it is history as life, as continuous formation of the present, and to engage in this Zeitgeist is to explore the cartography of knowing. To paraphrase from *The Story of Hai Ibn Yaqzan*: to engage in this journey is to become *Alive, son of Awake!* (Abu Bakr Muhammad bin Tufayl 1982).

The Spanish House

The next story I wish to discuss is the novella, *The Spanish House*. This is set partly during the autumn and winter of 1974–75, and partly in the year 2020, between London and rural Spain. The protagonist is a woman from London, Marjory Morris, who meets a certain Joe Leon at a Marxist meeting. She comes unexpectedly into a moderate inheritance from a hitherto estranged uncle, and they decide to take some time out. She spots an advert to rent a barraca, a very basic hut or cabin, in southern Spain. She telephones the number given and finds herself being interrogated by a certain irascible Doctor Levi, who owns the property. The story is contemporaneous with the dictator Franco's last illness, and it is told entirely from Morris's perspective and in her voice.

Joe Leon is of Jewish origin, though he has eschewed religion for dialectical materialism. The couple share a set of values, a view of the world. From the moment they arrive at the deserted barraca, however, they begin to react very differently to their new environment (a fictional setting, close to the village of Darra on the northern slopes of the Sierra Morena at the point where the three provinces of Castilla La Mancha, Extremadura and Andalusia meet). Marjory becomes fascinated by the local church and its priest, but the attraction, at least at first, is essentially a surface one. Joe, on the other hand, starts out the straight materialist, but by degrees falls into a state of intoxicated self-neglect. Their relationship steadily falls apart. The story is permeated by the *cante jondo* (deep song), one of the folk-song forms of southern Spain. Church and priest, it turns out, are far more than they seem, as is the elusive Dr Levi. Philosophically, the story is an exposition of the dialectic of the spirit in the pre-Marxist sense. Ideas of Sephardic and Arabic culture rise uncontrollably from the white, burned earth of the Inquisition-Conquistador trail, along with the unresolved axis of the Spanish Civil War (the second being an ultimate consequence of the first), until the narrative is driven to a screaming climax that is wordless in its intensity.

I see the Iberian peninsula (together with Sicily) as pivotal to the onset of the Modern era, as well as being a constant reminder of the interconnectedness of Judeo-Islamic-Christian culture and thought. In *The Spanish House,* this matrix manifests against the semiotic backdrop of an almost rabbinical dialectical materialism. The node in *The Spanish House* is the relationship between sex, politics and religion and the manner in which these three play out through the character of a woman at a particular time in history. The fugue lies in the link between love – Eros – and the aim of transforming the human condition. The poeticism of the piece becomes so intense that the fiction begins to bend; a process analogous to the effect on time-space of being funnelled into a cosmic black hole. The deliberate use of the folk-song idiom is a turning-on-its-head of the flawed and dangerous Romantic and post-Romantic concept of "a people", a self-contained tribe, a hermetically-sealed "folk", linked, bound and defined by the land on which they dwell. In a curious yet typical mirror-image of the eschatologies of some traditional societies where the people are seen as being an integrated seam in the landscape, the land becomes defined by these dominant groupings, their dominance being expressed through those ultimate farcical reductions of folk songs which we call national anthems.

The Spanish House plays out using folk songs, but here the agenda is the opposite, namely to elicit the lie, the inherent impossibility, of such a concept. Towards the end of the story, forty-five years on, the protagonist herself begins to question the veracity of the narrative, to poke faults in its fabric, to question its rules of engagement and even the existence of the other characters in the novella, and to point out obviously hackneyed literary devices such as the moderate inheritance, the newspaper advertisement, the peculiar phone conversation, until ultimately she is led to confront the tenuousness of her own existence, not simply as a mortal human being but also as a functional character in a fiction. This calls into question the range of possibilities of the novel/novella form in the long stream of storytelling and music that comprises the human imagination. Not so much angels on the head of a pin, as a balancing act along the invisible strings connecting diametric Kabbalistical poles stretched almost to breaking point. *Crack the vessels!*

The Aerodrome

The third story I would like to discuss here is entitled, *The Aerodrome*, and concerns a sixty year-old Indian man who arrives at a disused World War Two air-base in Lincolnshire. He sets up canvas and easel and begins to sketch the aerodrome as he imagines it might have been before it was bombed, all those years before. We learn that his father had volunteered to join the Royal Air Force and was posted to this aerodrome in eastern England. During a lunchtime hangar concert, the siren sounded, and the entire orchestra, together with the audience of RAF and WAAF (Women's Auxiliary Air Force) personnel ran to the nearest shelter, and this shelter took a direct hit. Many years later, our protagonist has cycled slowly, on his father's black bicycle, all the way from northern India, carrying with him the only possessions his father left behind: a cigar-tin, his airman's boots, and a small book. He notices a white line at the edge of the runway, follows it, and falls down a scree into what is clearly the remains of an old air-raid shelter. Unable to extricate himself, he sits down, takes out the book and begins to read. Just then, he notices, to his right, a small, wooden door...

We slip between three consciousnesses, all narrated in the first person: that of the sixty year-old son; that of the Luftwaffe pilot who bombed the aerodrome; and that of the upper-class English WAAF volunteer with whom the father was having an affair. The trajectory of the story flies towards the moment when the button is pressed, the fatal bomb released into the sky. Only once, at the very climax, do we hear the quiet voice of the artist's father, issuing from deep in the

English earth, before we return at last to the son whose quest, after all, carried us into this story.

The physical descent into the earth enables us to go backwards in time, as though we were not readers, but archaeologists. And in the same way that archaeologists piece together shards of pots and chains of necklaces, we, along with the protagonist, are induced to reconstruct internally this symphonic story of three individuals whose lives and deaths dance together on the point of a steel gramophone stylus. It is no accident that the German pilot is a failed concert pianist.

It has always seemed to me odd, and inaccurate, that in films and books about World War Two there are almost never any Indian (or African, Chinese, or Arab) characters, other than as "the natives", that ubiquitous and demeaning imperial denominator. There are rare exceptions: perhaps *The English Patient* by Michael Ondaatje may be one such, though even here the Indian soldier is used essentially as a catalyst in the main chemistry of the interaction between the three major white characters; in a sense, and particularly in the film medium, everything non-Western merely provides an exoticised backdrop. Has there ever been a feature film about the Burma Front that portrays Indian troops in character roles? And if such a yawning gap exists, then why is it so?

My maternal grandfather fought as a Field Officer, a major and adjutant, on that forgotten Front (forgotten, even in its own time). Thirty years later, after my parents had migrated to this country, as a boy I used to cycle past the many disused, deserted aerodromes of eastern England. I even learned to drive on one. In its obsolescence, the word "aerodrome" seems somehow sonorous and poetic, like the word "oracle". And let me tell you, they are eerie places, especially in the unbroken, blinding sunlight of mid-summer. (I never ventured into one at night!) Nowadays, some of them are still used occasionally for Sunday go-kart racing and suchlike, but they once held within their perimeters the bulk of British air power and the precariously balanced fate of this country at a critical time. So, in more ways than one, these places are part of my history too.

Perhaps it will have been noticed that the one common thread running through all three stories, is the presence – the immanence – of music. Perhaps like the mathematician-composer, the late Iannis Xenakis, I strive to perceive the correlation between architecture and sound, or that between geography and song, or that between society and the dissonant frequencies emanating from a plucked string or a blown reed. Energy equals illumination, twice over. A strange, somewhat heretical concept, this, especially nowadays when we are caught between glossy millenarian faddism and diehard, two-dimensional materialism. And what else but a bizarre hemi-hypothesis would lead me into the realms of an Anglo-Saxon Benedictine monastery, a stone shack on the Sierra Morena and the beige concrete of a deserted Lincolnshire aerodrome? At times, while writing (or should I say, composing?) *The Aerodrome,* I had the distinct sense of a presence over my shoulder. At the risk of sounding ludicrously Byronic, sometimes I do feel less like a creator and more like a conduit.

But perhaps this is simply an internalisation of compositional technique; the well-tuned athlete becoming unconscious of the shift and tug of each pace yet remaining supremely aware of the internal energy that causes every single movement. Yet I suspect that this is too linear an explanation. If, as in so many of the stories I write, time and space indeed flow in malleable parallels rather than sequentially, if the history and geography of reality are far more complex than even contemporary mathematicians or astrophysicists can conceive of, then who is to say what is, and what is not, possible? Indeed, who is to say what is, and what is not?

But this is all tied up with my place in the community – or in society, if you prefer – since no matter how much we may dissemble, it is frankly impossible for artists to really be dissociated totally from the people around them, those by whom they were raised and those who form their working/living milieu, as well as the people of the wider world. However, this is neither something which I regard as wholly definitive, nor is it a role which I try to avoid. Either attitude would be pointless self-delusion. The blade is double-edged, we must grasp it with both hands – and be prepared to open up, to bleed. Nonetheless, it is important to be wary of "ethnic" readings of all output produced by an artist who happens to belong to a group which is in the minority in a particular locus (but who, taking a worldwide frame, may very well belong to various majorities). One must avoid the ghetto-ising of talent, or the exoticising of that which was always intrinsic.

My approach, like the man with X-ray eyes, would be to try to see connections, whether historical, historiographical, literary or societal, or (more likely) a mixture of these, for such factors also exist in mutuality. In this regard, it is important to apply as many models of criticism as is possible to a piece of writing, and then some! Each work will throw up its own fractal of possible critical approaches, and an attentiveness to these, apart from giving the work its due measure of artistic respect, should also help to prevent the inappropriate genericising of work simply on the basis of the ethnic or religious origins of the author. It may be that some of the work of writers living in Scotland who are of South Asian, or mixed origin, writers such as (and even as I write this, I am somewhat loth to lump these very different writers together; I would hope that the ethos of this chapter demonstrates that actually I am striving for the opposite, for an opening-out, a recognition of the disparateness of the work produced by such artists) Shameem Akhtar, Kaiser Haq, Nasim Marie Jafry, Irfan Merchant, Saket Priyadarshi, Sheila Puri, as well as those who, for one reason or another, migrated here as adults from various parts of the world, such as Sarmed Mirza, Nalini Paul, Raman Mundair, Kamal Sangha (the first two of whom came from Pakistan and Canada respectively, and the latter two from India and England).

Their work deals with issues such as racism, migration etc., but these writers have also produced pieces which defy the definitions suggested by such narrow interpretations. Priyadarshi's assertion (in a personal communication with the author, 2003) that in his fiction he "specialises in white, middle-aged matrons" would seem almost to be a reiteration of the process whereby we see the wonderfully luminous film, *Elizabeth*, directed by Indian director Shehkar Kapoor. In addition, the cultural critique is not the only form of literary criticism that need be applied even to their poems, stories, articles, and essays. As a corollary, let us then apply such a cultural critique routinely to the work of white, middle-class male writers.

But it is important not to get hung-up on an identity politics trip; there are so many other kinds of interesting dynamics at work, whether those of class, gender, historical, geographical, metaphorical, metaphysical, perceptual, ecological, poetical or whatever. And the point is, they are all dynamics; like cultures, like notions of aesthetic, they alter. Writing is about change, for authors, for their readers, for the characters, all, and this can subvert the entire concept of fixed, societal edifices.

My agendas as a writer, or my muse, my daemon, my cathartic ecstatic anti-epiphanic need – whichever of these you prefer – are rooted in the science of being as well as in "pure" art, and in the local, the here-and-now, as well as in the geo-historical or historio-geographical politics of identity. Perhaps the reason I seem to hover around boundaries and borders, marches of the intellect, why figuratively speaking I seem to spend much of my time on street-corners, may be that I am striving for unity. You live, you die, and your loves fade away and are forgotten. Space is a vacuum, there can be no sound; the music of the spheres is an impossibility. Well, whatever. But I like stories. They're good for the time between. If we knew everything, we wouldn't need stories. The existence of, and our need for, fiction probably means that we will never know everything. Somehow, this is reassuring.

The (non) act of writing is the (non) seeking out of connections, of hermeneutic relationships. It is really a kind of intuitive, personal-into-societal magic, with words as alchemical symbols. But what I'm really reaching for lies beyond any language, even those of music or mathematics. The text is never all. I am wary also of equating language with concepts such as "freedom", "place", "a people" etc. To use a poetic terminology in a semiotic way, my stories strive, not so much for rhyme, as for assonance, or for even looser linkages, perhaps for Baudelaire's *correspondences* between superstructure and substructures. Much of my fiction is not so much allegorical, as employing symbols which operate on literal and allusive levels. In Sanskrit poetics, this process arouses in the reader that essence, *rasa*, which is central to attaining a state of knowledge. The reader becomes a *rasik*, a lover (Weightman 1999: 464–92).

In societal terms, such processes can engender the exploration by the reader of the area of tolerance and concepts of "The Other", not in the liberal materialist sense, but on the syntagmatic, metaphysical plane which has been so effectively delineated by, for example, Rusmir Mahmutćehajić in his *Sarajevo Essays* (Mahmutćehajić 2003). This entails a shift from obsession with the autonomous self to awareness of the transcendental which is at the heart of human society. I hear the reader as a musician, not a musician in the Western classical tradition, but a jazz musician who "breaks and enters" (Barbour 2002) the text at will and who, through the act of reading, redefines old modalities. I refuse to be a set designer for what Bernal calls "staged histories" (Bernal 1991). Like Isidore of Seville, I am searching for the prema-rasa, that tone evocative of love, which is the greatest of all the rasas.

Sufi writers considered that form, shape and analogy had the power to settle within the reader or hearer and transform the understanding: Rumi's "blood into milk" concept. The word "religion" means "that which re-connects". The mandala form of much of my work, connecting microcosm with macrocosm, is quite un-modern, and this may be the reason why such structures in the text can be hard to detect – we have forgotten how! Nonetheless, rhetorical analysis, which can help to evince such deep structures, increasingly is being applied not only to Biblical but to other texts as well. On the intuitive level, I believe that we human beings do have an innate sense of musicality and so the reader would be aware (even if subconsciously) of such micro- and macro-structures within the text as chiasmus and thematic parallelism. "This produces a higher order of significance from which it is often possible to see not so much what a text means but what it is seeking to do" (Weightman 1999: 481).

This is effected (or constructed) through the parallel use of outer and inner narrations, as well as through the ancient techniques of punning and word-play. As Weightman states, one such model might be defined by Aristotle's material, formal, efficient and final causes; or by Underhill's four stages in the mystical path: awakening, via purgativa, via illuminativa and via unitiva; or by the Neoplatonic terms, union, descent, ascent and reunion.

None of the three stories discussed is overtly political, in the narrow, colloquial sense of the word; none of them concerns purely contemporary events or forces. Yet among other things, on reading these stories, we are engaged in the minutiae of socio-political changes; in Renaissance and Reformation, in both World Wars of the twentieth century, in the ending of old empires, in various aspects of intra-colonial relationships, in the immensely fertile yet currently tragically unfashionable nexus of the Islamic-Jewish interaction, in the relationships between human beings and the land, in the linkages between past (whether recent or distant) and present, and in the interplay between dialectical materialism and spirituality. If all this does not represent some kind of overarching exploration of the relationships between literary culture and society, then I'm a Victorian curate!

Such a relationship is intrinsic, multi-layered, and undeniable. It emerges from the perpetual discourses of our mind. It is how we communicate with one another, with the past and with the multiple others that comprise our selves. To wander through the streets of literature, facing both ways, towards the past and the future, to move, as Hannah Arendt (1985) says, both dialectically, frenetically, analytically, and also undialectically like the proverbial village idiot, to allow random images, concepts and musics to filter into one's consciousness – is to effect a kind of linguistic transference which can result in powerful, multi-dimensional creative writing.

Perhaps because I spent a long time, in my young adult life, either failing to nurture any pre-existing literary talents I might have had, or else being forced by the rigours of petty-bourgeois economic and other expectations to not even be aware of these (Adam Smith showed that economic life cannot be separated from social life – how true!), and also because the entry of my work into publication (and thence, into a kind of acceptance, or at least recognition) has invariably been a hard-fought and, at least in the early stages, a solitary process of a thousand vicarious Eid-al-Adhas,[2] I constantly feel as though my lease on this talent, this ability to string words together so that their whole becomes greater than their sum, is a short-hold one, and that I am in perpetual danger either of it slipping away or of it being proven to have been illusory or slight in the first place. This seems to be a fairly common existential condition among writers, and probably other artists as well, and perhaps it is the need which

---

[2] Eid al-Adha: the annual Muslim festival celebrating the offer of sacrifice by Abraham of his son.

drives creativity. Perhaps, also, it results partly from the unspoken requirement placed upon artists by this liberal materialist society to hold together the sum of the symbolic meaning of all of its forms. Also, maybe because my work does not fit into a comfortably familiar ethic, it is by nature more difficult to breach those high white walls of the literary establishment. We're talking here about whether or not one gets a viable job. Those of us who remain historically excluded, or whose eventual inclusion is gained only after major struggle, tend to cast up from our nets the many voices of exile, the poetry of the lost and bewildered, the songs of the village idiot.

The windmill came from Asia; turning its giant arms has never been easy. Perhaps it is character-building or talent-honing. Perhaps, but it is also artistically and physically exhausting. An element of my relationship with society is grounded in this sense of perpetual fatigue, of trying to turn the unturnable. I believe this is the situation of many writers; indeed, it is probably the fundamental syntagma of the relationship between corporate, High Capitalist literary culture and society. If I go on – and at the time of writing this is by no means certain – it will be because I am good at nothing else and because I will have earned enough through selling my labour by other means to buy a few minutes, here and there. But this is not a recipe for great, or even good, art. It is the road to amateurism and, ultimately, to irrelevance. To abuse a George Mackay Brown analogy, if I were a carpenter I would have carved an aircraft-hangar full of wondrous tables, or if I were a dead rock musician, then my back-catalogue would fill an unpressed quadruple (presumably budget) album. But who would sup at the table, who would listen to the music? Those few who are not interested in the ASDA Top Twenty, those readers, perhaps, who like to dream their books into being, those who know how the red (soul) string is strung. *Ziryab singing in the dead of night.*

At the end of politics, at the end of the subway line, lies language. And so, it makes political sense, countering oppression, whether consciously or unconsciously, to begin with literature. The obliteration and denial of any referential or causative links between "European" cultures and thought (which includes European diasporic American, Australian, etc.) and those of the rest of the world was, and remains, a deeply racist, inherently colonial act. And it is based on wholly inaccurate assumptions. Yet these assumptions have led to the catalogue of denial and arrogance that passes for the Western Canon and to an overt and subliminal racism, a wilful ignorance, perpetuated through academic institutions, the sciences, the media and much popular culture that essentially precludes intelligent discourse and which serves to provide cultural-societal justification for continuing Western economic and political exploitation or colonialism.

The Western literary canon has been constructed over the past two centuries as a shimmering but false mechanism for bolstering the concept of Western (and by improper yet very real extension, Christian) intrinsic superiority and progressiveness of thought and action. To acknowledge that the works of "other" cultures have defined or formed those of one's own is to accept that there has always only been one culture with many narratives, and this carries definite and potentially explosive political connotations, both for those who deify/demonise the "West" and for those who fossilise/essentialise the "East". Such things can lead to "clashes" and wars justified ultimately by false literary edifices in which each punctuation mark is a closed bolt. Since I am a global village idiot, I refuse to accept such idols.

To explore the nature of fiction is to change it. The famous (or it ought to be) jar from the seventh century CE on which Europa is depicted in Oriental costume (Bernal 1991) is far more dangerous to this poisonous hegemony than the thousand bearded "fundamentalists" who owe their existence, their filled bellies, their political legitimacy and even to some extent their ideas, to the machinations of the corporate military-industrial West. What is not well-known is that in this old jar is a windmill djinn. To play in storm and stress (especially perhaps in Scotland, where in some senses a colonial mythology began with the reification of certain languages and peoples through folksong and storytelling) and to become a Walter Benjamite artisan-trader of the story, refusing to abbreviate or acquiesce in the dominance of certain mythologies, can be a dangerous pursuit.

And of course, I write (and dream, and sing) in English, which derives, in part, from Anglo-Saxon. So the old monks of Wurth Abbey are dancing around in my head and on my tongue through the cadences of the words that I speak, and upon the tips of my fingers, in the phrases that I write. In a way, through exploring and creating dialogues between the familiar and the exotic, in playing idiotically with concepts hitherto hallowed and internalised in society beyond the point of denial, I am trying to turn back the bolts, to swing open the doors. To turn the windmill, and free the djinn!

Bibliography

Aly, Abdel-Moneim. 2001. "The Theme of Exile in The African Short Stories of Muriel Spark" in *Scottish Studies Review* Autumn 2001: 94–104.

Abu Bakr Muhammad bin Tufayl. 1982. *The Journey of the Soul: The Story of Hai bin Yaqzan* (tr. Riad Kocache). London: Octagon Press.

Arendt, Hannah. 1985. "Introduction", in Walter Benjamin, *Illuminations*. New York: Random House.

Bernal, Martin. 1991. *Black Athena: The Afro-Asiatic Roots of Classical Civilisation, Volume I: The Fabrication of Ancient Greece*, 1785–1985. London: Vintage.

Barbour, Douglas. 2002. "Introduction" in Dennis Cooley, *Bloody Jack*. Edmonton: University of Alberta Press.

Mahmutćehajić, Rusmir. 2003. *Sarajevo Essays: Politics, Ideology and Tradition*. Albany: State University of New York Press.

Weightman, S. 1999. "Symbolism and Symmetry: Shaykh Manjhan's Madhumalati Revisited", in Lewisohn, Leonard and David Morgan (eds). *The Heritage of Sufism, Vol. III*. Oxford: Oneworld Publications.

Gay Writing in Scotland: An Interview with Edwin Morgan

This interview took place on 15 May 2003, in the poet's home in Anniesland, Glasgow. The interviewer, James McGonigal, had earlier sent him the questions outlined in the Notes at the end of the chapter.
Keywords: Robert Fergusson, Jackie Kay, David Kinloch, Ali Smith, Walt Whitman, Queer Theory.

Well, Eddie, in the context of gay writing in Scotland, was there anything before you?

Not very much, to tell you the truth, though it has to be said that a lot of investigation still has to be done. It's a very unexplored area, though someone like Christopher Whyte in his *Gendering the Nation* (1995) has begun to do that kind of thing. I'm sure we'll discover things as time goes on. You ask if there was anything by way of models, but I think, as far as Scotland is concerned, probably not. When I began writing love poems round about 1960, I wasn't aware of any models at all: I was just doing what I wanted to do.

If there were any models, they might have been some foreign writers that I'd come across. One name that does occur is the Greek poet, Cavafy. I thought that he was perhaps nearest to what I wanted to do. He wrote about many ordinary situations in Alexandria: a man going into a shop to buy handkerchiefs and being attracted by the assistant – that kind of thing. The sort of thing that had been happening to me in Glasgow. I knew his poetry and liked it a lot, and it seemed to me that there was something to be done here: an everyday urban context, but unusual things going on in that context.

Things that were permitted, perhaps, in other cultures but forbidden in Scotland?

Well, it was forbidden in his culture too. Modern Alexandria wasn't quite like ancient Athens and so he was doing something that was disapproved of, but nevertheless he was able to describe vividly the feelings involved in little incidents like that. So there was something there. I'd also read different kinds of poetry that might have had an influence – I don't know – Hart Crane in America, particularly. I liked his poem "The Bridge" a lot but that was different: that was a much more explicitly lyrical kind of thing that must have registered with me for other kinds of poem, not the short love poems. But on the whole I wasn't aware of a background of models; I was really just doing what I felt I could do. Especially with a poem like "Glasgow Green" – even now I can't think of models for that – it was something I felt I just had to write. It came out of very strong feelings about a number of things. It was set in a certain place which I knew I could describe. But I can't think of anything quite like it, can you?

I just wondered whether within your own reading there were certain writers where you recognised certain interests – a similar way of looking at the world?

I think so. I liked Whitman a lot. He was particularly interesting because it was a little bit like what I was doing. It was coded, up to a point. It was fairly clear to a man or woman of the world, but it was coded. He had to be very careful in his own time: he was criticised a lot but he was determined to write about things like that, often disguising them as something that might happen to anybody, as bisexuality or something of that kind. But there was something there that I felt was as real and as powerful in his attraction to men, much more strongly there than his attraction to women. I'm sure I must have learned something from that. But I don't know how far these things were *direct* – they are things that I read and enjoyed: they are seeping into your mind, but you don't know how they are going to come out until you start writing yourself.

Was there any sense in which you felt subversive or rebellious against normal codes, or were you just being true to the way you saw the world?

There was something rebellious, certainly, in "Glasgow Green" especially. People in later years spoke of a "gay liberation movement." This is an early poem asking for gay liberation. I was aware of that, and I felt it was a fairly strong thing to do, coming as it did at the beginning of the sixties, at the end of the fifties which was a very oppressive period, when there were some famous cases of people such as John Gielgud and Lord Montagu, Peter Wildblood – people caught and charged by the police, and there was a great deal of publicity about that. You couldn't hide. John Gielgud was caught and charged, and you couldn't hide it: it had to be reported.

But at the same time there was just the slight sense of the beginning of a change in the law. It didn't come for a long time; but there was just a feeling in the air (as Peter Wildblood wrote in his book about that period) that something could possibly be changed, and that this oppression of people's real feelings couldn't go on forever. I certainly felt that and, although there was no liberation movement as such when I was writing "Glasgow Green", I must have envisaged something like a movement, arising out of my feelings in that regard.

Was Scotland even more oppressive and darker, in that respect?

It probably was. It's very easy to say so, but I think it probably was. There was an oppressive atmosphere, and you had to be extremely careful about not being found out doing anything that might be frowned on or taken against you. It took a long time for things to change in Scotland. As you probably know, the actual law in Scotland was not changed until much later than in England. The law was slightly liberalised in England in 1967, but in Scotland this was not done until 1980, so that gave you an indication that things were difficult. I always think of it as a Calvinist thing. Maybe it wasn't – maybe it was the general religious background of the country. It was thought to be in some way very difficult to move forward in any reasonable way at all.

Have things changed markedly in your lifetime, then, or only in some surface areas?

Well, things have changed. If the law changes, then other things do change too. People feel slightly freer to go about their business and to do things they would not have been prepared to do before. After 1980 that was true. The atmosphere has changed, it's much less oppressive, especially among younger people in their twenties now, who are prepared to talk about things perfectly freely, and they're not shocked in the way that people in the 1950s were shocked. In the 1950s, people were genuinely shocked by Gielgud. How could a man who was a famous actor do things like these? He was charged with "importuning" in a public place. How could he possibly do that? People had to grasp at a new fact. It took a long time, in Scotland especially, for this to come across.

And I suppose you were in a public position too, within the University?

Yes, I was aware of that. I knew that if something like Gielgud's situation had applied to me, I would have been sacked. There would also have been a social ostracism at that time. It was a very difficult period altogether.

So your early poems were deliberately ambiguous and coded?

Yes, they were. "Glasgow Green" is not very coded at all if you look into it, but I suppose it was deliberately meant to be a nightmarish scene. You are not one hundred percent sure what is happening – even if you think it couldn't go on in Glasgow (so near the Cathedral!). But it was coded up to a point. And the love poems were always coded: I generally used the pronoun "you" instead of "he" for that reason. But they were coded in such a way that it left people to make up their own minds as to what was going on there.

I suppose some people would see that.

Yes, I knew that. People who had worldly experience, or a good imagination, or who knew me. I remember Tom McGrath round about that time (I knew him quite well, and he was going to interview me) made the point that it was clear to him that many of these poems were about men, not about women. I just had to say "yes". He was not gay himself, but a Catholic heterosexual person – but he saw straight away that these poems were in fact gay poems. That was the first clear indication I had. Tom Leonard too jaloused what was happening. I was in his house once, when he had a wee party there, and he just came up to me at one point and said: "You're gay, aren't you?" – just like that.

Was that the word he used?

Yes, that was a bit later, about 1970 or so.

When did that word first come in? I've heard it being used in 1930s American films, to describe a flamboyant way of living, beyond the norms.

The word goes back quite a long time in the theatre, for people acting. But the current use of the word probably goes back to when the *Gay News* came out (now called *Gay Times*) in the 1970s. By that time the word was quite clearly used to apply to homosexual persons. Before that, when I was a boy, the word normally used would be "queer". This has come back now (after many years as a terms of disapproval) as a sort of flag to be waved – as in Queer Theory. It seems a different resonance altogether. Either "queer" or "pansy" (which has pretty well almost gone now) was applied to gay men. The Scottish word "jessy" was not so bad as "pansy." A "jessy" was slightly ok: a "pansy" was over the top, just too much. A "jessy" might be saved.

And turned into a "jacky", or some such!

I remember, when I was in my teens, my parents wanted me to take piano lessons. There was a piano in the house, and that was the usual home entertainment, so my mother said, "You must learn to play the piano." They heard about someone living quite near us in Rutherglen. He was a student at Glasgow University and would be able to teach me the piano. He came up to the house, and after he went away my father said, "He's all right, but he's a bit of a jessy." He didn't mean it in a very negative way – just that his manners were slightly effeminate. He didn't say, "Don't darken our doorstep again." And he did come and teach me the piano. That gives a kind of idea.

And did the Scottish context of longer-lasting disapproval of homosexuality hold back the reception of your work at all?

I didn't think it did, probably because when poems like "Glasgow Green" and the love poems were published, they were approved of: people liked them and they got into anthologies and so on. They weren't *discussed*, and nobody really went into what they were actually saying. But they took them as good poems and accepted them in that sense. It was a long time before anyone delved into what they were actually saying – nobody has delved very much into them even yet. But they were just thought to be ok poems, and accepted from that point of view. I was surprised in a way. After I wrote "Glasgow Green" it took me quite a while to get it published, because it was different from anything that had been published before in Scotland, but it made its way, and was highly thought of, and now it's even taught in schools – which is to me very strange.

But I think often taught in an inexplicit way – in a generic way, as a poem of Glasgow's violent past.

Would they go into the whole thing? A lot would depend on the teacher and the class. Perhaps with Sixth Year.

In school contexts, a lot is left unexplained. There is a good deal of your earlier work in school anthologies, and teachers will work from those. There is also a sense that children at that age are not clearly defined, sometimes, in terms of sexuality, and teachers wouldn't want to be seen either as opening up an occasion for mockery of any particular youngster, or else seeming to foster something that maybe ought to be left an uncertainty. Teachers are cautious about that.

Certainly I have been asked at a school reading what exactly is going on in "Glasgow Green". I just said what it was: a homosexual rape. And the boy who had asked just accepted that all right. This was fairly recently. Nowadays people see so much on television in any case that they are aware of these things. He was not particularly shocked.

As your work became more open, and you were able to write more explicitly, what were you aiming for? Were you just exploring aspects of character or place, or were you conscious of trying to right a balance?

I'm not sure about motives in things like this. After I came out in 1989 or 1990, I felt that I would write about anything I wanted to. It was just case of whether I did or would do so. I had to make individual decisions all the time. There were some poems I wrote just because of the freedom, taking up subjects that would be regarded as improper or certainly not universal. I did think that there was an element of deliberateness about that – just to bring these things into poetry at all. There is one of the poems called "A Memorial" that is about cottaging, which is considerably disapproved of, because people who might accept a nice affair by two men living together in a house would not so easily accept someone going down toilets in search of prey (as it were), in search of partners. That would still be beyond the pale. But of course it goes on, it went on, and I just felt it's part of human life, let's have a look at it. It's a good poem, but I understand that some might find it offensive. It's a sort of celebration.

There's the poem "Head" as well.

Yes, even more so. In a way that's a kind of challenge poem. I say at the end: "I bring this head back here for all", and am challenging people. If it's a good poem, even though you hate the subject matter and disapprove, nevertheless you have to see it's well done, and there's human feeling in it. "What do you make of this?" I'm saying to the general audience. Obviously it means more to young people, but I'm trying to get both things together. I'm trying to talk about something that might be offensive, but to do it in such a way that it's good poetry. And if so, then it ought to survive.

And there's a very strong parallel with the artistic imagination that creates the image –

Yes, indeed.

– and somehow changes it by bringing it to light, so that it can be thought about and talked about. Is there a sense, though, that the traditional images and archetypes associated with homosexuality narrow the range? Or is that not true, or does that not matter? There's the association with darkness and duplicity, a sense that it

goes against the poetic norm in terms of symbolism and so on. Is that
a matter of regret, or is it just part of the palette that you work with?

I don't think it's exactly that. I understand what you say about a
possible narrowing, but it's just a part of the drama of the whole thing:
you write about things that are dramatic. And of course something that
is disapproved of, and therefore secret, does lead you towards a kind
of darkness, whether it's the darkness of a city street or a city park at
night. These are a natural background for poetry of that kind, just
because of the secrecy.

But this would not perhaps always be true. It depends on the time
and place you're living in. If it was ancient Greece, there would be
plenty of sunlight, and an older man and a younger man holding hands
against a beautiful column – it depends very much on your society and
what's allowed or disallowed. And the things that are disapproved of
in one society might be celebrated and enjoyed wholeheartedly in
another culture. So I was aware of all that in the background. I'd read
plenty of Latin and Greek poetry, and Japanese poetry for that matter
too – Samurai poetry – so I know that there were many different
avenues towards this.

I suppose that is always at the back of your mind, but you come
back to your own place and your own time, and the fact that
(especially when I was younger) Glasgow itself was a very dark place,
and I suppose a much more dangerous place at night. There are still
plenty of bad things happen in Glasgow, but not as many as when I
was a boy. You are aware of that darkness, and maybe do see it as
symbolic, with a sort of dark interesting drama about it. (But it's not
entirely that: I mean I would write poems that are sunny and in the
open air, and not dark at all.) Much of modern 20th century writing, in
any case, has that sort of thing. What would be most typical? The
American novelist, John Ritchie? He's gay, and his novels are about
gay characters in the American city. Night scenes are very vividly
done; night is his environment. For me it's not *entirely* that, but it's
part of it.

And then there are other ways in which you use bands of warriors or
explorers, bands of brothers, and quests of various kinds. These are

very ancient poetic devices, and they can be refreshed or moved forward in that way.

Yes, I think so. The idea of a band of fairly close-knit persons – maybe that's why I like *Beowulf* so much – appealed to me, although I'm not myself a great joiner of anything. I'm not much part of a band – except in the army, when I very much had to be. So it's an ambiguous notion. But I liked that idea of either a band of soldiers or explorers, and the sense of going in search of something – maybe I'm not sure what – but you have the sense of a quest very strongly. Perhaps if it's a gay poem then the quest is for the impossible perfect partner. (Quentin Crisp used to write about that.) The idea of searching is certainly there. My own experience comes into this in ways I haven't quite worked out. My five years in the army were pretty awful in some ways, but in other ways, in a male society, there were certain kinds of friendship that were very strong, a strong bonding.

And in some ways a sense of being part of something bigger, both of the larger enterprise of war and also of being with a group of people, like brothers, whom you worked with and lived with.

I think both. As an only child I didn't have brothers, so that may be why I did get something from the army. In a wider sense too: I had registered as a conscientious objector and then asked for that to be removed, and I registered for the Royal Army Medical Corps. I think at the back of my mind I didn't want to be left behind sulking as an objector. I could see that it was going to be a big and important thing, and I didn't disagree with fighting against Hitler. I thought at the time that he was going to have to be stopped, and I could take part in it. I know this surprised some people. They thought that I should have remained a conscientious objector: Norman MacCaig, for example, remained one. But I thought not: I could admire him up to a point, but not wholly. This was too big to stand outside.

And then, after the war, there was the whole business of opening up outer space, which was mainly a male enterprise (apart from monkeys and the dog!) and that must have registered quite strongly. Rockets

*came out of the warfare, of course, as the final weapon, and all that
was a male world.*

There were women too: the Russians made sure they sent women up,
like Valentina. But it was mostly male. I don't quite know how all that
fits in. I was fascinated by it and watched the whole of the
development, the men landing on the moon and so on, with
tremendous interest. I didn't give huge thought to its implications, but
I can see that there is something there.

*Well, there is the phallic rocket, of course! But do you think that it
might be the lack of boundaries that the loss of gravity causes, and the
sense of people being ill-defined by the suits they wear, and by the
fluid movement that is not a normal mode of walking?*

That could well be true, because your existence as a gay person is
more ill-defined, and more full of unexpected risks, and so on, so
there probably is a connection there. And I did put my name down for
a rocket flight – one of the first civilians to put my name down. The
interest waned when there were various disasters but it seems to have
come back again (for very wealthy people). But the fact that I did that
shows I'm really very much concerned by it.

*There's maybe something as well about "seeding for the future". The
sense of the sort of investment that parents would make in a child is
the sort of investment a man might make in the future, with all of that
uncertainty as to what will happen. And yet the very commitment
almost ensures it?*

I think there's something in that probably. Even the interest in the
future, which is quite strong in me, must have something to do with a
certain dissatisfaction with the present, presumably. You hope that
there will be better things in the future, and one of them might be
space travel which is very open indeed – no one knows what will
happen. I hope it continues. Given the fact that I managed to get on
the Concorde – that poor plane that is now grounded. Concorde was a
plane of the future, and it was interesting because it was European, not

American. For various reasons I liked that: going up without the certainty of landing.

Has all that a link at all with the fallen angels of Paradise Lost: *the cosmic movement, the free fall, freely risking everything? Various other descriptions in your poems, such as the planet Io in "The Moons of Jupiter", seem to be almost archetypes of hell, the sulphur mines that are being prospected there. Or is that to take two different elements and try to elide them?*

I'm not sure about that. It links up a bit with Milton's *Paradise Lost*, which I always liked, and lectured on at university for many years. The fall of Lucifer and the angels is very powerful and makes a big impression. The idea is very strong, whatever you think of the treatment you get from the deity. His fall is very interesting, and his reaction to that, and his determination not to let it defeat him forever, even though it probably will. The mixture of defeat and heroism is very interesting, and might apply to space travel as well. Norman Mailer has written about that in his book on the moon landing, the symbolism of the whole thing. There is a sense of transgression, in a way. "This is our planet here: let's solve our problems here, and let's not go up there to the moon or stars. Let's get our own lives sorted before we have any kind of assault on the heavens, from which we'll retire defeated." Some people probably do feel like that. But I would feel that our environment *is* the universe, and has to be explored. Basically we are an exploring creature, and I think that this has to continue. Any warnings we get from theology about doing that (say in the story of the Tower of Babel, for instance, which falls through pride or hubris) I don't accept. The thing has to be explored, and if there has to be a fall, well, so be it. Let us knock on the gates of heaven, as it were.

You mentioned "transgression" there, and of course this is a current jargon term, depressingly. People get very excited by it: it seems to validate any critical comment that they make, without need for any further argument. Is gay writing to be read like that, or should it just be read as writing? Is there any parallel with the struggle of women to be read differently?

Well, so much ground has to be made up in every way that there is an element of transgression about it, of forcing things out into the open, at the risk of offending some people. But I think it has to be done. It's the same the women's writing or black writing, I'm sure. These are initiatives that have to be looked at and given a hearing. And eventually these become part of the mainstream.

You can't go on being transgressive for ever, but you have to go through that process I think, and gay writing is probably half way to being accepted. There used to be either gay bookshops or gay ghettos in big bookshops. But on the whole now gay novels tend to be seen just as novels. And some of them are very good. Allan Hollinghurst or Edmund White are writing good novels, and I think these two probably have a general readership apart from any special readership they might have. So you possibly begin by being deliberately transgressive, but if what you do is any good then it will become recognised and generally accepted. I think it's still not wholly approved of, but it's moving towards a non-transgressive effect.

And what of Queer Theory, then, or queer readings of texts? Do you find that useful, or just fashionable?

It's fashionable, but I'm not sure how useful. Perhaps it's making up for lost ground. There's still so much to be discovered, that has been either forgotten or deliberately forgotten: so it has to become a part of research. Maybe not "theory", but certainly part of research. We'd like to know more about certain writers of the past who either are gay or whom we think might be gay. Queer Theory certainly has a place.

One of the main Queer Theorists is Eve Kosofsky Sedgwick (you'd better read her!). She's written a lot about this in general context of human relationships. She uses different words: words like homosexual, homoerotic and homosocial. It's a sort of ladder from homosexual to homoerotic (is it homosexual or is it not?) down to homosocial, which is just boys together or men together, in an army or in a band or whatever. I suppose the *Beowulf* society would be regarded by her as homosocial. There are overtones of something, perhaps, but you're not quite sure. Or the Samurai class in Japan. Very often in the Samurai period, in the seventeenth century especially, an older warrior would take a younger warrior under his wing, as it were. That sort of relationships would be homosocial, possibly homoerotic (we don't know). So it's quite useful to make distinctions of that kind.

Does it apply to Scottish literature? Are there writers that you think were gay?

The one I've always thought about is Robert Fergusson. It seems to me, just going by instinct, that he must have been gay. I can't prove it. In my essay in Christopher Whyte's book, *Gendering the Nation*, I mention some names, but to me Robert Fergusson is the most obvious one really. His life and his sexuality have never been fully investigated. It's very strange. There have been books about Fergusson that never say anything at all about his relationships: as far as we know, there were no women in his life, no close relationships. On the other hand, he had a very close relationship with the Italian singer, Tenducci, who was a castrato. What about that? Maybe they went about singing duets!

And came to a bad end!

These are just speculations, but you can't help thinking things like that. Going further back, there are no obvious figures, really. I always thought William Dunbar might have been, but again there's no evidence. I'm sure Henryson was not, but Dunbar might have been. But these are pure speculations. It's in the historical and modern period that you get clear evidence.

And whom did you value there?

Maybe of the older generation there was Fred Urquhart, the short story writer. He came out very late, but he was definitely gay. But it's more young people now, like David Kinloch in his poetry, which is very good and open, and Christopher Whyte himself, of course. And among the women writers, Ali Smith and Jackie Kay, both I think extremely good and prepared to be open about their sexuality. It's not something that worries them: they use it in their books fairly naturally and very expressively. I think they've reached a peace with themselves, they're able to write about it, they use gay themes or non-gay themes. And, of course, there's Thomas Healy, the novelist – a very strange man, but he has written about that. There are quite a lot now – not supporting a case or being transgressive, but just writing about things that they know to happen or be possible.

Is it harder to write as a member of a minority within a minority (Scottish) literature?

Well, I suppose the first acknowledgement of it in Scotland was that anthology by Toni Davidson that came out in 1989: *And Thus Will I Freely Sing: An Anthology of Gay and Lesbian Writing from Scotland.* That was the first open collection of gay writing, and they asked me to write the Preface to it (this was before I came out in the newspapers) and I said yes, I'll do it. There have been various anthologies since then: the Mainstream book of Gay Scottish Writing. So now it's open and you can read about it. There's a collection of essays, too, by Bob Cant (I forget the title now) about the experience of gay Scottish writers growing up. So it's in the open now. But still scholars will want to look back at earlier writing and discover things that we don't know. It may be difficult, but it's still possible. David Gray, for example, a minor, but a very good minor, poet.

What might gay writing be said to offer to Scottish literature, do you think?

It might just be something about honesty; about recognising aspects of experience that have been suppressed or submerged. A kind of opening up of sympathy in areas which have often been regarded as being very unsympathetic or recalcitrant to sympathy. That would be important, if it could be done.

Whether there's anything more unusual or mysterious, I'm not at all sure. I've thought about this. I think there are some books written by gay writers on gay themes that are not part of a mainstream, and you have to get into them by some means that not everyone, perhaps, could use. The best example is Jean Genet in France: these are really gay books. Proust is mainstream with a gay substratum, but Genet is only and openly gay, he uses gay slang – and I didn't know what the ordinary reaction to this would be. When I came across them, I thought this was most extraordinary. What the ordinary person makes of this I don't know. They are in print now in a bowdlerised version from Galliard in Paris, and they are presumably taught in France: but I don't know how they do that. That would be one case where you would have to reckon with the fact that this is not mainstream, but somewhat different.

What about Trocchi?

He was an ambiguous figure – ambidextrous, ambi-everything. I don't know. I think he was mainly heterosexual, though I'm sure he had other things on the side. He became, to some extent, not a gay icon exactly but fitting into the interest gay writers have in thinking about other writers. There's probably a lot more to be written about Trocchi yet.

What purpose do gay writers serve, do you think? There's the notion of a "gay gene", but why does it persist?

I don't know the answer that. It's a very interesting question. As far back as you go, into ancient Egypt and Mesopotamia, it's there. In ancient Sumeria, they had male prostitutes as well as female prostitutes. So it goes back into ancient history. Is it just simply a flaw, a fault in the human make up? If so, it's strangely persistent. You'd think that the weight of normality would have driven the gene out. So presumably it must have *some* use, though no-one knows what this might be.

I can't think of any answer to it, really, though the idea appeals to me that it's like in the best Persian carpets, where there's a deliberate flaw left in the design, barely visible, that just makes them distinctive. Something about the importance of a little flaw, in case things became too smooth, and work too well. I don't know. Is that a ridiculous idea?

The most interesting comment I've seen is that it enables human society to go beyond the basics: that the decorative, the different and the artistic are somehow sensed in evolutionary terms to be worthwhile, and that therefore some people need to be freed, as it were, from the bonds of manual work or of providing for a family to think different thoughts and to live a more aesthetic life. That seems very odd, even as I say it, but there seems always to have been a desire among human beings not to be merely functional, but to decorate spears or jars more finely, beyond what is simply required.

That is true, I think. And in so many early societies there is a shaman, who gets a place in that society: a mysterious person, he might be a gay person.

You see it in the shaman's clothes, which are male or female. And in Shakespearean comedy there's the deliberate confusion of male and female identity, as if this is something which it's maybe necessary to explore or think about. So perhaps there's more of a need for this in human societies than at first seems to be the case.

Even when it's most disapproved of, it just goes underground. In the Middle Ages, in Holland in particular, they had mass burnings of sodomites (as they called them) – a really dreadful period of history – even that did not stop it. So there must be something that keeps it going. Whether good or bad, useful or not, I don't know. But there must be *something* useful about it (he said hopefully!).

Well, let's leave this question defiantly unresolved!

Notes

1. *The context of gay writing in Scotland*
    Who were precursors or models for you in particular, as a gay writer? Were they contemporary or historical, European or American? Were they seen/read by you as rebels, misfits, subversives within Scottish culture or British culture? What of the role of religion within Scotland in creating an atmosphere or underclass? To what extent has that atmosphere altered over your lifetime?
2. *Within the context of your own writing*
    Where in the earlier work is gay identity/perspective most visible, and how was this read and received at the time of publication? Was your progress and place within Scottish literary culture helped or hindered by this? As gay identity becomes more open in the later work, what is it about the characters described that you want to express as valuable?
3. *Symbolism of gay writing*
    What about its archetypes and identification with the dark city, the demonic, the ineffectual? Is this to be accepted or countered, and how is this done (through domestic and other human detail)? To what extent in "The New Divan" sequence have you overcome such symbolic limitations? What of the other archetypes of outer space, the voyage, the warrior band, and the push towards the final escarpment in your work? Were you deliberately conscious of redressing an imbalance? Where does the *Demon* sequence fit within this perspective?
4. *Reading gay writing*
    How is gay writing to be read? Is there a parallel with women's writing at all? Is it written in a coded way that is truly open only to a certain section of the population, or is it more confidently generalisable into human aspects of love or destructiveness? What of Queer Theory? Is that useful as a way of reading, or is it in some sense exploitative? Can Scottish Literature be usefully re-read in those terms? Who might come more to the fore in such a reconstruction of literary history? What other minorities or identities or individuals do you find worth considering in any redress of history?
5. *The public role of gay writers*
    What use is gay writing in any culture? To surprise, deny, outrage, subvert? Is it an aspect of entertainment, and does this "explain" its persistence against the biological odds in an evolutionary sense? Is there any particular role for it within the sort of society we have in Scotland? What is your attitude to the "gay gene" and aspects of genetic programming/inheritance? Does this help or hinder gay people in their sense of identity?
6. *Gay writing in Scotland now*
    Which gay writers in Scotland do you value? Is gay more than a "lifestyle" word? What qualities or awareness does it uniquely offer within contemporary writing?

"A Different Kind of Natural": The Fiction of Jackie Kay and Ali Smith

Kirsty Williams

Contemporary Scottish writing has begun to reflect the social and sexual diversity of its society. Jackie Kay and Ali Smith, in exploring some of the ways in which homosexual love can be expressed in a predominantly heterosexual culture, do not simply assert difference, but rather use their fiction to invert the notion of difference itself. The corporeality of gay love is stressed by each of these novelists through a structured multiplicity of voices and play of language, but their evocations of relationship and desire are so authentically realised that the fact that this love happens to be homosexual becomes almost inconsequential.
Key words: Jackie Kay, Ali Smith, identity, gender, lesbian, the body.

The fiction of Ali Smith and Jackie Kay shares common ground. Both use thematic clashes between language and corporeality as a basis for exploring notions of gendered identity. Both depict gender and sexuality as unstable concepts and both negotiate lesbian love within the context of a society still largely constrained by the idea of sexual opposites. At the heart of their fiction are deep and fundamental senses of "other" love. Evoking these, they critique the notion that sexual and gendered identities are fixed and immutable by transcending them, stepping beyond the margins of mainstream society to the vast openness of free love.

Jackie Kay

Jackie Kay's novel *Trumpet* (1998) circumnavigates a character that is dead from the outset. Joss Moody is a famous jazz trumpeter with a wife and adopted son; and, inspired by the real life and death story of jazz musician Billy Tipton, the narrative pivots around the revelation that Joss was anatomically female. Whilst people like the doctor who examines Joss, his undertaker and his musician friends and colleagues provide a variety of reactions to this "unusual" situation, there are three principal narrative voices: Millie Moody, Colman Moody and

Sophie Stones. By refusing the reader a fixed position from which to judge Joss, Kay underpins *Trumpet* with a fluid and subjective sense of identity.

Each of the main voices perceives the aftermath of Joss's death in a different way. Amidst the scandal, Millie is primarily a grieving wife: "My husband died, I am now a widow. Why can they not understand how ordinary that is?" (Kay 1998: 205). The revelation of his father's gender adds to the combination of issues with which Colman's sense of belonging is already wrought. He is a black Scottish male with adoptive parents (one black, one white) and a cockney accent. Discussing the differences between his English and Scottish words and worlds, he says: "I was practically schizophrenic" (Kay 1998: 53). Colman feels betrayed and, at times, flabbergasted by the discovery that his father was biologically female, returning again and again to the corporeality of this. Sophie Stones is a tabloid journalist with her mind set on writing Joss's biography, authorised by and ghost-written for Colman. Sophie never attempts to empathise with Joss; as another rung on the career ladder and as a way of making her "big money" (Kay 1998: 129), he is dehumanised.

Kay plays upon the disparity between Sophie's exploitation of Joss and Colman's struggle to come to terms with his father again. Sophie's eager manipulation of others, from Colman to Joss's childhood friend, is so overt and lacking in humility that she is undoubtedly cast in a negative light. She embodies a critique of tabloid journalism, and, by extension, her role as onlooker and voyeur is a critique of the tabloidisation of British society writ large. Even though Britain has transvestite comedians and entertainers who successfully sell to mainstream audiences, tabloid culture still thrives on selling us "scandalous" stories about gay couples with children and transvestites with lesbian lovers. Such sensationalised interest foregrounds continuously their exclusion from and otherness to mainstream society:

The nineties are obsessed with sex, infidelity, scandal, sleaze, perverts. The nineties love the private life. The private life that turns suddenly and horrifically public. The sly life that hides pure filth and sin. The life of respectability that shakes with hypocrisy [...] The dirtier the better. The more famous, the better. [...] Lesbian stories are in [...]. And this one is the pick of the bunch. The best yet. Lesbians who adopted a son; one playing mummy, one playing daddy. The big butch frauds. Couldn't be better. (Kay 1998: 169–70)

Sophie's attitude never really shifts during the novel; if anything, her scruples diminish. It is Colman that undergoes the biggest mind change, moving from anger and a failure to understand his father's femaleness to an implied acceptance of this. In her depiction of Sophie, Kay renders the way that transitory subjects are dehumanised and turned into media spectacle. But by juxtaposing this with a humane exploration of Joss and Millie's love, Kay unpicks and challenges the gender limitations imposed by social boundaries. Discussing Kay's poetry, Alison Lumsden similarly asserts that "Kay encourages her readers to embrace [multivalent difference] suggesting that it is a failure to acknowledge multiplicity, either in our selves or in our society, which is in fact the real ailment" (Christianson and Lumsden eds 2000: 87).

Joss's corporeality is central to *Trumpet*'s narrative, but differing perspectives on it are juxtaposed (pointing to the fluidity of gendered identity itself). Whilst so many characters are preoccupied with their encounter with Joss's dead body (and, in particular, his breasts), Millie's narrative is free from the desire to know or understand the physical workings of Joss. The reader's context for, and point of identification with, Millie is her experience of loss. For Millie, Joss's death is not marked by the absence of a penis or the presence of breasts. Rather, it is the presence of his absence that marks her narrative: "The space next to me bristles with silence. The emptiness is palpable. Loss isn't an absence after all. It is a presence" (Kay 1998: 12). Millie renders their love as a form of symbiosis:

I feel pain in the exact place Joss complained of for months. A stabbing pain on my left side […]. I don't know what is real and what is not, whether the pain in my side is real or imagined. The terrible thing about pain is that it doesn't matter, it still hurts. It hurts like hell. (Kay 1998: 1, 4–5)

What Millie has lost is not an object or spectacle but a husband. She sees herself so intertwined with Joss that his cancer is felt within her. The fact that she cannot distinguish whether the pain is "real or imagined" posits the notion that the body itself, whilst being a physical entity, is subject to the imagination. Joss's maleness is palimpsestic: upon his corporeality he engineers another gender. To Millie and Joss, Joss is utterly masculine; his primary sex is inconsequential because they believe, or imagine, him to be male. This is emphasised by the way that Joss and Millie deal with Joss's biological sex. Millie notes that for Joss, his past life as a girl is a thing apart to him: "He always spoke about her in the third person. She was his third person" (Kay 1998: 93). A similar distance between Joss and his female body is rendered in the way Millie describes learning about Joss's sex. Rather than tell her, Joss shows Millie his femaleness, taking off his clothes until he exposes the bandages that strap down his breasts:

> I feel a wave of relief: to think all he is worried about is some scar he has. He should know my love goes deeper than a wound [...] I go towards him to embrace him [...] I am still holding out my hands when the first of his breasts reveals itself to me. Small, firm. (Kay 1998: 21)

Grammatically, Joss's breasts are the active agent; they reveal themselves to Millie, creating a gap between Joss as an active (male) subject and his (female) body. By prefiguring Joss's vagina in Millie's assumption that he is uncovering a wound, Kay points not only to Millie's misunderstanding about what was under Joss's bandages, but also to the fact that, regardless, Millie's love goes beyond corporeality ("my love goes deeper than a wound").

As with other characters, Millie's language implies a disjunction between the social and the biological Josses, but Millie's description points beyond the body and reaffirms her love for him. It is, however, this perceived disjunction between his female body and male subjectivity that haunts some of the other characters. When Holding, the funeral director, unravels Joss's bandages, his breasts are personified:

> Even though Holding was expecting them, he still gave out a gasp when he saw them. There they were, staring up at him in all innocence – the breasts [...]. Pert, alert [...]. Holding had a strange feeling staring at those breasts [...]. It was as if they knew they had hardly been seen by anybody. As if they knew they were secrets. (Kay 1998: 110)

Once again, rather than objectifying Joss's body, his breasts are grammatically active. Despite the melodramatic gasp, the initial relationship between object and viewer is inverted here: it is Holding that becomes the spectacle whilst Joss's breasts assume the empowered role of surveyor. The combination of them staring with "all innocence", fully aware that "they were secrets", in some way challenges Holding to question their legitimacy. By blending innocence and knowledge, the breasts silently refuse responsibility for the truth they hold. It is Holding who must choose to withhold or expose their secret. When Colman recalls Holding showing him Joss's body, no direct mention is made of his breasts, instead the act of naming them is explicitly evaded:

The funeral man shows me some surgical bandages that he says were wrapped tightly around my father's chest to cover his "top". I take a quick look. But that look is still in my head now. It has stayed in my head – the image of my father in a woman's body. Like some pervert. Some psycho. I imagine him now smearing lipstick on a mirror before he died. (Kay 1998: 63)

The fact the Colman sees "the image of [his] father in a woman's body" holds within it a complex relationship. What is recognisable to Colman is still described as belonging to him ("my father"), but there is a grammatical disjunction between this and the randomness of "a" female that has overtaken his body. Once more it is the body that holds power, but only temporarily, as Colman's cultural associations about gender-crossing overlap with his father's image: "I imagine him now smearing lipstick on a mirror before he died". Ironically, Colman's innate sense of Joss as male remains here as this image actually suggests a man dressing up as a woman. Whilst Colman's point of view reflects a sense of shock and betrayal with which many would empathise, it also reflects the posthumous violation of Joss himself.

Voiceless, Joss's personality and body are reinterpreted: the mismatch between his male appearance (and adult life-story) and his female body create a space within the concept of Joss. Open to interpretation, Joss's motivations, desires and sexuality all become subject to debate and wonder, and the idea of what Joss is becomes a depository for each observer's sexual imaginings. Whilst Colman's reaction to viewing Joss naked shows this by inverting Joss from a woman who has assumed a male persona to a man who "smear[s] lipstick on a mirror" (Kay 1998: 63), there are other characters whose reactions carry overtones of titillation. When, for instance, Dr Krishnamurty (who comes to sign his death certificate) discovers Joss's true gender, there is a subtle juxtaposition:

Doctor Krishnamurty felt as if she was removing skin, each wrapping of bandage that she peeled off felt unmistakably like a layer of skin [...]. When she first saw the breasts (and she thought of them again driving home, how strange they looked [...]) she thought that they weren't real breasts at all. At least not women's breasts [...]. Also, the doctor was struck by how young these breasts looked compared to the rest of the body. They hadn't aged. It took her pulling down the pyjama bottoms for her to be quite certain. Doctor Krishnamurty wondered at the woman waiting for her downstairs. (Kay 1998: 43–4)

Before she reveals the breasts hidden beneath, Dr Krishnamurty registers an intimate connection between Joss and his bandages. By likening them to skin, the idea that the bandages are an extension of Joss is emphasised; this reiterates the naturalness of Joss's maleness to Millie. However, this is violated once Joss's breasts are discovered. Not only by the parenthetical contemplation of Joss's breasts as she travels home and the doctor pulling Joss's trousers down, but also by her desecration of Joss's death certificate:

She got her red pen out from her doctor's bag. What she thought of as her emergency red pen. She crossed "male" out and wrote "female" in her rather bad doctor's handwriting. She looked at the word "female" and thought it wasn't quite clear enough. She crossed that out, tutting to herself, and printed "female" in large childish letters. Then she put the medical certificate in the envelope [...] and closed the door on the dead woman. (Kay 1998: 44)

By writing and rewriting Joss's biological gender, she removes from Joss his life's identity and leaves behind a "dead woman". The sense of violation here is emphasised when Mohammed Nassar Sharif registers Joss's death. Seeing the change from male to female on a death certificate is an unprecedented experience for him: "On the grounds of pure aesthetics, Mohammed found the last minute change hurtful. The use of the red pen seemed unnecessarily violent" (Kay 1998: 77) and Mohammed goes some way to restoring Joss's identity by consenting to Millie's request to name him Joss rather than Josephine on his death certificate. Holding (the funeral director) expects that he may "be duty bound to correct" Joss's death certificate if it mistakenly registered him as male: "He almost wished it would happen. If he could have the satisfaction of brutally and violently obliterating 'male' and inserting female in bold, unequivocal red, then at least he would have something to do" (Kay 1998: 112–13). The crude way in which both Holding and Dr Krishnamurty deal with what, for Millie, is a delicate and painful situation, suggests a lack of humanity. Their underlying desire to violate the concept of Joss (symbolised by the legitimation of his life in his Death Certificate) suggests that, because he has chosen to transcend his biological gender, his memory is worth less than an unambiguous corpse's.

Colman's struggle to come to terms with the ambiguity of his father's body rests upon the bridge between what is and what is not ambiguous. His reaction to seeing Joss as female is violent, reflecting not only a retrospective sexual abhorrence but also his struggle to address the fact that his father never revealed himself fully to him. But from early on in the text, Colman does make a distinction between the female body and the male person, finding a sense of identity and peace when he reflects upon Joss as he was:

It was the weirdest thing, but the man in the coffin and the woman that I saw in that funeral parlour really did seem to me to be two different people. My head was even more done in. He looked all right in that blue suit. He looked normal again. Dead; but normal. Better. (Kay 1998: 72)

For Colman, his father makes sense when he remains within a male role. However, when he tries to merge Joss with the female who has stepped beyond the male-female polarisation, Colman is unable to comprehend who or what his father is. Moreover, the immensity of his discovery calls into question his very being:

I hope I can find some. If I saw a photograph of her, I could convince myself that I'm not living some weird Freudian dream, some fucked-up dream where I don't know my father, my mother or myself. I don't know any of us any more. He has made us all unreal. It doesn't matter where your father came from, Colman, he said. Like fuck it doesn't. (Kay 1998: 60)

The need to strip Joss back and view him as a female, points toward the primacy of seeing and suggests that, fundamental to the subject, is his or her body. This association between self and body is undercut when the self refuses to be constrained by gender. Colman seeks impotently to remarry the two. In his emotional journey from anger and disgust back to love, Colman asks the kind of questions that circulate around those who refuse to remain within the rigid social distinctions of male and female:

He wonders how come his father shaved. How the hair got there. Or was there never any hair. Did he just pretend? Did he take hormones to make himself hairy? Fucking Jesus. What did he do? (Kay 1998: 122)

Sophie asks and seeks to answer similar questions, but for her this is fundamentally because the possibility of fully comprehending Joss's sexuality and motivations is a potential money-spinner. Thus Kay juxtaposes two desires for knowledge. Colman, whilst complicit in Sophie's actions, is essentially attempting to regain his father, exploring the gap in his sense of Joss created by discovering his biological gender. Sophie, on the other hand, wishes to find out enough superficial information to satisfy her readers' hunger to be titillated over the torrid sexuality of the other:

The question of Mill Moody's attraction to Joss intrigues me. She married a woman who pretended she was a man. Why? A woman who stuffed wet cotton wool into a condom and tied on a couple of walnuts to fake the balls and penis. (Well, I don't know if Joss had a so-called "three piece suit" or not; but I've read about that somewhere.) Wild! It will do. (Kay 1998: 126–7)

Millie is all too aware of the kind of biography Sophie seeks to write, and her thoughts point to this when she thinks that neither she nor Joss can be understood within society's categorisations:

My life is a fiction now, an open book. I am trapped inside the pages of it. Anything is possible. My life is up for grabs. No doubt they will call me a lesbian. They will find words to put on me. Words that don't fit me. Words that don't fit Joss. They will call him names. (Kay 1998: 154)

Joss's blurring of gender divisions does indeed foreground the problematic nature of categorisation itself: if he is not a man, then what is he? Dave King argues that the dominant medical and psychological view "sees transvestism and transsexualism as properties of individual persons over which they have little or no control, for which they should not be punished" (King 1993: 184). But, as someone who occupies a male space in order to ensure their musical talent is recognised, Joss's choice is loaded with a certain shrewdness. This questions the underlying notions in mainstream society that transvestism and transsexualism are either deviant states or conditions thrust upon someone without choice and for which they should be pitied. I have chosen to refer to Joss throughout as male and as a transvestite, but do so while recognising that such categorisations remain prickly and unsatisfactory. The discovery in 1989 that Billy Tipton was anatomically female whilst living his life as a male is a case in point. Whilst the gay community reclaimed Billy as a woman, referring to her as a lesbian, the *Transsexual News Telegraph* saw him as a transsexual man (Romaine 1999: 46). As persons occupying a grey area, both Billy and the fictitious Joss are subject to a variety of interpretations and classifications.

Whilst Kay portrays Sophie from the outset as a hard, selfish character, her ultimate critique of the tabloidised world that Sophie represents comes during *Trumpet*'s final movement. Millie describes Joss dying:

So I kissed his hand and took some initiative. I said, it's all right now, darling. You can go now. You can go now. It is all right. You can go now. I kept stroking his hand, stroking it smoothly in the one direction. Feeling the ghost of a pulse still beating. I left the room. I went to the toilet. When I came back his pulse had gone [...]. He told me to remember the bandages, to remember and put the bandages back on. So I unbuttoned the pyjama jacket, managed to pull it off. It was hard work. I wrapped the bandages around his chest for the last time. The bandages that were part of our life together. I wrapped them round and round tightly till his small breasts flattened underneath the cream-coloured bandages. I did not cry when I was doing this. I had no way to express this feeling I felt. (Kay 1998: 202–3)

Here Millie lays herself bare for the reader; the sheer humanity of her living and reliving this moment erases sex and gender, pointing back to the early sense of loss and pain in which the novel opens.

Kay's coup, however, is twofold. Subsequent to this passage, Kay answers the questions that Colman and Sophie have pondered, but she answers them via Millie:

I wrapped two cream bandages around his breasts every morning, early. I wrapped them round and round, tight. I didn't think about anything except doing it well. Doing it well meant wrapping tight [...] I did it without thinking about it. He put a white T-shirt over the top. Over that another T-shirt. Over that, a buttoned shirt. He put on his boxer shorts and I turned away whilst he stuffed them with a pair of socks [...] His breasts weren't very big. They flattened easily. Nobody except me ever knew he had them. I never touched them except when I was wrapping the bandages round and around them. (Kay 1998: 238–9)

It is thus through Millie that the intrigue into how exactly Joss assumed the body of a man is satisfied. But, rather than rendering this as a display of otherness, it is posited simply as a part of daily life. Kay actively denies Sophie's desire to sensationalise the physical relationship between Millie and Joss, emphasising the sense that Joss's female body is inconsequential in their love for one another.

Consequently, when the opening of Sophie's biography is quoted thirty pages later, the person she describes is unrecognisable to the reader (and now also to Colman, whose voice she has assumed):

I found out my father was not a man but a woman ten weeks ago. [...] On the person who I thought of as my father, the breasts and pubic hair looked disgusting. Freakish. He might as well have turned into an albino. That would have been less shocking. His pubic hair and breasts looked grotesque, monstrous. I was so shocked [...] that I decided to write a book. [...] I know that not many people will ever find themselves in my position (count yourself lucky) but on the other hand unusual things happen to many people and anybody that has had anything freakish happen to them will relate to this book. I had to write this book so that I could understand my father and so that I could understand myself. (Kay 1998: 265–6)

Sophie makes a clear distinction between her assumed reader ("normal", heterosexual) and the kind of "freakish" other she observes and dissects. Through the process of unfolding the daily routines which allowed Joss to assume a male role, her reader would confirm his or her own sexuality and social status as both natural and superior. Thus, what Sophie's readers would find is not Joss at all, but themselves. But we, on the other hand, read Kay's novel, and what she ultimately portrays is not a freakish transvestite, but a loving husband and father whose words in a letter to Colman resonate: "You will understand or you won't. You will keep me or lose me. You will hate me or love me. You will change me or hold me dear" (Kay 1998: 277).

Ali Smith

Where Jackie Kay's *Trumpet* takes the concept of hidden love and exposes it in order to evoke its naturalness, Ali Smith's first novel *Like* (1997) explores the way that other love can be lost or broken within a dominantly heterosexual society. As in *Trumpet*, language and belonging assume a complexity. Told from various narrative positions and in two parts, *Like* explores the lives of two women, Amy and Ash. The first part, "Amy", looks at Amy's present in which she and her daughter move house, go on holiday and visit her estranged parents. The second part of *Like* is told from Ash's perspective, and retraces her friendship with Amy, who is now estranged from her. Slipping from Amy and Kate's present to a past that Amy and Ash shared, the narrative remains unsettled, anachronistic and in flux throughout, and at best the reader absorbs a series of subjective readings (and re-readings) of events and encounters.

This narrative style is accentuated by the fact that Amy, an ex-lecturer with a PhD in literature, can no longer read. Smith plays on this theme in *Hotel World* too. Sara, the first narrator, is (like Joss) dead on arrival, and through the course of her narrative forgets words: "Seeing birds. Their wings. Their beady   . The things they see with. The things we see with, two of them, stuck in a face above a nose. The word's gone. I had it a moment ago" (Smith 2001: 8). And Elise, a homeless girl who begs outside the Global Hotel, does not use vowels: "(Spr sm chn? Thnk y.) Chn. Spr sm. F y cn rd ths mesg y cd bcm a scrtry n gt a gd jb.)" (Smith 2001: 46). This points not only to her physical condition, freezing and wasting away on a street, but also to what appears to be suppressed and abusive past experiences. Unexplained, Amy's lack remains resonant during the second part of

Like, as the significance of language as a thematic and symbolic tool is fully explored.

In *Like*, words are either something intangible with no fixed meaning, or they provide individuals with powerful access to their own emotions. In the second half of the novel, Amy and Ash mirror these theories of language, Amy assuming the former and Ash the latter role. But, Amy is also a fractured character, and the Amy that is represented in the first part of *Like* is almost utterly at odds with the younger Amy whom Ash recollects. Where the younger Amy plays with language, manipulating its fictitious nature, the older Amy's struggle with its written form marks out her alienation from mainstream society. Because *Like* inverts chronology, portraying the older Amy first, her loss of language as a written form colours the way that the younger Amy is perceived. Moreover, the fact that Ash portrays the younger Amy through an exploration of her experience of loving means that the principal way of understanding the older Amy is through the resonance of this love. Ultimately, Ash's narrative consumes both senses of language, as she folds the link between language and bodily desire back into the fictitious nature of words. There is, however, also a symbolic connection between language, Amy's lack and the love experienced between Amy and Ash. Ash's love is explicit whilst Amy's is implied and even suppressed; nevertheless, a homoeroticism is posited between them. The ambiguity surrounding Amy's life and sexuality (underpinned by the various narrative points of view) feeds back into her loss of language as a written form. She sits on the cusp of sexual orientation; lost amidst forms of categorisation, her neitherness is encoded in her defunct relationship with language, the form which ultimately binds and labels her. Smith's thematic engagement with questions of language thus points to the interplay of these two experiences of love and the way homosexuality is, or is not, absorbed and embraced in a predominantly heterosexual society.

Throughout the first part of the novel, Amy starts to be able to read again. At times a link is forged between naming and being: Amy's inability to read is dated back to: "Kate's name around her ankle and on the card at the end of her perspex cot. The last written words to mean anything" (Smith 1997: 53). But, at other times language emerges as arbitrary once again:

Vesuvius, she sifts the word through her head. The word and the thing it means, the barbed dark between the word and the world; nothing but a rope bridge hanging by knots across a ravine, dropping loose slats as soon as you put your weight on it. A path around a chasm, that's all there is. (Smith 1997: 96)

Whilst this explicates the gulf between signifier and signified, it simultaneously appropriates the metaphorical power of language to imagine and project its own tenuous association to the material world. The image at once announces language's failure and its triumph. This points to the younger Amy rendered later in *Like*. But as an academic, Amy's outlook is postmodern. Ash recalls one of her lectures:

I remember what she said. That language was meaningless, that words were just random noises. The twentieth century, she'd said, was, more than ever before, the century of testimony, because it was more than ever before the century of questionable meaning. But since language was all an act, a performance, since words were by nature all fiction, words could never express anything but the ghost of truth. (Smith 1997: 269)

Theoretically Amy argues that language is a meaningless indecipherable void or an infinite play of fictions. However, Amy's position is undercut by Ash. At the same moment that Ash renders Amy's argument, she inscribes and re-inscribes one word: "I looked down at the piece of paper in my own hand; I saw I had written in the margin over and over, like one long word all the way down the page, her name" (Smith 1997: 269). Where the title of Amy's lecture, "The Body of the Text III", suggests a link between language and corporeality, it is Ash's narrative that actually identifies and explores it. Ash recounts her actions on her return home from the lecture:

I went round opening and closing drawers, putting things into a plastic bag. Then I sat on the bed. Then I took things out of the bag again and put them back on the table, back in the drawers, back under the bed, sat on the bed again, unfolded the piece of paper in my hand.
Amyamyamy. (Smith 1997: 270)

For Ash, Amy's name, signifying her being, is a potent and powerful symbol of Ash's intoxicating passion for Amy. So, rather than language being devoid and uncertain, as it is from Amy's academic perspective, language embodies something for Ash. In symbolising Amy, the word "Amy" itself focuses and enunciates Ash's corporeal passions.

In Melanie, Ash's sister, Smith makes this relationship between language and bodily consumption more explicit. Melanie physically consumes the written word: "She was always eating paper. You had to hide the *TV Times*, it'd be torn to bits" (Smith 1997: 274). Similar themes recur in Smith's work. In "The World with Love" from Smith's first collection of short stories, *Free Love*, Sam reminisces about a school-girl crush she had on Laura Watt: "You thought of her with words that gave you an unnameable feeling at the bottom of your spine and deep in your guts. [...] Words you could only imagine, words like caresses, *les cuisses*" (1995, 146–7). Whilst language may fall short of naming everything, for Sam and Ash it is so bound up with physical desire that the enunciation appears to prefigure the sensation.

In "Kasia's mother's mother's story" from *Other Stories*, the religious overtones apparent in Melanie's consumption of words are echoed. A woman burns her own and her family's identity papers, but before destroying her husband's she tears his name out and puts it in her mouth. She "lets the old ink, dried for years and all of them his, season after season of him, dissolve into her tongue" (Smith 1999: 161). Here, and in both Ash's and Melanie's relationships with language as a written form, Smith plays with the notion of transubstantiation. Melanie consumes and embodies "the word" as if it were the host, whereas Ash inscribes and recites it. She seeks to engender the real thing within the word, turning to the word itself over and over again in the impotent hope that this incantation will produce a compliant and reciprocating Amy. Eventually Ash succeeds, because in the creation of her narrative (which is written as a memoir), she effectively inscribes, creates and possesses Amy.

It is, however, Amy who first inscribes and possesses Ash through language. One morning, after Amy has spent some of her summer holidays in Scotland and befriended Ash, Ash receives a letter from her. The letter moves from a dictionary definition of Ash to a list of quotations pivoting around the word Ash. Whilst Amy almost evades any direct address, retaining an atmosphere of poetic distance, the quotations are rich with sexual overtones and her final lines evoke something of the girls' symbiosis: "*My grained Ash, / are you running like sparks through the stubble?*" (Smith 1997: 224). Just as she does as an academic, Amy plays with the notion of language as code here. Where Ash is explicit and specific about her emotions and her use of words, Amy's word choice is far less definite. She plays on the openness of language, pointing towards possible interpretations, but never defining her meaning. Nevertheless, by enunciating her, Amy's letter to Ash possesses her:

> Because in telling me my name like she did, in letting me know what it meant, my friend Amy carved her own name in me like a scar. After that, every time she looked my way, and every time she didn't, though I didn't know or notice, something was branding her deeper into me. If I were to snap open now at an arm, a leg, anywhere on my body, I could look down and there would be the a and the m and the y of her, visceral and elastic, stretching with the flesh; look in the bones, the cross-section of the honey-comb marrow, and there it is again written all through me, sweet and sticky, a souvenir from Amy. (Smith 1997: 228)

Amy's letter mirrors the effect of Ash's "Amyamyamy" (Smith 1997: 270) and whilst the roles are reversed (it is Amy who enunciates Ash), the power relation remains the same. The semantic links between Ash's name, trees and fire recur as do the motifs of notes, diaries and letters.

For Ash, language embodies meaning. The effort she takes in describing the letter itself emphasises this physical link: it was "a thick letter [...]. The writing on the envelope was fountain pen ink, neat, round, light blue. The paper was rich and rough to the touch" (Smith 1997: 223). And, given the value Ash places on the intertwining relationship between language, meaning and its physical inscription, the devastation of finding that her name does not appear in Amy's seven diaries is supreme. She sets fire to Amy's room, fleeing with the diaries:

> I had found out that her handwriting got touchingly younger as the years rewound.

I had found out that she wrote beautifully.

I had found out all number of trivial facts, hundreds of forgettable details, the slightest ripples across her surface. I had read the names of people I'd never heard of, and some I had, and I had followed every flicker of her attention round them.

Most of all I had found out something about myself, which was, after all, my main interest in reading them.

Not a word, not a thought, not a syllable. Not once did I get a mention. I wasn't there, anywhere. She'd left me out.

Now I turned and saw the sky was lit up behind me. The sight of it. The smell on the wind. The charred pages. The historic place of burning, I'd done that, me.

That'd get into her diary, then, if nothing else did. (Smith 1997: 305)

Ash externalises and objectifies the discovery of her absence by setting fire to Amy's things, effectively erasing them, reciprocating Amy's original act of violence – her denial of Ash. The fact that Ash is made symbolically absent in Amy's life through her diary mirrors Amy's withdrawal from language as a written form. Both lacks play on the boundary between language and being. For Ash, Amy's failure to inscribe and document her absence ultimately erases the significance of their shared experience. On the other hand, Ash's absence in Amy's diary potentially points to Ash's significance as something hidden or repressed within Amy herself.

Retrogressively this is touched on when a journalist calls Amy out of the blue to speak to her about Ash. During their conversation Amy recollects a journey she and Ash made to see a place in a T.S. Eliot poem. Rather than it being a beautiful landscape, they find themselves looking at a defence base, the consequence of which is being locked up, then being driven and dumped in "the middle of nowhere" (Smith 1997: 134) and finally having to sleep in a ditch until morning. Amy does not tell the journalist this story, but recounts it internally. Her narrative perspective shifts from first person plural to singular, moving between shared and individual elements of the experience:

We hadn't a clue where we were. I remember I was terrified, I was terrified because they'd taken our names [...]. But it was warm, it was mid-summer, I slept in a ditch that night, it was very exciting, I'd never done anything like it in my life before. (Smith 1997: 134)

This recollection is mirrored at the end of *Like*, when Ash returns to the same memory. The two compare significantly and the comparison effectively delineates the difference between repressed and open love which *Like* explores. Initially, Ash posits the tale in the third person, distancing both herself and Amy from it:

> And it's high summer. The sun is up. Two friends are watching it rise, hunkered down in a dry grassy ditch in the middle of nowhere. [...] one will see the other out of the corner of her eye as she sits in the warm air [...] and think how she looks like a different person, her hair everywhere, her face smudged with dirt.
> But for the moment, they're still lying there in the dry ditch, keeping out the night's slight chill under a jacket. One of them has her hand on the other's chest.
> I can hear your heart, you know, she says.
> You can what? the other says [...] she is startled by how close they are, so close that she doesn't know where to put her hands [...]. But her friend doesn't move, she stays with her ear pressed against her. (Smith 1997: 341)

The intimacy of this moment is emphasised not only because Ash's choice of personal pronouns blurs the distinction between herself and Amy, but also because it refigures Amy's version of events, infusing it with a physical and emotional intensity. As the narrative continues it becomes clear that Amy is lying listening to Ash's chest:

> It's saying the words, go on, she said.
> Then she asked me to tell her what hers was saying, and I put my ear to her chest and listened.
> What does it say? she said.
> It's like, like – I said, and I stopped. I couldn't think what it was like, it was Amy's heart, it wasn't like anything else. But she misunderstood me; that's good, she said, like, that's a good word, and she looked so pleased I didn't want to spoil it so I didn't [...]. (Smith 1997: 342)

This is the only explicit rendering of their physical bond in *Like* and, as the intimacy of this moment continues, it is syntactically rendered through long, sprawling sentences that move between describing their passage from ditch to train to describing the less tangible emotional shift in their relationship:

> we waited at the early morning station for the first train, go on beating inside me, keeping time over and over, and I dared to clean the smudge off her chin with the

corner of my shirt, I took her face in my hands and turned it up towards me like a child's and put the corner of my shirt in my mouth and cleaned a grass-dust smudge off her skin with my spit. [...] and we didn't say anything, nothing out loud, you could hear the summer for miles around us.
    That was something. I liked that then, yes, I did. (Smith 1997: 342)

This marks out a difference between Amy and Ash explored throughout *Like*: where Amy is pivotal to Ash's narrative, Ash is marginalised and even excluded from Amy's.

However, Ash's experience of marginalisation is, to an extent, resolved as she writes out her memories. Ash remains bound up with Amy through metaphor and linguistic play. If, as Amy argues, "language was all an act, a performance, since words were by nature all fiction, words could never express anything but the ghost of truth" (Smith 1997: 269), then it is in the shadows of her language that the significance of Ash is palpable. What is significant in Amy's conversation with the journalist is her whispered desire to reconnect with Ash: "You know where she is? Amy hears herself say [...]. You don't know where she is, Amy says. She sits down [...]. Is that – are those all the stories there are about where she might be?" (Smith 1997: 131, 133). This implicit desire is rendered once again in the conclusion of Amy's narrative, which is a subtle play on Ash and the correlation between her name, paper, trees and burning.

Pre-figuring (in the novel) Ash's burning frenzy, Kate and Amy build a fire on a snowy beach and burn "the things they don't need to keep anymore" (Smith 1997: 148), including some of Amy's diaries. Simultaneous to the actual, material scene, is a metaphorical imprint of Ash: "[Kate] shoves her head under Amy's arm. Amy looks down at her. Ash all over her. Her face, her hair, her mouth, her eyes":

Kate was stubborn about it. You shouldn't burn diaries in case they were important for history, she said. Amy explained; they're like when you draw something or write it for the first time and it's not what you wanted, so you throw it away and start all over again [...] Amy waits with what's left of her burning words. The fire is collapsing in on itself now. Soon, Amy thinks, there will be nothing left of it, Ash, that's all. Nothing else. (Smith 1997: 151–52)

Perhaps, then, the lack in Amy, which surfaces as her inability to read, symbolises her loss of Ash, and Amy's final erasure of her diaries points to her connection with and affirmation of Ash. Whilst this remains implicit, and Amy never explicitly draws Ash out of the margins, Ash's narrative does re-inscribe her within Amy's world. In effect, Ash's narrative does what her friend Malcolm advises her to do in their (imaginary) conversation. Being in Scotland, she says, is "a bit confusing. Ghost-ridden" (Smith 1997: 338). "All ghosts need is a good story," he suggests. "Give them somewhere to love that keeps them happy."

Ash and Amy remain bound together by their absences, and it is this loss that binds and colours the narrative, just as one of Smith's prefatory quotations by Emily Dickinson says: "My story has a moral – / I have a missing friend". *Like* is a love story about the need to be accepted, the desire to love and be loved and the price paid when we try to erase or ignore love's impulse. Ultimately neither has succeeded in erasing their love for the other: echoing Amy's desire to know where Ash is, there is Ash's telling shift from past to present tense as she conflates the heart-beat tale with Amy herself: "go on beating inside me, keeping time over and over". Whilst she concludes with the more final "That was something. I liked that then, yes, I did" (Smith 1997: 342), and whilst the act of telling and inscribing her story of their world effectively provides the ghosts of their past "somewhere to love" (Smith 1997: 338), the continuous presence of Amy keeping time within Ash resonates.

Ultimately, *Like* explores the way that lesbian love is excluded, marginalised or erased in mainstream society, and this experience is not new to Ash (indeed the whole reason for the journalist's call to Amy is to write an article on famous people who have dropped out of the public eye). During her final year at school, Ash finds herself in the middle of a conversation about lesbians. The majority of the girls and boys discussing it dismiss it as "disgusting" (Smith 1997: 216) and "unnatural" (Smith 1997: 217), but Ash rebukes this: "No it's not, the voice said, and it was coming from me. Not unnatural, I said. Just unexpected. It's just a different kind of natural" (Smith 1997: 217). But the last words on the matter come from Donna, who, up until this moment is Ash's girlfriend: "People aren't meant to act like that. Otherwise we wouldn't be made like we are. It's not natural. It's not normal. It's really sick" (Smith 1997: 218). Donna's statement, like

Amy's diary and her recollection of their overnight stay in a ditch, pushes Ash out of the picture. And whilst Ash re-inscribes herself in a central role, she remains a character whose desire to love is marginalised.

Before *Like* and *Trumpet*'s publications, Caroline Gonda suggested that writers like Smith and Kay had a stark dilemma: they could either "stake out a place in the margins, boldly asserting [their] difference(s) in the face of a hostile society which alternatively trivialises and demonises" or they could "sink [their] differences in the hope that the dominant culture will kindly overlook them" (White: 1995: 2). *Like* and *Trumpet* mark out a different moment in the forging of a Scottish literary heritage that embraces diversity. Smith's writing often happens to be about homosexual love and the way it functions in a predominantly heterosexual culture. But her triumph lies not in asserting difference, but in inverting the notion of difference itself. Because Smith's evocations of the (universal) desire to love and be loved are so beautifully realised, the fact that that love happens to be homosexual becomes inconsequential. As Douglas Gifford asserts of *Free Love*, gender is transitional and the stories "can almost be read according to preference" (Gifford and McMillan eds 1997: 588). Whilst this remains true for much of Smith's short fiction, her novels are more explicitly lesbian. However, the "kind of lyric prose-poetry" which Gifford describes as "transforming the conventional worlds of women into new, evocative and dream-like states" remains to the fore. What is ultimately significant, then, is the depiction of love itself and the homosexual imprint of the love explored is so subtle as to be almost transparent. She thus succeeds in marginalising the issue itself.

Likewise, in *Trumpet*, Kay foregrounds the physical distinction between male and female, but the logic of the love and experience she evokes transcends corporeality. In stories like "Shell" and "In Between Talking About the Elephant" from *Why Don't You Stop Talking*, Kay continues to step beyond conceived notions of love and identity, exploring through stories infused with magic realism and metamorphoses, a diverse range of loves (Kay 2002). In *Trumpet*, the distinction made becomes a matter of language – the difference between "freak" and "husband" – and that, Kay shows, is a matter of choice. Ash says gay love is just a different kind of natural, but I would argue that Smith and Kay undercut this. In their lyrical realisations of it, there is nothing different about this kind of natural: they speak about and for our most basic instinct – the desire to love and be loved. And what, after all, can be more natural than that?

Bibliography

Christianson, Aileen and Alison Lumsden (eds). 2000. *Contemporary Scottish Women Writers*. Edinburgh: Edinburgh University Press.
Gifford, Douglas and Dorothy McMillan (eds). 1997. *A History of Scottish Women's Writing*. Edinburgh: Edinburgh University Press.
Kay, Jackie. 1998. *Trumpet*. London: Picador.
—. 2002. *Why Don't You Stop Talking*. London: Picador.
King, Dave. 1993. *The Transvestite and the Transsexual: Public Categories and Private Identities*. Aldershot: Avebury.
Romaine, Suzanne. 1999. *Communicating Gender*. New Jersey: Lawrence Erlbaum Associates.
Smith, Ali. 1995. *Free Love and other stories*. London: Virago.
—. 1997. *Like*. London: Virago.
—. 1999. *Other Stories and other stories*. London: Granta.
—. 2001. *Hotel World*. London: Penguin.
Whyte, Christopher (ed.) 1995. *Gendering the Nation*. Edinburgh: Edinburgh University Press.

Beating, Retreating: Violence and Withdrawal in Iain Banks and John Burnside

Scott Brewster

This chapter traces the preoccupation with masculine violence, the ambivalent relation to the father, and the fascination with alternative modes of being in the fiction of Iain Banks and John Burnside. While both writers depict various forms of retreat and withdrawal from the external world, they also highlight the limits and consequences of such ethical disengagement.
Keywords: Iain Banks, John Burnside, Emmanuel Levinas, Gothic, male violence, the Other.

The rare, intense, unsettling beauty of John Burnside's poetry and prose gives us a momentary glimpse of a magical realm that runs parallel to the everyday world. Yet this fleeting disclosure of "the beauty of the impossible" (Burnside 2001b: 29) is often counter-pointed by a sense of threat and danger that lurks under the surface of things, a sense that Burnside has termed "the stoat in the soul: its pink-eyed wonder, its wistful desire for blood" (Burnside 1992: 4). This blend of lyrical grace and sinister violence has become particularly characteristic of his fiction, which depicts brutal, alcoholic and sociopathic masculine worlds. I use "lyrical" advisedly here, since Burnside remarks that "the lyrical impulse begins at the point of self-forgetting" (Burnside 2000b: 260). The disparate elements that constitute the stoat in the soul – the wonder of the natural world, the unassuageable longing for transcendence, and the ever-present potential for startling cruelty – are woven together by an increasing fascination with retreat and (self)obliteration. As he acknowledged in a recent interview, "The men I've thought were worthwhile were always people who had exercised some kind of surrender – the surrender of the security of their own power to a kind of openness" (McDowell 2003).

While this chapter will focus primarily on the interlinked concerns of masculinity and violence, alternative worlds, ethical responsibility and disengagement in Burnside's work, it will also trace a striking if unlikely affinity between Burnside and Iain Banks.

Indeed, in its sinister brutality, ambivalence towards masculine power and the paternal, fascination with taxonomies that shut out the external world and seal in their protagonists, exploration of "other" modes of being and reflection on openness and "surrender", Banks's *The Wasp Factory* (1990a) might be said to foreshadow the preoccupations of Burnside's fiction. As we will see, both writers depict various forms of retreat from the other, but also highlight the limits and consequences of that retreat.

Iain Banks

The Wasp Factory seeks to displace the paternal metaphor, but merely translates it another form. Frank Cauldhame is driven to devise systems and ordering patterns by his desire to escape the Law and the shadow cast by the Name-of-the-Father, but his willed separation can turn suddenly into a destructive isolation and madness that must in the end be resisted. Frank's passion, even mania, for naming (the Wasp Factory, the Sacrifice Poles, the Bomb Circle and so on), the maintenance of the Measurement Book, the fastidious cleaning routines and compulsive shop-lifting, the "paranoid imaginings" (Banks 1990a: 109), ritualistic behaviour – typified by the excavation and totemic veneration of the skull of Old Saul, which grants power over the "old enemy" supposedly responsible for Frank's castration – and the Factory itself all constitute closed, self-referential systems. The Wasp Factory is Frank's instrument of judgement, torture and destiny, an intricate, implacable Gothic machinery worthy of Poe. True to the Gothic dialectic of order and transgression, the Factory's grisly, insistent operation proceeds independently of the designs of its creator. Although its decision is always final for the hapless wasps it traps, the Factory refuses certainty, inviting instead ever-deepening layers of interpretation:

Despite the fact that I keep all the door mechanisms well oiled and balanced, and repair and test them until the slightest tremor sets them off – I have to tread very lightly when the Factory is doing its slow and deadly work – sometimes the Factory does not want the wasp in its first choice of corridor, and lets it crawl back out on to the face again. (122)

This mesmeric, capricious uncertainty, whereby the pursuit of truth is a matter of play (in several senses), reproduces Frank's paternal relation. His father, like the Factory, withholds the truth, but he nonetheless offers the lure of revelation, a game that Frank plays with apparent knowingness:

> Only these little bits of bogus power enable him to think he is in control of what he sees as the correct father-son relationship. It's pathetic really, but with his little games and his secrets and his hurtful remarks he tries to keep his security intact. (16)

Yet the study represents another chamber of the Factory: it cannot be entered freely, and its secrets are defended by force. The family home plays with Frank, a fate that recalls Quiss's game-playing in the labryinth-like Castle of Bequest of *Walking on Glass* (Banks 1985). In his wild freedom, the son seems to be a child outside the system, yet he lives in the shadow of Paternal Law: Frank enjoys evading the Father's watchfulness, but he remains enmeshed in the field of the Other. Frank's "education" is based on a farrago of his father's lies and whimsical jokes, and in the search for truth he turns to the Factory for information, and to his complex, totemic sign systems: "From the smaller to the greater, the patterns always hold true, and the Factory has taught me to watch out for them and respect them" (Banks 1990a: 37).

It is in the failure to read signs, however, that Frank finally sees himself. The crisis provoked by the return of Frank's dog-killing brother Eric undermines their father's authority, and grants Frank the opportunity to discover the secrets of the study: the shorn genitals, the male hormones. Ironically, it is through an act of misinterpretation that Frank discovers his Father's secret. Frank's initial conclusion is wrong – his father is not female – and the "real" secret is that Frank is actually Frances, a deception born of his father's wilful "misreading" of his child. *The Wasp Factory* is faithful to the Gothic tradition in that the novel sways between conviction and delusion: to demystify anomalies and uncover apparently unfathomable secrets, Frank/ Frances must confront arbitrary, untrustworthy signs. It is only by opening to this uncertainty that Frank/Frances can break the Factory's hold over his imagination. This break is accompanied by a growing awareness of, and emerging sense of responsibility to, others: Frances mourns the dead, reflects on her crimes, and comforts her disturbed brother in quasi-maternal fashion. The "murder" of Frank – which initially prompted the unwitting son to acts of spectacular vengeance, and a substantial body count amongst the family circle and the island's wildlife – is the birth of Frances's "involvement".

As Victor Sage has argued, Frank lives for most of the novel in a "self-defining Gothic reality", his/her "superstitious world of death [...] a simplified compensatory fiction, a counter-dream born of the historical fiction of being socially, geographically, and anatomically, 'cut off'" (Sage 1996: 27). Frank's fascination for building dams is a response to the "petrified fiction of his own maleness" (Sage 1996: 25), but it also acts as a barrier against any encroachment, against the split that marks the relation of self and other and foregrounds the non-identical, against the doubling that constitutes the "I". Yet Frank/ Frances is made and unmade by this split, in spite of the defensive mechanisms that he (by maintaining his fortress) – or his father (by surreptitiously feeding Frank male hormones) adopt. Frank's relationship with his father revolves around a battle with, and disengagement from, the masculine: the relinquishing of Frank's masculinity is coterminous with the relinquishing of his spatial and psychological defences. When Eric escapes from hospital, and declares his intention to return home, Frank reluctantly abandons his plans for another War on the island in order to "start dealing with the real world" (Banks 1990a: 24). Once his father's deception is revealed, Frank must relinquish the boundaries he has constructed, the rigid fortifications that have failed to sustain his retreat from the "outside".

Labyrinthine topographies and enclosures that at once protect or isolate individuals yet offer an escape route are a central feature of Banks's "mainstream" novels, and his science fiction. For example, the elaborate architectural designs in *The Bridge* (Armitt 1996: 103– 11) mark out a point of departure, and an anchoring point, in a text split between "real" and "delusional" worlds. The protagonist Orr is in part imprisoned by structure: confined to a hospital bed by a serious car accident, he "escapes" to a dystopian futurist landscape in which the bridge "is not only the central reference point but also the limits of existence" (Armitt 1996: 104). Orr faces the possibility that "the bridge might eventually meet itself, form a closed circuit" (Banks 1990b: 130). Yet the very negotiation of this intricate architecture of restraint also enables Orr to gradually return to consciousness. Thus the act of withdrawal eventually transmutes into a form of re-engagement. The Wasp Factory represents Frank's bridge to involvement, a release from determinism, from remorseless and self-absorbed struggle:

> The factory was my attempt to construct life, to replace the involvement which I otherwise did not want.
> Well, it is always easier to succeed at death.
> Inside this greater machine, things are not quite so cut and dried (or cut and pickled) as they appeared in my experience. Each of us in our personal Factory, may believe we have stumbled down one corridor, and that our fate is sealed and certain (dream or nightmare, humdrum or bizarre, good or bad), but a word, a glance, a slip – anything can change that, alter it entirely, and our marble hall becomes a gutter, or our rat-maze a golden path. Our destination is the same in the end, but our journey – part chosen, part determined – is different for us all and changes even as we live and grow. I thought one door had snicked shut behind me years ago; in fact I was still crawling about the face. Now the door closes, and my journey begins. (Banks 1990a: 183–4)

The Factory represents opening rather than fateful closure, the incalculable rather than the destined. It suggests that living involves separation and relation, and the surrender of security.

John Burnside

With its icy detachment, scandalising cruelty and macabrely self-enclosed world, John Burnside's *The Dumb House* (1997) bears a close affinity to *The Wasp Factory*. In both texts, system becomes faith, and reason and its obverse merge into one another, and the main protagonists have a vivisectional fascination to uncover the secret order of things. In *The Dumb House*, however, security is never relinquished. In order to find "the locus of the soul" (Burnside 1998: 3), the designer of the Dumb House, Luke, incarcerates his twin boys in his basement, depriving them of speaking contact and observing their mute interactions. In doing so, he replicates the experiments of the dyslexic Mughal Emperor, Akbar the Great. To test the theory that language is innate rather than acquired, Akbar built a mansion for new-born children, who were surrounded by mute attendants. Luke's experiments serve a greater design: "Each of these events was an inevitability, one thread in the fabric of what might be called destiny, for want of a better word – a thread that neither I nor anyone else could have removed without corrupting the whole design" (3). The treatment of the boys is marked by a total withdrawal of affect:

I knew from the first that it was an error to think of the twins as *my* children, whatever the biological reality. It's only a flaw in the language that confuses kinship with possession, and in this case the kinship was accidental. I had no real connection with these creatures who lay in the basement room, crying and fouling themselves, clinging to a life that I could easily have ended with a basin of water or a length of twine. (145)

Similarly, the mute Lillian, who gives birth to the twins and dies immediately after, lingers briefly as a stain over the makeshift cot until she fades away, uncomplicatedly and "almost imperceptibly" (145). Luke remarks that every human transaction is a question of control, and that "choice is destiny" for both the powerful and powerless. It is Lillian's choice "that made her my possession" (107), and his relationship with Karen Olerud begins with a moment of dream-like invitation or recognition, "where you touched them and they responded, surprised by their own complicity, amazed by a moment of unexpected surrender" (52). In each case, the women's "surrender" is not reciprocated by Luke. He espouses the "true scientific ethic, which is total commitment. The scientist is the one for whom everything is a hypothesis, the one who is wholly dedicated to the experiment. There can be no exceptions" (140).

Luke's love of classification (a recurrent feature of Burnside's poetry and fiction) is a defence against the loss of control:

nothing seems more beautiful to me than language when it creates the impression of order [...]. What disturbs me now is the possibility that language might fail: after the experiment ended so inconclusively, I cannot help imagining that the order which seems inherent in things is only a construct, that everything might all into chaos, somewhere in the long white reaches of forgetting. (11)

For Luke, "[h]appiness, or fulfilment, or whatever else you choose to call it, seems to me to consist of a glimpse of the world as a patterned and limited whole" (23), and "an ordered illusion is necessarily preferable to the chaotic truth of the world" (112). Yet he fails to see the whole picture, fails to discern "a symmetry, a deeper order, a more complex and subtle world" in the twins' wordless relationship (156), and he cannot break into their complicit, exclusive world (175). They possess an unreadable language, their uncanny, telepathic intimacy representing a private system of communion and empathy that frustrates the "objectivity" of Luke's experiment: "in my heart I knew by the end that they were talking to one another about a world I could not see, or hear, or touch, and the language they were using was so perfect, so fully attuned to their being, that it was beyond any analysis that I might attempt" (152).

It is not the first time that Luke tries to analyse an impenetrable language – he remembers the private, invented language of a "foreign" woman from his childhood (45–6), and the alterity of his mother's last attempts at communication: "she made a sound – a kind of sob, though it was more than that, more deliberate, almost articulate, like a word in some foreign language that I didn't understand, rooted in some dark, wet place, the beginning of decay perhaps, the beginning of annihilation" (75). The abusive, aphasic relationships with Karen Olerud (the O of her mouth ruled), and the rescued vagrant Lillian, reproduce this silenced maternal voice, whose stories can no longer be deciphered. The nameless twins sing their indecipherable songs, transcending "the gap between human and animal [...] plugged into a current of instinct and blood-knowledge" and aware of things that Luke cannot detect. Each twin surrenders, opens absolutely to the other, and Luke can only breach, not enter, that bond since his relation to the twins is predetermined, self-justified. They remind Luke of his cat, Rusty, whose pitiful need and vulnerability disgusted and enraged him. He batters the cat with a spade, determined "to expunge that scrap of living misery, to destroy its pitiful soul" (173).

The twins provoke a similar sickness, and Luke's sense of deprivation and exclusion places him temporarily in his own Dumb House. He can only confront that exclusion by first performing laryngotomies on the boys, then poisoning them, a destructive act that confirms the failure of the experiment. It is Karen Olerud who returns at the end of the novel as an "all-seeing" intruder, not the vengeful ghost of the vagrant Jimmy, whom Luke has horribly murdered. When he locks Karen into his mother's bedroom, he "experienced a sudden thrill of joy, as if I were locking away some hidden treasure that I'd been waiting years to find, the one thing I had never expected: a necessary gift, an indisputable moment of divine grace" (191). This is a grace granted by possession and power, rather than openness, however; after this deeply unsettling first novel, the tension between security and surrender increasingly characterises Burnside's fiction.

The Mercy Boys (Burnside 2000a) has a more quotidian setting than *The Dumb House*, but it portrays another dysfunctional world, one scarred by alcoholism, disillusionment, loneliness and latent violence. The four central characters meet each day in a Dundee pub, the Mercy, to swap stories of ghosts, torture and brutality, and to avoid sharing their own tales of disappointment and loss. The brittle camaraderie of the pub masks a deeper aphasia and isolation. The narrative begins, and ends, with a character retreating from violence. One of the drinkers, Alan, periodically wakes with the conviction of having committed murder, and keeps "seeing flashes of violence in his mind's eye". He wards off these half-memories by halting time, and imagining "his life had been suspended, not finished, but held in abeyance, kept in reserve forever, like a soul in limbo" (5). Alan no longer wants to mingle with the crowd; he observes his neighbours without a sense of superiority, but instead with "a soft, detached pity for them, and for himself, and a sense of the coldness, the neutrality of the world they inhabited" (22). Alan recalls "some philosopher" who took a daily afternoon walk at "exactly three o'clock", a monotonous routine that Alan imagines gradually acquiring colour and variety: "a life full of landmarks, a life of endless detail. It was something to believe in, this life of observed moments – an escape, somehow, from time" (22).

The grace of routine is similarly discovered by the central character of *Living Nowhere* (2003), Francis Cameron: in sweeping leaves in the grounds of a Cambridge college, he finds a "steady rhythm" in which "I felt everything slip into place around me" (Burnside 2003: 277). Perhaps fittingly, when Alan helps another of the Boys, Rob, to flee from justice after murdering his wife and neighbour, it is a farmer with such a routine – "if there was any grace in working, any sense of pride, it surely resided in this – in cleaning, keeping, maintaining, oiling, repairing" (224) – who discovers their forest hideout. Alan finally floats free of time by drowning himself in a sea loch:

With every step he took, he felt lighter and cleaner, as if his body was dissolving, leaving him only spirit and light […] he went on, the lightness growing in his body, bright and cool and perfectly balanced, the weight he had carried for so long dissolving between his shoulder blades, in the pit of his stomach, in the ache of his groin […] he kept on walking, stumbling over the rocks, but moving on, moving on, emptying, becoming weightless. (265)

In various ways, each of the other main characters seeks such weightlessness. Rob's violence – particularly the mugging of "fat boy" (105–9) and the listless, detached killing of his wife and their neighbour (171–3) – is partly born of frustration and humiliation, but it is also strangely casual and relieving. His philosophy is that a man must avoid surrendering himself, either out of generosity or fear: "If you were prepared to give it away, that was your own look out" (149). Sconnie, the drifter, also learns that men must not reveal any weakness. He concludes that to be a man in the eyes of the world is to be like his father: "You had to conceal yourself, you had to pretend things weren't really happening to you" (44). Yet he glimpses an alternative mode of being, a weightlessness that eludes social expectation: "That was a special skill that some men possessed: nothing more than an intuitive understanding, an acceptance of gravity that allowed them to pass through the world with a certain grace. Sconnie was certain it was there in everyone: a hidden essence, a secret other" (52). He seeks this grace in travelling to random destinations, eschewing "company": on the train, he feels "absolved: weightless and clean, like a new man" (53). His final, aimless journey sees him sacrificed in a cultic killing.

The fourth Mercy Boy, Junior, learns to trust through a sadistic, humiliating trick played by father, which is intended to teach him to "Trust nobody". Junior, however, wants to "take people on trust, and to trust himself" (40). His desire to trust is about surrender, about laying oneself bare rather than about denial and defensiveness. In contrast to the other Boys, Junior enjoys a dignified retreat: when his chronically ill wife Estelle dies suddenly, he feels immense relief to be free of the burden of care: "For the first time in years, he was alone, and he was surprised at how glad he was. [...] It felt good. He was glad the other boys weren't there. It was his moment, a moment he'd been waiting for – he realised now – for as long as he could remember" (177).

The epigraph of *Burning Elvis* (Burnside 2001) – Donne's "No Man is an Island" – resonates through the narratives of isolation, violence and loss that follow. The collection is Burnside's most austere exploration of self-forgetting and anonymity: most of the stories have self-annihilation at their heart. In the title story, the narrator observes a picture of Elvis "fading away into nothingness at the edge of the page. It's hard to describe – it sounds like the morbid imaginings of a teenage girl but for me there was more, a surprising poignancy, a glimpse of vacuum" (Burnside 2001a: 10). This fading of the iconic image is mirrored by the aftermath of the murder of one young woman by another:

People will kill for the sensation of being, just to see themselves in the story. Lindy used to say that everybody wants to be special; but Cathy wasn't special at all, she was nothing. Her fragment of history had passed and nobody knew or cared who she was. Life had moved on. It was a banal and surprisingly comforting thought, and all of a sudden it made me unaccountably glad, like the stillness of a city graveyard, or the first thick fall of snow, that obliterates and renews everything it touches. (27)

Burning Elvis is peopled by bereft sons and husbands, strange counterparts and inadequate father-figures who play sadistic games and whose stories cannot be believed. In "What I Know about Myself", the narrator is angry "that my real father didn't exist and had to be invented", an anger that is harboured like a "private virus" (38). Similarly, in "Dada", the eponymous individual may or may not be a real father, but the son's anger and abuse is eventually transformed into surrender and a form of reconciliation. He preserves his father's body in the downstairs bathroom, and fruitlessly interrogates the corpse: "he'd say the truth was staring me in the face, only I couldn't see it. He said the truth is always there, just staring us in the face. I ask him about that sometimes, and I look at his mouth, as if he could answer." Dada's "listening", however, may give the son "the chance to figure things out for myself" (172). He traces his father back "to an origin I must have forgotten was there", the "bright afternoon" when he was taught to swim. He recalls the feeling of "amazing lightness" and weightless freedom which comes from "an unexpected abandonment". In this moment – remembered or imagined – his father was "so knowing, so generous". The narrator's act of imagination is correspondingly generous, making his father "the gift of a new life: I'm teaching him to be something he never even dreamed of becoming" (183).

There are numerous examples of "lightness" and self-absenting in the collection. The narrator of "The Invisible Husband" (a counterpart of Junior in *The Mercy Boys*) yearns to escape his mentally ill wife, who no longer recognises him as she moves away into a realm of "universal uncertainty" (61). It is the emergence of this alternative partner that allows the narrator to disappear: "I owe him a debt of gratitude [...]. I have never heard his voice, but I like to imagine, from time to time, that he looks and sounds like me or, if not me, exactly, then someone I might have become, once upon a time" (64). In "Folie à Deux", the survivor of murderous twins exists in "a kind of limbo, an eternal summer of my own, where I watch and wait, free of identity, beyond all human jurisdiction" (132). In "Bebop", the young narrator is introduced to jazz by an older man whom he befriends: "the music was all air and distance and infinite possibility" (192). The sense of freedom, and the concealment of loss that the records offer, is counter-pointed by the childhood murders, gruesome nightmares and unspoken grief that dominate the story. The yearning for escape in the final story, "Graceland", is accompanied by the sinister threat represented by a character called Elvis. As the narrator is recovering from his disturbing experience in hospital, he imagines Graceland as "an idea of home" even if this is an "illusion": it is "an ordinary house in the suburbs" pervaded by the smell of "cheap lilac soap and the radio playing in the kitchen". However, typically of the collection, this idealised domestic space combines anonymity, security and menace: it has "as a kind of joke, a Hallowe'en night of horror films in a darkened room, and a mouthful of trick blood on the bathroom floor, to keep the night at bay" (224). Against a dark backdrop of violence, suspicion and failed relationships, *The Locust Room* negotiates its way towards a willed isolation, "the grace of the forgotten" (Burnside 2001b: 276). Through its meditation on solitude, psychological disturbance and sociopathic male behaviour, the novel offers various models of separation, self-containment and connection (Brewster 2005). The novel's protagonist Paul, a photography student, progressively withdraws from family, lovers and friends during the summer of 1975, when a rapist is creating a climate of insidious fear with a series of violent attacks in Cambridge. Paul's lonely photographic work discloses a certain "shadowy, nervous kinship" with the rapist: he, like the rapist, is a night-inhabitant, a revenant drawn by "urgent" curiosity to explore the dark (91). (This unnerving kinship typifies the discomforting fraternal bond forged between a number of male characters and the rapist: in the pervasive atmosphere of distrust and denial, one woman declares that the rapist could be any man in the area.) Both Paul and the rapist long for invisibility, although for very different reasons. During his reign of terror, the rapist believes he can assume the contours of the rooms he invades, and after his capture, he meditates on his desire for invisibility:

Because he had been in danger, always: side-streets, city; night; a man walking in the rain, watching, listening, choosing. It wasn't the danger you saw on television, or read about in a book. This was something else, something to do with a different sense of loss, of the moment when he too would become conscious, not only of himself walking those dark, deserted streets, but also of that invisible assembly of movement and steps and even breathing that matched him in every way, but was not himself – like that invisible presence the Arctic explorers described when they came home from being lost, walking for hours or days in the snow and the dark with a single, unseen companion. It would be impossible to talk about this to anyone else and make himself understood, but he had known all along that this other was always waiting to arrive. (148–9)

He is "a man walking in the rain", unremarkable, and yet under threat: his separation is a burden rather than an escape, and leads to a different form of aberrant detachment. His violent assaults constitute an attempt to evade the counterpart who haunts his every step. The rapist refuses to surrender to the other, to open up to this "unseen companion". His security depends upon his ability to inhabit the other's space, and to resist any encroachment from his own surroundings.

Paul too seeks a form of retreat and estrangement: "He was capable [...] of a kind of absence, a self-abandonment that led to visions, streams of words, images, ideas that almost translated themselves into something meaningful, something he could see or name. Yet these private hours were less satisfying when he thought someone else might be in the house" (24–5). He views photography as "a continual re-estrangement from the given" (176), a picture of the world stripped of "invested memory", and he seeks an art of revelation that he terms magic or alchemy. Tony, the lab scientist at the field station where Paul takes up casual work, and which houses the eponymous locust room, is just such a shy, remote man who resembles "an old-time alchemist, assisting in the rituals of decomposition and transformation" (254–5). The murmur of the insects resembles an incomprehensible language (164), and is reminiscent of the "hum" in Emily Dickinson's "I heard a Fly buzz". P. H. Fry comments that this hum constitutes the ostensive moment of literature, whereby literature is a sign of the pre-conceptual, "disclosing neither the purpose nor the structure of existence but only existence itself" (Fry 1995: 11). For Paul, the creative act involves "seeing, and making seen, the true nature of the world, a world that had seemed given, and finished, and entirely nameable until that moment" (Burnside 2001b: 175). His theory of the photographic encounter is structured around the pursuit of impossibility and invisibility at the "borderline of habitation" (207):

you had to go beyond the social, you had to refuse the given role, in order to perform a kind of alchemy that would be at once a disappearance and a way of remaining utterly still. As a photographer [...] Paul had fallen in love with the idea of an impossibility, half-knowing all along that the beauty of the impossible would cast its shadow over everything else, every possible fact, showing it up as the temporal, contingent thing it really was. (29)

Paul eventually realises that art is about invisibility rather than disappearance, a realisation that follows the death of his father. His father is his counterpart, another version of the rapist's "unseen companion": "It was the father hidden in every man's mind, a father Paul had carried with him all his life: a good phantom composed in part from the man he had known and, in equal part, from a figure he himself had invented" (271). This good phantom recalls the "secret other" whose weightless grace Sconnie discerns, even in his "ordinary, heavy" father, in *The Mercy Boys* (Burnside 2000a: 52). Paul's father hovers "at the edge of some region of unlikeness", his solitude a "dwelling, a refuge" (Burnside 2001b: 211). His father possessed the "solitude of a craftsman, the isolation of someone who had traded the social, traded the human, for something else, something he couldn't explain or share" (231). He had retreated to a psychological space voided of clamour: "It was familiar and strange, empty and full, private and, at the same time, wholly impersonal" (178). Paul discerns that such estrangement is the necessary prelude to invisibility:

It was a surrender, it was a relinquishing of power – to become, for one's own sake, a helpless, tender, unvictorious human being. That was why they had taken themselves away: men like his father, the boy in the woods, all those quiet shifting figures that had hovered around the edges of the social. They had understood that the only way to become themselves as they could be was to be alone. Each of them, in his own way, had come to understand the need for surrender – which was not only different from, but even the opposite of submission. Surrender was an act of will, a relinquishing of visibility and power, in exchange for the tenuous moment of grace. (274)

Like his father, Paul begins to "surrender something": he belongs to a "world of silence and light", and feels a "dangerous" nostalgia for "the unnamed world of other creatures, that made him homeless in the world" (275). Yet this homeless longing leads him to recognise that "he was always at the point of freedom": "Generations of unfathered men had picked up their unseen burden and moved on into the same darkness, the same accommodation with homelessness that he had begun to imagine from himself" (275–6). This recognition means that his existence is not a matter of establishing a barrier between inner and outer life: it is instead "a necessary choice between estrangements" (276). The novel ends with a moment of accommodation: the unfathered, homeless Paul returns to the family home, where his mother is preparing Christmas lunch.

Living Nowhere represents Burnside's most intense exploration of homelessness, surrender and responsible disengagement. The novel begins, and ends, in the unhomely space of Corby, where Burnside grew up. He has reflected on how this industrial environment shaped masculinity: "In Corby, if you were a man, you were always closed, you were always defensive. That's what male power is about and you lived with it every day" (McDowell 2003). The main characters attempt various forms of withdrawal: drugs, drifting, art, and dreams of elsewhere. The opening section depicts Alina Ruckert's acid trip; she moves through the wintry landscape as if protected by an invisible bubble. In this withdrawn state, everything is "filled with energy, filled with some bright, receptive power"; the poison of the outer world can be swallowed and transformed "into something good and true, the way an alchemist would transform base metal into gold" (6–7). Alina imagines a space of retreat beyond Corby: home for her "is a country which did not exist" (13). A different sort of outside intrudes when the young boy Micmac enters Alina's bedroom, the underlying menace of his proximity shattering her sense of apartness and recalls the rapist's invasive presence in *The Locust Room*. Alina can only escape imaginatively into another icy realm, the "inhuman paradise" of the Fairy King that she recalls from a childhood story.

Alina's brother Jan, and Francis, seek escape through photography. Jan takes pictures of emptiness and "unrelenting greyness", an aesthetic vision that corresponds to his withdrawal from other people. He is "always slipping away from them [...] stepping out of their line of vision", disappearing from school photographs and adding

the alchemy of studied absence to snapshots of first communions and confirmations, a blur at the edge of the picture like snowfall, or like the wisp of nothingness that storytellers mistake for a summertime ghost. (57)

Unlike the displacement experienced by his Latvian antecedents, Jan's distance is a willed separation. This separation cannot protect him from a vicious murder at the hands of a sadistic local gang: ironically, it is Jan's intervention to help another victim attacked by the group that leads to his death. Throughout the novel, the desire for detachment is often thwarted by arbitrary events, and the longing for separation derives from ambivalent emotions. The compulsive violence of Francis's father Tommy arises from the same sense of dismissive withdrawal as that of Jan. Soon after his arrival in Corby, Tommy's involvement in a fight reveals "a thick tide of exhilarating anger he'd not been aware of till now, something cold and steady, a new readiness to judge and find lacking and strike down, like some Old Testament God disappointed by the human race he had wanted so much to love, erasing whole cities with a single, arbitrary word" (76–7). This is the perspective of the tyrant or the psychopath; Tommy can take action for its own sake, and needs no further justification. He can only challenge this tainting anger by using violence responsibly; when he fears that Francis will retaliate after Jan's murder, he decides to pursue the killers himself. Francis's brother Derek has a different response to force: he responds to the "natural", commonplace assumption of male violence with "an appropriate refusal" (165). He also espouses a distinctive ethical code, one that resists the conception of neighbourly love and forgiveness:

> there was something impossible about Christianity itself, about living by these particular commandments, about turning the other cheek, about loving everybody. Christ, how could he – how could anybody – love his neighbour as himself? Why would he want to? He didn't want anybody's *love*, he just wanted to be treated with some basic decency. [...] If they'd had another system, another set of rules based on the ordinary, possible decency of which people were capable, everything would be different. People wouldn't be set the impossible task of loving their neighbours, they would just have to treat them as human beings. There would be no excuses. (172–3)

Nonetheless, Derek's "fairytale" fraternal love (333) for Francis suggests an ethical obligation to the neighbour: Derek's attachment to his brother leads him to avenge Jan's murder before Tommy can enact justice. Equally, it is Tommy's absolute dedication to his grandson that defuses his anger and allows him to cope with his terminal illness.

When Francis exiles himself from Corby after Jan's death (he is believed, mistakenly, to be fleeing the law after one of Jan's assailants is found dead), he eventually drifts to an acid-inspired cult who take up residence at Westwater, a Scottish manorial squat. The brainwashing tapes played at Westwater preach self-invention, but they encourage lethargy rather than transformation in Francis (262–3): in spite of his affinity with the idea of absolute retreat, he fights against the loss of energy and autonomy that the insidious voice induces, and finally rejects the communal pursuit of "another world". The radical transformation and self-obliteration that the tapes promote lead to mass suicide at Westwater, yet when Francis sees the dead bodies, and the followers' farewell videotape, on the television news, he pays tribute to their delusion, their conscious withdrawal:

As I began working, studying the pictures I'd cut from the paper, rereading the reports, I found myself on their side. I'd started to wonder why nobody was saying that, in a world like this, there was a logic in wanting to leave, especially if you believed another, better life was possible elsewhere? (321).

Francis realises that the Westwater tapes were "almost right". To be "rid of the self" is not about giving up the world, but giving up one's "presence in the world" as "a social person":

I did it willingly, thinking that I would receive nothing in return. But when you give up one thing, you have to gain another: it's a law of nature, a fact of life. The process isn't one-way. In exchange for my absence as a person, I have to be given a presence in a wider world, a presence alongside the weather and sky and light, alongside birds and seals and the horizon, alongside water and the stars and you, receding one moment at a time into infinity. (307)

Retreat here is also a process of opening-up and, in relinquishing the social self, Francis enters into another form of exchange with the "wider world". This is the distinction between "people" and "persons": the latter are "the ones who moved through this territory, on whatever journey they were making, leaving almost no trace". They acknowledge their place in the world "as transients, as mortals" (356).

Francis decides to seek another elsewhere, to find his place through transience, by returning to Corby, and re-establishing a tentative connection with his family. Home is a matter of simultaneous engagement and withdrawal, "a sense of the moment, of the now. [...] Always *now here* and always nowhere" (359–60). The novel ends with Francis on the point of departure, but he is resolved to return, and will not be "a stranger" to his kin: "No matter what happened, they were connected, all of them. They were all connected, and they were all alone with their phantoms, but the phantoms were warmer and less unknowable than Francis had thought." The connection of earth and sky, mortal and transcendent, past, present and future in the closing passage, with the son tending the father's garden in the family home, evokes Heidegger's "fourfold" in "Building Dwelling Thinking" (Heidegger 1993: 352):

> Francis looked up at the sky and he saw the high blue of it, empty and clear and still, and he could feel something moving, receding into the distance, returning to its origin. It was gone now, it was elsewhere. Everything changed so that this – the sky, the earth, the summer light, a man working in a garden – could continue. For the moment, he was that man and this was the garden. It was his light, it was his sky, it was his body that worked, tuned to gravity, assured and careful and skilled. Then the thought passed, and he went back to work, forgetting himself: a man working in a garden, then a garden and nothing else. (372–3)

Immersion in the work, immersion in the surroundings: amid post-industrial decline and lost idealism, Francis's self-forgetting exemplifies masculine openness and surrender.

With a certain latitude, Burnside's fiction – and, to some extent, *The Wasp Factory* – might be construed as the search for the good neighbour, or the good fraternal/paternal phantom. (Indeed, Burnside's latest collection of poetry is entitled *The Good Neighbour*.) It is the search for a route out of self-obsession and defensive isolation. The oscillation from retreat to embrace, and from exclusion to surrender in Burnside, in particular, is reminiscent of Emmanuel Levinas's articulation of the ethical relation. For Levinas, the idea of the Infinite is to be found in the responsibility for the other: to be oneself is to be "for" the other (Hand 1989: 5). As he points out in "Ethics as First Philosophy", the responsibility for the other stems from a time

> before my freedom in an immemorial past, an unrepresentable past that was never present [...]. A responsibility for my neighbour, for the other man, for the stranger or sojourner, to which nothing in the rigorously ontological order binds me – nothing in the order of the Thing, of the something, of number or causality. (Hand 1989: 84).

Levinas argues that "the departure from the self is the approach to the neighbour", and this approach, which cannot be resisted, places the self in a relation of "proximity" to the other. Proximity is the responsibility for the other, a primordial responsibility that is a form of transcendence ("Ideology and Idealism", in Hand 1989: 246). Levinas stresses that "nothing is outside of the control of the responsibility of the one for the other" (Levinas 1991: 159). In the ethical encounter, proximity binds me to the neighbour through a relation of kinship "outside of biology, 'against all logic' [...]. A fraternity that cannot be abrogated, an unimpeachable assignation" (Levinas 1991: 87). The neighbour's presence, a presence that cannot be determined or categorised in advance, summons me to a responsibility without choice (Levinas 1993: 120). The neighbour is encountered at the vanishing point of singularity and community, distance and intimacy. This primordial responsibility without choice, an inescapable obligation that is also a radical freedom, marks a transcendence that is non-absolute. It is the choice emblematised by Banks's Wasp Factory. The necessary forgetting of the self, or the bearable lightness of being, in Burnside's fiction can be read as a response to the neighbour's summons: a moment of surrender in which the stranger, the sojourner, the unseen companion, can find a welcome.

Bibliography

Armitt, Lucie. 1996. *Theorising the Fantastic*. London: Arnold.

Banks, Iain. 1985. *Walking on Glass*. London: Macmillan.

—. [1984] 1990a. *The Wasp Factory*. London: Abacus.

—. [1986] 1990b. *The Bridge*. London: Abacus.

Brewster, Scott. 2005. "Borderline Experience: Madness, Mimicry and Scottish Gothic." *Gothic Studies* 7: 1 (May). 79–86.

Burnside, John. 1992. *Feast Days*. London: Secker and Warburg.

—. [1997] 1998. *The Dumb House*. London: Vintage.

—. [1999] 2000a. *The Mercy Boys*. London: Vintage.

—. 2000b. "Strong Words." In Herbert, W.N. and Matthew Hollis (eds). *Strong Words: Modern Poets on Modern Poetry*. Newcastle: Bloodaxe. 259–61.

—. [2000] 2001a. *Burning Elvis*. London: Vintage.

—. 2001b. *The Locust Room*. London: Jonathan Cape.

—. 2003. *Living Nowhere*. London: Jonathan Cape.

—. 2005. *The Good Neighbour*. London: Jonathan Cape.

Fry, Paul H. 1995. *A Defense of Poetry: Reflections on the Occasion of Writing*. Stanford, CA: Stanford University Press.

Hand, Sean (ed.) 1989. *The Levinas Reader*. Oxford: Blackwell.

Heidegger, Martin. 1993. *Basic Writings*. (ed. David Farrell Krell) (Revised edition). London: Routledge.

Levinas, Emmanuel. 1991. *Otherwise than Being or Beyond Essence* (tr. Alphonso Lingis). Dordrecht, Boston and London: Kluwer Academic Publishers.

—. [1987] 1993. *Collected Philosophical Papers*. Alphonso Lingis (ed. and tr.) Dordrecht, Boston and London: Kluwer Academic Publishers.

McDowell, Lesley. 2003. Interview with John Burnside, *Sunday Herald* (19 January 2003).

Sage, Victor. 1996. "The Politics of Petrifaction: Culture, Religion, History in the Fiction of Iain Banks and John Banville." In Sage, Victor and Allan Lloyd-Smith (eds). *Modern Gothic: A Reader*. Manchester: Manchester University Press. 20–37.

"Pathetic Reminders"? The Idea of Education in Modern Scottish Fiction

Beth Dickson

Education is such a defining feature of Scottish identity that it permeates the imaginative life of the twentieth-century novel in Scotland. Although literature does not always reflect education realistically, it does reflect on what education "means" in society. Recent more searching interpretations of Scottish education offered by historians – both idealistic and negative – are also present in literature, in possibly more problematic guise.

Keywords: George Friel, Robin Jenkins, James Kelman, Ian MacLaren, Muriel Spark, education, identity.

In this chapter I want to look at what novelists have made of education in late twentieth-century Scotland, and at what education has made of them. Such a survey has to begin, however, with the endurance of the myth of "the lad of parts" from the previous century, an idea that was widely taken as validation of such stoutly Scottish virtues as a democratic and meritocratic education system, community investment in talented individuals from that locality, and individual exertion in deploying that talent in the wider world. My title borrows its phrasing from Lewis Grassic Gibbon's description of early twentieth-century Scottish schoolteachers, but questions his negative view:

> They called the man the Dominie; there are many such curious words in the Scots dialects, pathetic reminders of the once-national worship of scholastic attainment. (Mitchell [1931]: 27)

The implication in Lewis Grassic Gibbon's "pathetic reminders" that by this time Scots no longer valued education is not borne out by the historical facts. Education was, and is, a defining aspect of Scottish national identity and as such has been the arena of national effort and reflection by teachers, educationalists, historians and sociologists (Paterson 2003: 201–22). As recently as the 1980s, Scots resisted the Thatcherite education reforms of Michael Forsyth because

they trusted educational professionals enough to leave decisions about
schools and schooling up to them (Pickard 2003: 233).

Why then should Gibbon have written so dismissively? Although
the values of democratic access and opportunity are often proudly
associated with education, the school system itself has had its
detractors: its stress on rote learning and corporal punishment, which
Gibbon also describes, constitutes a view closer to the conclusions of
T.C. Smout in *A Century of the Scottish People*:

> In short anything but the most basic curriculum taught in the most traditional way was
> regarded as superfluous in most schools until after the Second World War: most
> education was what it had always been, a drilling in the three Rs. If the child could not
> understand the lesson, the tawse was on the desk.
> Perhaps, then, it is in the history of the school more than any other aspect of
> recent social history that the key lies to some of the more depressing aspects of
> modern Scotland. If there are in this country too many people, who fear what is new,
> believe the difficult to be impossible, draw back from responsibility, and afford
> established authority and tradition an exaggerated respect, we can reasonably look for
> an explanation in the institutions that moulded them. (Smout 1986: 229)

It is ironic, however, that in the case of novelist George Douglas
Brown, cited below, a similarly bleak fictional vision of education
obscures some personally positive experiences of schooling that were
similar to the experience of the lad of parts in Ian MacLaren's
Kailyard short story "Beside the Bonnie Brier Bush". This dissonance
alerts readers to the fundamentally literary nature of the texts under
discussion. Gibbon and Brown rejected what they saw as the
complacent vision of Scotland expressed by Kailyard writers and
constructed their novels as literary weapons in an ideological war.
Later twentieth-century Scottish novelists continue to examine the
assumptions underlying the myth that education is indisputably
beneficial.

Ian MacLaren (the pen name of John Watson, 1850–1907) is the
writer cited most frequently in discussions of education in Scotland
because of his collection of short stories *Beside the Bonnie Brier Bush*
(1894). MacLaren, a Scottish minister in the Presbyterian Church of
England, worked in Sefton Park, Liverpool and was involved in
educational initiatives throughout his life, notably the founding of the
University of Liverpool. The title story provides the *locus classicus*

for the lad of parts. Geordie Howe is the archetypal figure of the talented young man from a modest background whose ability is nurtured by the local school teacher. The boy's access to university is funded by a wealthier member of the community and his subsequent academic success redounds to the community's credit. Historian Robert Anderson points out how this image was used to justify various educational changes, many of which were quite conservative in nature:

The myth of the lad of parts became part of the ideology of nineteenth-century individualism or meritocracy, in which a limited equality of opportunity was held to justify the reinforcing of structural inequalities. (Anderson 1985: 84)

For MacLaren the myth did function conservatively. *Young Barbarians* (1907), a subsequent novel, demonstrates that, though the lad of parts may be distinctively Scottish, Scottish identity can be as easily expressed as part of a wider British identity, particularly as that is expressed through military and imperial enterprise. Along with the lad of parts character in the novel (William Pirie, a pupil who becomes a Cambridge don), the daring boyhood exploits of two other pupils who become soldiers are explicitly linked to the service they later give to Britain's imperial cause: one dies defending settlers in Matabeleland. Such sentiments echo, with uncanny exactness, a contemporary Scottish Education Department document which discusses the importance of physical exercise in schools:

Indirectly they [physical exercises] bring the individual into contact with the principles which lie at the foundation of national defence, and they bring home to him his duties and responsibilities as a citizen of the Empire. (Anderson 1995: 2002)

At the onset of the Boer War, MacLaren preached that "every young man should now be drilled" (Nicoll 1908: 271). What his rhetoric ignored was the fact that so many young men were unfit for military service not because they had not been drilled, but because they had not been fed (Anderson 1995: 193).

In his sociological study, *Understanding Scotland*, David McCrone notes that, "The idealisation of the rural parish school began in the 1890s (in the Kailyard literature, for instance) just as it was vanishing in practice" (McCrone 2001: 94). While this is true of MacLaren's writing, it is possible to argue that, although the lad of parts was an eighteenth-century phenomenon made obsolete by industrialisation, nevertheless, because of the ability of the myth to stay outwardly constant while being applied to varying and even contradictory historical situations, it could come to be applied by MacLaren's readers to themselves, some of whom had benefited from the Education Act of 1872 which established mass elementary education in Scotland.

New readers, as well as established ones, provided a market for popular fiction and *Beside the Bonnie Brier Bush* quickly topped the best-seller lists. MacLaren received a note of approbation from Prime Minister Gladstone as well as receiving notes of thanks from working people. He writes:

By the same post [as Gladstone's thanks] had a letter from a working man, whose sweetheart had given the book to him on Christmas Eve with a pair of socks. Also a note praying that on their marriage they might live like the people in the glen. (Nicoll 1908: 171)

MacLaren's success drew readers from all social classes. The newly literate who read popular fiction might well have enjoyed the sentimentality and conservative vision while yet appropriating for themselves that element of the myth which, in the context of urban industrialisation, made sense to them – the idea of education as a great human pursuit to which Scots seemed specially attached, and which could perhaps lead to increased personal prosperity, summed up in the Scots fixation with "getting on". Education was an important feature of national identity for Scots generally and such ethical qualities as equality, associated with access to education and progress through education, could well have been appropriated on a grander scale than MacLaren's conservatism might have conceived.

MacLaren's sentimental vision of Scottish society caused some early twentieth-century writers, especially those who regarded themselves as the avant garde, to react violently against it. In George Douglas Brown's *The House with the Green Shutters* (1901) the teacher of the small school in Barbie (based on the village of Ochiltree, Ayrshire in the west of Scotland) is Archibald Gemmell, nicknamed Bleach-the-Boys because of his constant recourse to corporal punishment. As representative of the way in which education mediates national identity, Gemmell is detached and unresponsive to young John Gourlay. Gemmell knows that John has an excellent imagination which is undisciplined by intellect and tells the "bodies" – the men who stand in the street watching what is happening in the community and commenting maliciously on it – that it is a mistake to send John to university. Then he returns to his study to read Adam Smith's *The Wealth of Nations*: his own educational credentials are impeccably Scottish and intellectually sound, but he is indifferent to John's educational progress. At every point, Brown's narrative contradicts the myth: the boy does not even *want* to go to university; his father sends him so that he can provide for the family, not for education's sake; the villagers take a malicious delight in his eventual downfall rather than in his success. Brown is doing his utmost to characterise MacLaren's version of Scottish education as unrealistic.

Despite these bleak representations, Brown himself bears an uncanny resemblance to the lad of parts. For the illegitimate son of a farm servant, an education by sensitive, thoughtful teachers with high expectations offered entry into a way of life both interesting and financially secure. There is an acute dissonance between biography and fiction. Essentially Brown is involved in an argument about values, seeing himself as part of a protest against the religious and political values of the Liberal Protestant establishment. For MacLaren's overarching aim in *Beside the Bonnie Brier Bush* was to show how education is the servant of religion. By dying in a more liberal Protestant faith, Geordie Howe, the lad of parts, draws his agnostic teacher into the faith, thus repaying him for the efforts made to educate him. This version of Christianity, expressed through the feminising influence of Geordie's mother, contrasts itself not so much with a secularist view of society but with other Christian formulations such as the hell-fire preaching of Revivalists, or the severe spirituality of Scottish Presbyterianism: both are characterised negatively in MacLaren's story.

Brown's virulent reaction to MacLaren's conservative religious and political position is informed mainly by the social realism of earlier Ayrshire writers such as Robert Burns and John Galt whom he began studying closely at Ayr Academy. Imperfect elementary schooling, limited economic prospects, personal desire, parental expectations and the attitudes of other members of the community are all factors which are as likely to decide the outcome unfavourably, rather than producing the optimistic outcome associated with MacLaren.

Brown's fictional reflections on education also show how instinctively Scottish writers resort to comment on education as part of their comment on society more generally, and what passion is generated if ethical values about individual and social progress through education are felt to be at risk. The myth of the lad of parts assumes that education is beneficial, as are its implicit values of access and personal progress. Whether universal access does indeed produce these advantageous outcomes is closely scrutinised by subsequent writers, as this intense discourse about values continues through the later twentieth century: Robin Jenkins's *The Changeling* (1958), Muriel Spark's *The Prime of Miss Jean Brodie* (1961), George Friel's *Mr Alfred MA* (1972), and James Kelman's *A Disaffection* (1989) can help us chart the progress of this educational debate in fiction.

Robin Jenkins

Robin Jenkins is deeply aware of the vulnerability of the child as the subject of adult parenting and educational practice. *The Changeling* (1958) is set in one of Glasgow's senior secondary schools in the 1950s where proficiency in Latin is used as the basis of class setting. Charles Forbes, an English teacher, can see real intelligence in Thomas Curdie "born and bred in Donaldson's Court, one of the worst slums in one of the worst slum districts in Europe" and decides to take him on holiday to Argyll with his family (Jenkins 1958: 2). Initially Forbes's decision is presented as idealistic, if somewhat naïve. More realistic perspectives are provided by the headmaster and Forbes's wife, Mary, both of whom can see the problems inherent in removing a child from his background, especially one such as Curdie who is already on probation for theft. Eventually, Forbes finally admits to himself that he has an ulterior motive. Passed over for promotion because of his lack of judgement, Forbes hopes that his supposedly altruistic action "might reach the ears of authority" and improve subsequent promotion prospects (Jenkins 1958: 50).

Things go disastrously wrong. Jenkins presents Curdie as a clever boy headed for a life of crime. This assessment of Curdie is endorsed by realistic teachers: Mr Todd is instantly contemptuous of Forbes's scheme. The Headmaster, more thoughtfully, phones Curdie's primary school headmaster in order to seek a second opinion. The primary head's negative assessment coincides with his own and, although he gives reluctant sanction to the arrangement, he too feels that Curdie is a lost cause.

Curdie himself steals in order to maintain a consistently hostile approach to the society which allows him to live in Donaldson Court. On his way to burgle the school, he holds onto the bars of the railings around the playground "as he subdued that treacherous weakness. Not to give in had been his pride, his faith, his reason, his sustenance, and so far it had not failed him" (Jenkins 1958: 29). However, Curdie is aware of Forbes's attitude towards him and feels its unsettling intent negatively: "Forbes had been pestering him with kindness" (Jenkins 1958: 29). This indirect narrative of Curdie's thoughts and feelings is not accessible to any of the adults in the novel. Forbes's attitude is not without a measure of self-interest, and, although his kindness receives many setbacks as Curdie tests its strength and fidelity, it is just at the point where the desired change has taken place in Curdie that Forbes's patience and self-preservation, with tragic timing, run out. The awesome nature of this rejection, which occurs just when Curdie's well-honed defences have been overcome, contributes to Curdie's suicide.

Interwoven with psychological and social realism, Jenkins uses elements of fable to describe the parenting Curdie receives. Curdie, the name Tom shares with the eponymous hero of George MacDonald's fantasy fiction, *The Princess and Curdie*, alerts readers that he too has to fight against the goblins – not frightening creatures whose danger is neutralised by their inevitable defeat (a convention of the fantasy genre) but similarly destructive creatures roaming wild in another genre and therefore not necessarily subject to the same rules.

The grown-ups with whom Curdie lives consist of his mother, "A genuine horror. Crafty as Auld Nick's wife" and his step-father, "a cripple, from birth" (Jenkins 1958: 9). Jenkins develops the witch-like description of Curdie's mother, and towards the end of the novel the family appears very much like the malicious, disturbing fairy host when they impose themselves on the Forbeses' hospitality. Mrs Curdie "cackled goodnaturedly" and Forbes finds himself asking the question mortals ask when confronted by fairy visitants, "What can I say, what am I to do, how do I get rid of them?" (Jenkins 1958: 167). Mrs Curdie has come to blackmail Forbes with accusations of child abuse from which she hopes to gain financially. Connotations of the supernatural and Gothic horror, to be read tragically rather than comically, highlight the self-serving nature of parenting and the extreme vulnerability of the child.

Although Forbes is not described using supernatural description, there is a negative link with Mrs Curdie in that both are described as fat. Curdie thinks of Forbes as "the fat English master" and this allows him to think that "he could be laughed at" (Jenkins 1958: 20). Tom thinks of his mother as being "fat like Forbes" (Jenkins 1958: 21). This links the adults who take most responsibility for Tom – one a figure of fun, the other a figure of horror. Forbes, though well-meaning, is not perceptive enough to see the changes in Tom. His idealism makes him initially too innocent and when idealism is punctured by unpleasant reality, he moves to the sorts of cynicism associated with other teachers; he is incapable of correctly identifying the child's needs at any stage in the relationship.

Mrs Curdie's arrival at Towellan throws Tom into acute distress:

As soon as his mother had begun to speak [...] he had with his right fist struck the tree several times, deliberately, with all his force, so that his mother had shrieked and blood had spurted from his knuckles, staining the trunk [...]. (Jenkins 1958: 175)

The novel reaches its grim conclusion by employing religious language in order to highlight the human culpability it demonstrates. When trying to shrug off his own generosity in taking Tom on holiday, Forbes gaily announces that "this is my chance to atone" (for what is not clear) and "if there is to be salvation there must be sacrifice" (Jenkins 1958: 6–7). The image of Tom punching the tree contains significant elements of crucifixion imagery (blood, tree, wounded body). The missing element, the nail, appears in the suicide itself where Tom ties his rope to a nail fixed into a rafter. Tom is sacrificed on the altar of his mother's neglect and Forbes's idealism. There is neither salvation nor atonement; only the destruction of a confused child. Gillian, Forbes's daughter, initially resents Tom but eventually understands his dilemma. The powerlessness of one child to help another is emphasised by hyperbole. When Gillian finds Tom she is unable to cut him down or untie him: "her fingers [...] became as weak as a baby's" (Jenkins 1958: 188).

This novel is severely admonitory about the consequences for children who are at the mercy of seemingly legitimate discourses of power within parenting and education that cannot, or will not, listen to children. If Tom had stayed with his family and the expectations of his "realistic" teachers, he would have become a criminal. Because Forbes is unable to deal with the forces he unleashes, Tom loses his life. Thus both intervention and non-intervention are criticised. The only hope lies in someone (a grown up Gillian?) being able to access the flow of Tom's thoughts and reactions as presented in the indirect narrative of his consciousness.

By the period in which Jenkins' novel is set, the battle over access to education is effectively over. All Scottish children go to primary school, and academic education is then available in senior secondary schools, while a more vocational curriculum is available in junior secondaries. However, this achievement has not brought about the educational paradise which believers in the myth of the lad of parts had perhaps assumed would result from widened access. Jenkins wants to probe the reality of progress through education. Curdie is clever, but his background makes him hostile to society and therefore to the schooling that is representative of organised society. Because the full implications of Curdie's deprivation are not understood by teachers, school, instead of being liberating or enlightening, becomes at best a means of maintaining an inequitable status quo – Curdie will progress to crime because the intervention of education is ineffective – or, at its worst, fatal: Forbes's well-intentioned but unrealistic intervention causes tragedy. The novel therefore anticipates the moves towards child-centred learning which characterised the mid- to late-

1960s, but it is also exceptionally alert to the ways in which any discourse which seeks to "help children" may be blindly corrupted into its opposite by the human forces at work within any institution which prioritises maintaining power before effective functioning. Education is still vital to Scottish identity but the complex effects of poverty challenge the notion that there is equality of opportunity.

Muriel Spark

Muriel Spark also reflects on the way in which the teacher-pupil relationship can be abused, being characteristically alert to the paradoxes which result from the human desire to educate. Miss Brodie sets out to influence her pupils with a personal set of values she associates with her life experience to date – this she calls "her prime". She regards this as being more valuable than the "authorized curriculum" which she regularly ditches in order to apprise her pupils of "the Buchmanites and Mussolini, the Italian Renaissance painters, the advantages to the skin of cleansing cream and witch hazel over honest soap and water, and the word 'menarche'; the interior decoration of the London house of the author of Winnie the Pooh had been described to them" (Spark 1961: 5). These juxtapositions, by turns bizarre, realistic and entertaining, seem to identify Miss Brodie as endearing but eccentric. However, when one of her pupils, Joyce Emily, from a wealthy but dysfunctional family, applies Brodie's rhetoric about the romance of fighting for Franco's Fascists to herself, goes off to Spain to fight and is killed in an attack on the train in which she is travelling, Miss Brodie is seen to be so dangerous that the headmistress is able to achieve a long-held ambition to sack her.

It seems quite obvious, therefore, that Miss Brodie is illegitimately influencing her pupils. Yet Spark is adept at demonstrating the fluid nature of power. Is Miss Brodie as influential as she thinks? It is clear that that Brodie's influence depends on the personalities of the girls. Rose is Miss Brodie's favourite pupil. Brodie hopes to consummate a love affair (which she desired but withdrew from because the man was married) by using Rose as her proxy. Paradoxically, the wrong action she turns away from is of less significance than the one she continues to work for. Because this aim is never made explicit to Rose, it does not enter Rose's head that she should conduct such a relationship: "She shook off Miss Brodie's influence as a dog shakes pond-water from its coat" (Spark 1961: 119).

Sandy, an intelligent and introverted girl, close to Miss Brodie, is subconsciously jealous of Rose's pre-eminence. Miss Brodie confides in Sandy more than in any of the other girls but this is not enough for Sandy. When she realises what Miss Brodie's ambitions for Rose are, she thwarts those ambitions by becoming Lloyd's lover herself. She finally "betrays" Miss Brodie to the headmistress by explaining why Joyce Emily went to Spain. Later Sandy becomes a nun, embracing Roman Catholicism, a faith Miss Brodie regards as superstitious. Although this seems like a comprehensive rejection, Sandy "clutched the bars of her grille more desperately than ever" as she is visited in the convent and when asked what the influences were on her penetrating work of psychology, she says, "There was a Miss Jean Brodie in her prime" (Spark 1961: 128). Ironically her obsession with and rejection of Miss Brodie demonstrate that the teacher's influence determined the course of her life.

Spark produces one paradox after another. Brodie's influence on Mary McGregor is debateable. On the one hand her contemptuous responses to this pupil's clumsiness seem to re-inforce the pupil in the belief that she is clumsy – and this clumsiness leads to Mary's death in a hotel fire. Yet on the other hand, other teachers also found the girl clumsy. Did Miss Brodie make her clumsy or was she clumsy anyway? Certainly Mary does not think to blame Miss Brodie but remembers the only days in her life when she was truly happy as the ones she spent listening to Miss Brodie's stories. Yet even Miss Brodie thinks "Perhaps I should have been kinder to Mary" (Spark 1961: 77). Spark is able to show that power is not static within the school nor does it inhere within the charismatic personality, rather, it is fluid and exists in relationships.

Spark then broadens the discussion from the role of the teacher to the role of the politician and the priest. Brodie's admiration for Fascist politicians is clearly a limiting factor – "Hitler *was* rather naughty" simultaneously reveals and damns Miss Brodie (Spark 1961: 122).

However, this political system which has everyone marching in step and which Miss Brodie tries to emulate as her girls walk through the Old Town, fails as a political system because of the profoundly unpredictable nature of influence. While the blackshirts appeared to be walking in formation and acting as one, in reality the individuals comprising these units reacted as variously to the imposition of ideology as do Miss Brodie's girls. Among the priests Sandy meets in her progress through the church, there are "quite a number of Fascists much less agreeable than Miss Brodie" demonstrating that the desire to impose institutional values is a generic feature of institutions (Spark 1961: 125).

Although Miss Brodie thinks of herself as in conflict with the school, offering a separate sense to the children of what knowledge consists of, Spark is aware of the extent to which all Miss Brodie does is replace one paradigm of how power and knowledge reinforce each other with another. What blocks the seemingly invincible power of an institution to mould and produce creatures in its own likeness is not the imposition of another force, such as Miss Brodie's personality, but the sheer variousness of life itself. This is why the novel can be regarded as a tragicomedy, because in the end things work out according to the processes of life rather than death. Two girls do die, however; Spark does not flinch from the detrimental effects of power.

For Spark, education is a usefully limited arena in which to observe how the entities of power and knowledge manifest themselves within institutions and through personalities. Her tragic observation is that this can be fatal. Her main comic observation is that humanity's ability to order and control life is very slight. Things do not always work out as planned and can have consequences totally unforeseen or unintended by the planner. Even when they do work out as planned, this is often fortuitous. Miss Mackay had wanted to get rid of Miss Brodie for a long time but unless Sandy had betrayed Miss Brodie, there was no necessary link between Miss Brodie's actions and the consequence of being sacked. Yet – again paradoxically – she displays exactly the same features as the institution does in trying to mould her girls according to her vision. Just as her temperament subverts the school ethos, so their temperaments stymie her stated intentions.

Is Spark arguing that education is a waste of time? Not quite. A fluid rather than a mechanistic vision pervades the novel. There are the grey teachers like Miss Mackay who deliver the curriculum reliably, if unimaginatively. She represents a tendency, of whom the Gaunt sisters are more extreme examples, who teach by rote and coercion. However, they have the signal virtue of not killing their pupils. Influence does enable people to learn, but what they learn is beyond curricular control. Miss Brodie's regime may look more "enlightened" or "emancipated", yet she uses power and knowledge to influence pupils and she operates without the checks which the school has evolved so that it can maintain its existence as an institution. What causes Miss Brodie's regime to fail (as with the German and Italian dictatorships she loves) is a lack of awareness of how institutions regulate their power and knowledge so that they can function. Spark also shows that any institution is at risk from people who set out deliberately to undermine it; Miss Brodie simply refuses to subject herself to these processes while maintaining an outward show of conformity.

After Sandy has betrayed Miss Brodie she is quite certain that she has done the right thing. However, this view alternates with another in which Sandy remembers "the first unbetrayable Miss Brodie" (Spark 1961: 60). It is this figure who stands, not only in Sandy's memory but in the memory of generations of readers, as the character who, more than any other, symbolises the way in which a teacher can open up new worlds of cognition, imagination and freedom for pupils. And the extent to which we want to believe in this figure is the extent to which human beings desire education, subjecting themselves to its discourse because they believe that it enables them to understand themselves and to formulate ways of living for themselves which are not bounded by "the way things are" but which have a point of reference in the "way things could be", a way which has been opened out for them by a teacher. Like Jenkins, Spark is not entirely sanguine about the assumption that education is an unalloyed benefit. Miss Jean Brodie is the fictional character in whom the Scottish desire to link identity and education is internationally recognised. Given the fatal impact she has on some of her pupils, this is merely the last, and, perhaps, most salutary, of the ironies surrounding this novel.

George Friel

Spark's novel is set in Edinburgh in the 1930s when teachers enjoyed a measure of social respect. As the century wore on, attitudes to authority changed and the waning of automatic respect for teachers is a feature of George Friel's *Mr Alfred MA* (1972), set during the early days of comprehensive education. In 1965 a decision was taken to implement a fully comprehensive system of secondary education by which all primary pupils progressed to the nearest local secondary school and were not sent to different types of secondary school on the basis of ability. Friel's novel is a sustained attack on mid-century changes in education as perceived by the eponymous main character in the novel, Mr Alfred, but which can be read in ways which only serve to show how profoundly just these changes were.

Mr Alfred is proud of the fact that he has a Master of Arts degree but feels cheated that, because of his mother's illness, he was unable to afford the extra year to take his study to the higher level of an Honours degree. This means that he is never given the most academically able boys to teach. He is sure he would have been able to inspire them with his own love of literature because he wrote poetry at university. The school in which he teaches in Collinsburn has recently changed from "a local Academy to a regional Comprehensive" (Friel 1972: 42). Thus instead of selecting pupils on ability, it now accepts all pupils in its catchment area which includes Tordoch, an area of social deprivation. The school has a new range of pupils but does not have a curriculum which meets the needs of all pupils. Mr Alfred has a disagreement with one of his pupils, Gerald Provan, who according to his headmaster is "hardly a candidate to stay on for O levels. He's learned all he'll ever learn at school. And God knows that wasn't much" (Friel 1972: 54). Gerald is a difficult pupil:

> "Wipe that silly smile off your face," said Mr Alfred.
> Gerry raised an open hand to his face and drew it down over his nose and mouth. Took the hand away to reveal a straight face. The bland insolence of the

obedience provoked Mr Alfred. He smacked Gerry across the nape. He knew at once he shouldn't have done it. (Friel 1972: 15)

What is so strange about this narrative is that the reader is being asked to sympathise with Mr Alfred in a supposedly justified act of violence when Mr Alfred's consistent complaint is about increasing levels of violence in society. Although corporal punishment was not abolished in Scottish schools until 1987, in a discussion later in the novel Friel anticipates the arguments against abolition, mainly that there is no point in making a personal and unilateral decision not to use corporal punishment because in such a situation an individual's classroom discipline would disintegrate (exactly the same argument is put forward in MacLaren's *Young Barbarians* published sixty years previously) and if the decision was made nationally schools would become ungovernable. Order in school and society, then, is predicated on the threat of violence. This is what makes it "acceptable" for Mr Alfred to strike a pupil – teachers know better than pupils and corporal punishment coerces pupils into accepting the prevailing social order.

However Gerald will not accept this. After another incident where Mr Alfred attempts to administer corporal punishment because he had seen him draw a knife in a fight, Gerald argues that because the fight took place outside school hours, Mr Alfred has no authority over him and he refuses to enter into discussion about it or to take the punishment. The incident escalates and Gerald is suspended. Finally the local education committee declare the suspension invalid – a sign of their complicity in falling standards as far as Mr Alfred is concerned.

Mr Alfred's subsequent wrongdoing is even more worrying to later generations of readers. He is given a class of twelve and thirteen-year-old girls, one of whom, Rose, he begins to make a favourite and this leads to her emotional and sexual exploitation. The girl so treated is presented in the narrative as being untroubled by his behaviour. Mr Alfred again knows he ought not to be doing this but because of own loneliness and social inadequacy, he does not prevent the relationship from becoming more physically intimate. Intercourse does not take place and in that sense the girl is not raped. However, to a modern reader, more aware of the horrors of abuse suffered by children, the idea that the girl was entirely undisturbed by such behaviour seems to reflect the complacency which used to surround this subject, in which imagination is as deeply mired as other aspects of humanity.

Mr Alfred is ill-disposed to social change. When Gerald's mother comes to the school to argue for his re-instatement, she points to the fact that not only has he lost two days education to which he has a "right" but he has also lost his "right" to free milk and free meals. She contacts journalists who entitle their subsequent story "Teacher Has Spite Says Mum" (Friel 1972: 55). While Friel is alert to the misuse of rights claimed without responsibility and prescient about the mother's subsequent recourse to litigation or press coverage as a means of settling differences, he does not describe any advantages of social change. Friel presents the introduction of welfare benefits for children as a privilege which should be withdrawn if they are disobedient. Teenagers intimidate old people and the local café owner to the extent that he moves away and the police do nothing to check such anti-social behaviour. To Mr Alfred these trends signify the end of civilised society as he conceives it. He defines civilisation as the ability to appreciate "high" culture such as poetry and is irritated by a primary school teacher who does not show the children examples of classic poems but encourages them to write their own poetry which she accepts with grammatical and spelling errors. "This is the day of the child-dominated classroom" she says as Friel attacks the idea of child-centred learning (Friel 1972: 171).

Unable to adapt to this new world, Mr Alfred begins to lose touch with reality and surreally meets a figure called Tod who claims to be responsible for the appearance of graffiti in Glasgow, the first sign of the anarchy he intends to unloose on the world:

> It is the end of the printed word. Everything's a scribble now [...]
> "You think you're God perhaps?" said Mr. Alfred.
> "No, the other One," said Tod. "The Adversary [...]
> "I say No to you and your likes. I'm nibbling away at the roots of your civilisation. I'll bring it down [...].
> "Life is more important than civilisation. Life is a comprehensive school."
> (Friel 1972: 195–97)

Engaged by his enthusiasm, Mr Alfred is found writing on the wall (the pun is intentional) and taken off to an asylum by the police. The novel does chart the way in which teachers ceased to be regarded as the figures of authority – for good or ill – represented in earlier fiction. Mr Alfred has only his own skills to fall back on and his love of poetry has to be backed up by a level of violence, justified by society as a whole, in order for him to be an effective teacher. The demoralisation and sense of worthlessness of the character caught in the transition between one culture of teaching and another makes him pitiable and Friel is ahead of his time in pointing out some of the ways in which a rights-based culture can be abused if there is not a balancing emphasis on responsibilities.

However, is apocalypse the necessary consequence of an awareness of possible abuses? There were advantages in progressive educational legislation which Friel clearly does not acknowledge. The comprehensive system clarified the need for a more appropriate curriculum in Scotland. The Standard Grade curriculum, introduced in 1984, aimed to provide certification for all at sixteen, the earliest age at which a pupil could leave school. The award had six divisions which reflected achievement across the ability range. This meant that pupils such as Gerald Provan were given a curriculum appropriate to their abilities. Corporal punishment phased out then finally abolished in 1986, and in 1997 the Sex Offenders Register was introduced to record the names of those who posed a sexual threat to children and young people.

In the light of these developments, which more effectively addressed the same problems that Mr Alfred faced, it becomes possible to read the novel as one which demonstrates the atavistic way in which the old may fear the young because they feel threatened by their lively and sometimes chaotic energy. When Gerald rebels against the system, Mr Alfred immediately wants to suppress Gerald violently and expects that the school authorities will not blame him for hitting the pupil. For Mr Alfred the alternatives seem to be civilisation based on violence, or anarchy. The relationship between teacher and pupil can be humanly nourishing for each, but instead of creating conditions where that relationship could be safely expressed within professional boundaries, Mr Alfred ends up perverting Rose's innocent friendship. Scott Hames comments:

> Confusing the authority of knowledge with his own professional authority [...] Mr Alfred's education makes up the protective "bars" which shield him from a menacing, lawless society which has forsaken the civilising power of the word. (Hames 2004: 63)

While it is possible to feel pity for Mr Alfred, whose inadequacy makes him dangerous, he can also be seen as one of the split personalities which occur so frequently in Scottish fiction. He rails against violence but hits a pupil. He idealises Rose, "Rose upon the rood of time. Red rose, proud Rose, sad Rose of all my days" while allowing an improper relationship to continue (Friel 1972: 90). In his speech to Tod quoted earlier, although it is ostensibly Tod who is the Devil, it is Mr Alfred who calls him "the devil seeking whom he may deflower" (Friel 1972: 197). This alludes to the Biblical description of devil who is a "roaring lion [...] seeking whom he may devour" (1 Pet. 5). The change is a symptom of Mr Alfred's guilty conscience. Despite his protestations about violence in society and falling standards of behaviour, he is as complicit as Tod.

It is hardly surprising that all the false rationalisations in the world (by which I mean principally the cleverness of the ideas about language and Friel's punning, allusive style for which the novel is generally known), which Mr Alfred feels education and its discourse should inscribe for him, cannot prevent him from being overcome by the fear of violent retribution. Read against its ostensible meaning, this novel offers the optimistic possibility that political and educational leaders were capable of responding to the needs of pupils in ways which protected them from teachers who, for their own personal comfort, wanted to cling to what they perceived to be "traditional" methods and attitudes.

James Kelman

The 1980s, a period associated with the government of Prime Minister Margaret Thatcher, tended to unite Scots against a set of policies which closed heavy industry and saw unemployment rise steeply. There was a great deal of resistance to the Community Charge, a new form of local taxation, derisively known as the "Poll Tax", which was imposed on Scotland before becoming law in the rest of the United Kingdom. This depressing period provided Scots with the impetus to campaign more vigorously for greater political autonomy, finally resulting in 1999 in the devolved Scottish Parliament. Unlike Mr Alfred, Patrick Doyle in James Kelman's *A Disaffection* has a political understanding of his role as a teacher. A creation of the 1980s, Patrick Doyle explicitly repudiates the role of teacher as enforcer of social control, while sharing with Mr Alfred a lack of professional self-esteem. Patrick regards himself – and other teachers – as failures: "we're all secondbest for a kick-off, that's what I canni go" and the novel charts his descent into despair. Doyle is explicit about the link between the state and education. He believes that teachers are agents of the Establishment who by turns coerce and cajole children into being submissive citizens. He complains about unaware parents who "let their weans' heids get totally swollen with all that rightwing keech we've got to stuff into them so's we can sit back with the big wage packets. It's us that keep the things from falling apart. [...] We're responsible for it, the present polity" (Kelman 1989: 149). Doyle tries to make these values explicit to the children he teaches by conducting discussions on "essential 'side issues'" (Kelman 1989: 23).

His "disaffection" has come about because of his own experience of education. A bright, working-class boy, he was able to go to university but for him it seemed that it was his family that "wanted him to go to uni and no him, his parents and his fucking big brother. [...] He had not wanted to go" (Kelman 1989: 53). This quotation displays the predominant narrative mode of the novel – an extended interior monologue where Doyle by turns berates and interrogates himself, rambles, fantasises and rails against life. The richness and subtlety of his thought expressed in pared-down demotic Scots contrasts vividly with the rather down-at-heel, inadequate exterior he presents to the world. Doyle resents the way middle-class people he met at university seemed blind to the social injustices on which their privileges rested and he feels that university stopped him from doing what he wanted to do. What that is, is difficult to formulate: he only knows it was "something massive" (Kelman 1989: 53). As a result of his politics and his own experience, he shows contempt for other teachers who do not share his intellectual interests, "Far better remaining silent in the midst of such crassness, in the midst of such utter cant and hypocrisy" (Kelman 1989: 7). He is contemptuous, too, of the remnants of the older academic traditions of Scottish education still visible in the school: "There was Old Milner below, stalking the ground floor in his MA gown" (Kelman 1989: 27). Most of all he is contemptuous of being tempted to become drawn in to a comfortable middle-class lifestyle, and of the fact that he has a common scholastic identity with Old Milne: "It is definately [sic] the case that Patrick Doyle MA (HONS) has definately [sic] no plans for nestling in the lap of married person Mirs [sic] Bryson who occasionally seems to be giving him the eye [...]" (Kelman 1989: 64). The juxtaposition of academic achievement with sexual fantasy devalues the former.

It is worth noting that this is a deeply ironic anti-climax in the fortunes of the lad of parts. Access to tertiary education which many socialists had struggled to secure was widened under the Wilson governments of the late 1960s and access was not as dependent on means as it had been previously because of the introduction of a system of student grants. Yet just when this social objective has been achieved, it is found wanting by someone who was supposed to benefit from it.

It is possible to read *A Disaffection* as a lament for the disappearance of the working-class autodidact. That figure had to wrest his own education from the harsh conditions of long hours, tiredness produced by heavy labour, and the paucity of resources available to someone whose income was slight and who sought support in evening classes, local reading rooms and public libraries. Such an education allowed its students to construct their own curricula which then enabled them to formulate a position from which to critique the way in which the state benefited from the labour of many of its citizens. Doyle feels that his university education prevents him from criticising the state. By participating in an educational system which aspires to achieve the great middle-class objectives of a secure and stable state (for themselves) rising prosperity (for themselves) and thus the fulfilment of the self (for themselves), Doyle feels that his objections to the state have lost their ideological purity because they come from within the mainstream, rather than from outside it. Certainly his brother sees teaching as synonymous with middle-class identity.

He himself, however, sometimes acknowledges that this argument is not entirely valid. Like Mr Alfred, he is guilty of trying to conduct a contemporary argument about education by using anachronistic ideas. Sometimes Doyle does seem to realise that the argument has moved on, as here when he thinks about taking up an explicit political role: "he could take to the streets and become an urban terrorist, an urban fighter for freedom. Who was stopping him. No bastard" (Kelman 1989: 78). Thus it is not educational discourse as presently formulated which prevents Doyle from saying, thinking or pursuing what he wants, but personal inertia. His weakness is widened to an accusation of self-indulgence by a girl in Doyle's sixth year class:

I want to say something else to you, to Mister Patrick Doyle, to you, I really don't think you're being fair because what ye do ye start all these things and then ye don't finish them or even just in a way follow them through properly. Properly. (Kelman 1989: 196)

A final road traffic incident results in Doyle's death, but whether this is accidental or deliberate is unclear. Like Mr Alfred, the tension between inner monologue and external society leads to incoherence and silence.

Within this hopeless outlook, there are scattered hints of another possible view of teaching. Doyle does feel the need to impart information about a coercive government to children and attempts through Socratic discussion to teach critical thinking skills (Kelman 1989: 24). He admits to being "fired by the Spirit of the Great Teachers" (Kelman 1989: 33) but his initial enthusiasm has dimmed. "He believed in teaching, he also believed in being a teacher, the spirit of that, of what it was – what was it?" (Kelman 1989: 34). Here his ideas fade out and he drifts off into sexual fantasy. Doyle also remembers Old McGeechan, a colleague from the first school he worked in, "a great auld guy whose attitude was spot on and P. Doyle would aye have emulated him, if anybody [...]. A genuine socialist [...]. He used to say, Doyle, you've got to tell more jokes in the classroom [...]" (Kelman 1989: 143). It is the opinion of Doyle's brother that "He doesni really hate being a teacher at all [...]. He fucking loves the bloody job! He loves it!" (Kelman 1989: 281).

However, Doyle's problem is that the argument no longer exists in the terms in which he wants to constitute it. While he has a ready battery of socialist arguments against a capitalist state, he is only intermittently aware of the fact that the context has changed and therefore he needs to work out how to combat a capitalist state whose workers have embraced the values of the consumerist marketplace, where class distinctions are blurred and there is a pick-and-mix attitude to values rather than an allegiance by a significant section of the population to the totalising arguments of any ideology. He has no clear idea of what a positive purpose for education could be and that proves fatal. Great teachers belong to the past and all that is left for contemporary teachers is a managerial function on behalf of a state which needs educated consumers in order to exist. While education can be accessed by everyone, Doyle is very pessimistic about the kind of life opportunity it actually offers.

In conclusion, it can be seen that the testimony of imaginative writers concerning Scottish education alters as schooling itself has altered in the twentieth century. MacLaren's fiction clearly valorises Scottish education, linking education to the good citizenship necessary to maintain Britain's imperial rule (Anderson 1995: 202). However, later writers interrogate the optimism associated with the lad of parts. Brown presents a much darker vision. Paradoxically, their use of education as a metaphor for the parochialism and complacency of Scottish society belies their own positive educational experiences. In *The Changeling, The Prime of Miss Jean Brodie, Mr Alfred MA,* and *A Disaffection*, the representations become even darker as writers explore the extent to which schools pose a threat to pupils. Abuse and death are not supposed to be the final destination of the lad of parts; not even imaginatively. Through indirect narration, teachers and pupils are confined to inward thoughts, often unable to express themselves openly in the language available within the institution. This leads to the stifling atmosphere of this fiction and shows clearly that discourses of power and knowledge can silence voices as well as release them through the teaching of reading and writing, talking and listening – their ostensible function.

Thus the voices at the end of the twentieth century seem much more doubtful about the value of education, although the fact that Scottish writers' imaginations habitually turn to it as an arena in which key ethical values are examined shows how deeply it is still linked with national as well as personal identity.

Bibliography

Anderson, Robert. 1985. "In Search of the 'Lad of Parts': the Mythical History of Scottish Education" in *History Workshop Journal* 19: 82–104.
—. 1995. *Education and the Scottish People 1750–1918*. Oxford: Oxford University Press.
Brown, George Douglas. [1901] 1923. *The House with the Green Shutters*. MacDougall Holmes.
Friel, George. 1972. *Mr Alfred MA*. London: Calder and Boyars.
Hames, Scott. 2004. "Fightin' Dominies and Form: Politics and Narrative in Some Modern Scottish Novels of Education" in Alexander, N., S. Murphy and A. Oakman (eds). *To The Other Shore: Cross-currents in Irish and Scottish Studies*. Belfast: Clo Ollscoil na Banriona. 56–67.
Jenkins, Robin. [1958] 2000. *The Changeling*. Edinburgh: Canongate.
Kelman, James. 1989. *A Disaffection*. London: Secker and Warburg.
MacLaren, Ian (aka Watson, John). 1894. *Beside the Bonnie Brier Bush*. London: Hodder and Stoughton.
McCrone, David. 2001. *Understanding Scotland: the Sociology of a Nation* (second edition). London: Routledge.
—. 2003. "Culture, Nationalism and Scottish Education: Homogeneity and Diversity" in Bryce, T.G.K. and W.M. Humes (eds) *Scottish Education (second edition): Post-devolution*. Edinburgh: Edinburgh University Press. 235–43.
Mitchell, James Leslie (aka Gibbon, Lewis Grassic) 1931. *The Thirteenth Disciple*. Edinburgh: Paul Harris.
Nicoll, W.R. 1908. *"Ian MacLaren": Life of the Rev. John Watson D.D.* London: Hodder and Stoughton.
Paterson, Lindsay. 2003. *Scottish Education in the Twentieth Century*. Edinburgh: Edinburgh University Press.
Pickard, Willis. 2003. "The History of Scottish Education, 1980 to the Present Day" in Bryce, T.G.K. and W.M. Humes (eds). *Scottish Education: Post-devolution*. Edinburgh: Edinburgh University Press. 229–38.
Smout, Christopher. 1986. *A Century of the Scottish People 1830–1950*. London: Collins.
Spark, Muriel. [1961] 1965. *The Prime of Miss Jean Brodie*. London: Penguin.

Translating God: Negative Theology and Two Scottish Poets

James McGonigal

To discuss religious influences and concerns in the poetry of contemporary and "post-religious" Scotland, it may be necessary to examine the persistence of two casts of mind that have influenced Scottish thinking for many centuries. Here voluntarist and intellectualist approaches are linked with insights from negative theology to explore the differing impact of Protestant and Catholic upbringing on the writings of two major contemporary poets.
Keywords: John Burnside, Edwin Morgan, intellectualism, voluntarism.

The unknowable is difficult territory for poets, but they return to its borderlands time and time over. Religious faith is perhaps an even more challenging terrain. In this chapter I want to explore contemporary religious poetry in Scotland, and attempt somehow to capture its engagement with agnosticism and unbelief, its residual Calvinism and anti-Catholicism, and also the quieter insistence of a "Celtic" spirituality, filling spaces where a more confidently reformed Scottish Christian discourse used to be, and yet not without its own pagan echoes in this twenty-first century of the Christian era.

Ethics and religion exist in complex relationship, changing in response to each other as well as to their social and political contexts. Religious insight and practices of a particular protestant kind have had a significant effect on the ethical beliefs of Scottish people, of course, but people's moral insights over time have also brought change to the forms and function of religion, and this is reflected in Scottish poetry, past and present. In this chapter, I will address some ethical concerns of two poets through an exploration of the "voluntarist" and "intellectualist" casts of mind that have persisted in Scottish thought, also in complex relationship, across centuries. Such religious and theological concerns as persist in their poetry are examined through a type of negative theology that may be particularly suited to our relativistic or agnostic age.

The word "religious" presents some problems when applied to poetry, and various anthologists of religious verse (for example, Davie 1981, Levi 1984) have defined it differently, led by the Christian and indeed English emphasis of their collections. In this chapter, my definition is closer to that of the Welsh poet and priest, R.S. Thomas, who attempts to broaden the meaning of the term religious "by sitting somewhat loosely to orthodoxy", and by recalling Keats's advice on "negative capability": poetry being born from the poet's ability to be "in uncertainties, mysteries, doubts, without any irritable reaching after fact or reason" (Thomas 1963: 11). While it is difficult to ignore the shaping impact of a reformed Christianity on Scottish culture, my focus will be on the middle term of Keats's trinity, "mysteries", and the often troubling presence of the numinous, the spiritual or awe-inspiring within the contemporary world. I will try to anchor this wide exploration by a focus on two poets from different generations, Edwin Morgan (b. 1920) and John Burnside (b. 1955). In the Scottish context of historical and residual sectarianism, it also seems appropriate to have one poet raised in the Protestant tradition and one in the Catholic.

Not that childhood religion is a sure guide to poetic readings. Bringing his 1983 series of Gifford lectures to a close, the critic David Daiches looked back to his Orthodox Jewish boyhood in Edinburgh, and reflected that he came to appreciate the poetry of Psalm 126 only once he had ceased to sing it as part of family religious observance. He went on to suggest that religious poetry "gets behind belief to the human dilemmas that belief arose to cope with" and that it is perhaps best for us as readers "to stand outside all closed systems of belief if we wish to be able to respond to the way the poet builds up meanings out of the system he believes in" (Daiches 1984: 211).

Or disbelieves or half- or misbelieves in, it might be truer to add now. Revisiting Daiches' themes some twenty years on, in a new century and a renewed nation (in a political sense) we are more conscious of what Callum Brown (1997) terms Scotland's "haemorrhage of faith". Between 1939 and 1997 religion seemed to lose its place in Scottish society, despite its fairly successful earlier adaptation in the late nineteenth and early twentieth century to an urbanised and industrialised capitalist Scotland:

[...] new research in the late 1990s is suggesting that an ultimate stage of secularisation may now be in progress in which the people – having shunned churchgoing, church membership and the religious rites of passage – are now losing their Christian faith; only just over 70 per cent of Scots in a 1997 opinion poll expressed a belief in God, a figure lower than those of ten and twenty years ago. (Brown 1997: 174)

That this opinion poll was first published in the national newspaper *Scotland on Sunday*, however, reminds us that religion can still make news in Scotland. This is particularly so in its connection with sectarianism. Drawing his three hundred year survey to a close, Brown judges that:

Scottish national identity has never fully integrated Catholic and Protestant. In the late twentieth century, there is still evidence of religious-based ethnic division which confounds a common identity. [...] For Protestants the Church of Scotland in the late twentieth century has failed to arouse enough interest or passion to "defend" it against perceived threats. Yet, if secularisation has undermined popular presbyterianism, it has thus far not destroyed sectarian identities in Scotland. (Brown 1997: 195–96)

Can writers and critics help their country to move forward in this regard? It is possible to evade a tendency to dichotomise religion along sectarian lines (McGonigal 2000: 55–76) by adopting the overview of Alexander Broadie in his *The Tradition of Scottish Philosophy: A New Perspective on the Enlightenment* (1990) and *The Shadow of Scotus: Philosophy and Faith in pre-Reformation Scotland* (1995) where he explores the ongoing tensions in Scottish thought between broadly intellectualist and voluntarist approaches to moral and theological issues. Briefly, he argues that, opposing the traditional medieval intellectualist vision based on a confidence in the mind's ability to know the good, there seems to be a traceable contradictory Scottish tendency from Duns Scotus onwards through the Scottish Calvinist theologians of the Reformation and on to David Hume in the Enlightenment, to take a much more instrumental view of practical reason, where reason's proper function is to identify the best means to achieve a goal fixed by our own desires and preferences (rather than, in the intellectualist view, serving to identify or determine which are the proper ends of human action). In Hume's phrase, reason is "the slave of the passions", and we are driven by our inclinations and desires, for good or ill.

What is positive in Broadie's analysis is its recognition of the gradations and interconnections in these seemingly dichotomous views of the nature of the mind. Both were in operation in Scotland as tendencies of mind in exploring complex religious and ethical questions. They overarch the pre- and post-Reformation divide that still echoes in sectarian tensions of the present day, suggesting that here may be a creative way of considering the role of poetry and poets in a secularised society that still seems caught in the half-life of largely abandoned theologies.

To circumvent such factional sensitivities, I also want to use the ideas of negative theology here to consider how religious poetry may be written in contemporary Scotland. Medieval thinkers could deploy intellectualist or voluntarist perspectives to deal with both ethical and theological issues. By the end of the twentieth century, however, it might seem for many Scots that God is barely conspicuous by his absence. Ethical issues may continue to be answered by one or other tendency of mind, but theological issues are now better explored through a different approach. Negative theology has been deployed by contemporary theologians as an answer to the problem of a discourse about God that need not be bound by metaphysical assumptions considered untenable in a postmodern age. The negative theology of Pseudo-Dionysius or Meister Eckhart, for example, is able to combine "a vigorous denial of absolute knowledge with a theological import that goes beyond the critical negations of postmodern philosophy" (Westphal 2000: 699). It offers an approach that may also be appropriate for discussing religious poetry in the context of a modern multicultural Scotland, developing as it did within Muslim, Jewish and Christian theism.

Broadly, negative theology can be seen as an attempt to avoid misrepresenting God, by emphasising his unknowability. To talk meaningfully about God, we can only say what he is not. The enormous difference between God and creatures means that a phrase such as "God is wise" cannot be used in the same sense of God as of a wise woman or man. Again, "if his presence is always of his whole being and life all at once, in each place in space and time, he must be non-spatial and non-temporal in being and nature and clearly he must be unimaginable" (Braine 2000: 621). John Burnside's apparent dismissal of the presbyterian God of his neighbours in *The Asylum Dance* (Burnside 2000a: 41) becomes rather more nuanced when read in this light of negative theology:

My neighbours passed me on the road to kirk
and thought me odd, no doubt, though I could see
their omnipresent God was neither
here nor there.

Staying close to the transcendent vision of an unknowable God that is part of protestant faith, negative theology does not veer towards the all-powerful determinism of Calvin's theology but rather leaves a space of poetic freedom where the human voice and imagination can begin again to explore the divine.

Edwin Morgan's Voluntarist Vision

Engines unheard of yet will walk the Clyde.
I do not even need to raise my arms,
My blessing breathes with the earth.
It is for the unborn, to accomplish their will
with amazing, but only human, grace. (Morgan 2002: 11)

Edwin Morgan's reputation is so identified with his poems of the technological city that it is easy to forget the apocalyptic tone of his earliest work: "the blaze and maelstrom of God's wrath" in "Dies Irae" (Morgan 1990: 21, hereafter CP), or the agonised movement "beyond despair and redemption./When matter has uttered its last sound" in "Stanzas of the Jeopardy" (CP: 25).

The sources of this tone were partly the presbyterian churchgoing and Sunday school classes of childhood: "Bible imagery stays in your mind whatever your beliefs eventually become" (Nicholson 2002: 32). But there may also in this early work be echoes of the Anglo-Saxon poetry that Morgan was translating in the post-war period. Demobbed from the army in 1946, he had completed his degree in English Language and Literature at Glasgow University, and then accepted the offer of a lectureship there. His translations of "The Ruin", "The Seafarer", "The Wanderer" and several Anglo-Saxon riddles appeared in *Dies Irae* (1952), in the same year as his verse translation of *Beowulf* from the Hand and Flower Press.

These first translations reveal Morgan's characteristic tendency to use a negative trope in poetry and speech, and to link this to the inscrutability of fate. W.J. Sedgefield points in his early annotated *Beowulf* to its author's "preference of allusion to direct statement, for the negative rather than the positive. The favorite figure of speech is consequently *litotes* or understatement, which may be seen in such phrases as [...] *duguth unlytel* [...]" (Sedgefield 1935: xvi). This edition of the poem was on Morgan's bookshelves, and he himself cites examples of the figure in the Introduction to his own translation (Morgan 1952: xxx ff.).

Negatives can be a positive aesthetic factor, then. But Kevin McCara has also pointed out the contrasting, and unheroic, "measures of guilt, despair and self-loathing" in the poems of those early years, which "conceal more than they communicate" (Crawford and Whyte 1990: 5). The double life that Morgan led at this time, as a homosexual man in an era and in a country where traditional moral, professional and legal sanctions bred caution and a sense of duplicity or "otherness" may well have created the revealingly negative patterning in lines such as these:

I keep thinking of your eyes, your hands.
There is no reason for it, none at all.
You would say I can't be what I'm not,
Yet I can't not be what I am. (CP: 369)

Litotes (from the Greek *litós*, single, simple, meagre) is capable of a wider range of effects in Morgan's work than its understated origins suggest:

When you left, it was my studious
avoidance of you that said goodbye.
It was the body, not the heart. (CP: 329)

Can this negative potential in grammar reach beyond physical or emotional need? I am thinking here of the function of ambiguous negativity as a literary way of handling conflicting religious interpretations. Brian Cumming in *The Literary Culture of the Reformation: Grammar and Grace* (2003) points out the characteristic use of the double negative in Thomas Wyatt's translations of the *Penitientiall Psalms*, composed in the 1530s, as a way of evading the dangers of heresy. In his line "Nor in his spirite is ought undiscovered" for example, Wyatt "sets the tone for subsequent writers, working between 'revelation and concealment, between freedom and bondage, between epiphany and damnation'" (Hadfield 2003: 31).

We find Morgan using a similarly elusive technique in *The New Divan* (1977) just after he has introduced a mystical eastern perspective into the turmoil and aftermath of warfare – a celestial vision that is immediately reversed in the riddling apocalyptic negatives of the following poem where the soldiers' perspective on death and judgment floods back:

We never thought we'd never die
but there it was at the moment of death,
the greatest fear we'd ever known [...]
We never thought we wouldn't burn
if that was all our lives had done
but oh it was sharp all the same. [...]
We never knew we'd have no more
to feel expect one pain, one glow
memory blows us to, like coal. (CP: 323)

Such spinning of the coin of affirmation and denial reaches elusive speed in "The World", in the same collection:

I don't see the nothing that some say anything
that's not in order comes to be found.
It may be nothing to be armour plated.
I don't believe that what's been made
clutters the spirit. Let it be patented
and roll. [...] (CP: 346)

This affirmation of human design characteristically modulates for Morgan into the work of the future, with its defiant seizing of the positive from the negative:

We're here. The past is not our home.

I don't think it's not being perfect
that brings the sorrows in, but being soon
beyond the force not to be powerless. (CP: 346)

There is a deal of difference, I suppose, between the will to power and the will to avoid powerlessness, and yet the latter is a "force" all the same, and one that takes Morgan in a trajectory beyond the world as he knows it. The hundred verses of "The New Divan", based on his war experience in the Middle East, are immediately followed by "Memories of Earth", an imagined taped report of extra-terrestrial voyagers to Earth, another group using new technologies to explore the boundaries of the universe. There is a continuum in Morgan's double negative's trajectory, then, from Anglo-Saxon marauding war-bands to intergalactic astronauts and even to the defiant warrior angels and demons of his own (and Milton's) hellish visions. The lunar landscape of Io in "The Moons of Jupiter", for example

Burned,
not that it never burned before, but this
was roaring, sheeted, cruel. [...]
Sulphur blew to choke the very soul. (CP: 391–2)

To borrow Morgan's characteristic phrasing, we cannot say that this past and future quest is wholly irreligious in its transcendent reach.

However, the description in "Memories of Earth" (CP: 333) of Pacific islanders who voyage "forward in ordinary fortitude" also recalls the "amazing, but only human, grace" of the epigraph to this section, from *Cathures* (2002), and the conjunction there of grace with the human will of future generations. The speaker in this poem is the heretic Pelegius, Morgan's namesake ("I Morgan, whom the Romans call Pelegius" runs the defiant opening line) and, significantly, he was a layman not a priest. The thesis mainly associated with his name is that "human beings have it in their own power to avoid sin and achieve righteousness" (Kirwan 2000: 664). This tendency to magnify human powers is a challenge both to human beings and to God. Morgan/Pelegius does not shrink from that, as we will see in some of his final work.

Technology also magnifies human powers, of course, and machines can be seen to merge with our physicality and will: "Engines unheard of yet will walk the Clyde". I am reminded here of the marine engines cared for by the Scottish engineer in Rudyard Kipling's "McAndrew's Hymn", anthologised by Morgan (1963: 646–52), that seem to catch the very rhythm and remorseless power of his Calvinist ethic:

From coupler-flange to spindle-guide I see Thy hand, O God –
Predestination in the stride o' yon connectin'-rod.
John Calvin might ha' forged the same, – enorrmous, certain, slow –
Ay, wrought it in the furnace-flame – my "Institutio".

These engines are very possibly Clyde-built: the poem refers specifically to districts of Glasgow (ll. 20, 65). Interestingly, McAndrew appears somewhat tempted towards Pelagianism (l. 185), which Morgan as editor glosses as disbelieving in original sin, while also making the link to *pelagic*, "an inhabitant of the open sea". The late poem about Clyde engines in *Cathures*, then, may be a last commentary on Kipling's voyager and Morgan's partial identification with him. Childhood experiences of Clyde marine engineering clearly had an emotional impact on him, as Kevin McCara records (Crawford and Whyte eds 1990: 1–2).

Moving from nineteenth into twentieth century technology, we find Morgan poetically at home with the new powers of electronic machine life and of particle theory in *Star Gate: Science Fiction Poems*, even although it leads him deep into dark apocalyptic worlds beyond this world, as in "The Mouth":

heavens and paradises popped like sea weed eternal laws were never
  seen again
angels' teeth were cosmic dust and cosmic dust was angels' teeth
  all's grist
to that dark mill where christs and godbearers were pulped
  with their domes ikons vanes
their scrolls aeons and reigns (CP: 389)

Considering the religious dimensions of his poetry, we might read its quasi-positive double negativity and its archetypes of technological quest as his attempt at building a Scottish sublime for modern times. Not this world, merely, but its potential other far beyond our bounds. W.N. Herbert refers to Morgan's hypothesizing of a Scottish tradition of other-worldly grandeur in his 1979 Warton lecture "Provenance and Problematics of 'Sublime and Alarming Images' in Poetry", where he suggests that Macpherson's *Ossian* might usefully be considered "in terms of a Tolkien-like creation of an imaginary but self-consistent world", and further perhaps that "the sublime is being reborn in science fiction, and the last refuge of the sublime is the stars" (Crawford and Whyte 1990: 66).

Morgan is uneasy with orthodoxy ("the christs and godbearers" and their sacred architecture that are "pulped" above), although it could be said that heterodoxy follows naturally from the voluntarist protestant tradition in which he was raised. The radicalism that appears in Calvinist political theories of the people's right to resist a monarchy, is also evident in Morgan's radical and riddling Christ of "The Fifth Gospel":

It is not those that are sick who need a doctor, but those that are
  healthy. I have not come to call sinners, but the virtuous and law-
  abiding, to repentance. [...]
    In my kingdom there are no temples. Work,
  and pray.) [...]
Give nothing to Caesar, for nothing is Caesar's. (CP: 259)

Such resistance draws Morgan equally to the Devil's party. The connection between his astronauts and Milton's fallen angels in their cosmic journeying has already been hinted at. His argument in lectures at Glasgow University for Satan as the hero of *Paradise Lost* was said to have aggrieved more traditional colleagues. *Demon* is a powerful late collection of twenty poems defiantly written when facing death from cancer, and outfacing it imaginatively in the demon's guise and voice, that is by turns seductive, mocking, knowing, witty and cruel. In the final poem, "The Demon at the Walls of Time", the demon climbs a final barrier by fingertip holds on lines of a mysterious text cut in the wall:

Feeling and following
The life-lines of unreadable inscriptions
Cut by who by how I don't know, go
Is all I know. (Morgan 1999: 115)

A similarly remorseless drive towards survival had been earlier celebrated by Morgan "when two swans flew like spirits past my window": but what remains of their powerful passing in "A Flypast" is merely a

wonder that we ever thought them spirits,
those muscles working, those webs, that eye, that purpose. (Morgan 1994: 74)

This sense of purposeful shaping motion is what I have identified with the voluntarist tendency, present in Scottish thought long before predestination claimed to apportion either doom or salvation. In these late Demon poems, Morgan remains determined to wrest knowledge from what is negative, alienated and irredeemably obscure:

I don't come unstuck. I don't give up.
I'll read the writing in the wall. You'll see. (Morgan 1999: 31)

On occasion, it is true, he does seem to remain open to at least a suspicion that we are not quite alone. The final poem of "The New Divan" opens: "The dead climb with us like the living to the edge" (CP: 330). This edgy liminal vision is further detailed in "A Vanguard", when a group of tired soldiers who "came to the end of the world at midnight" find an "edge, rim, sick slope to vacancy" that might be hell or simply a ravine, with its "windy caves and flues like voices", although it sounds like a "yelling abyss [...] the terrible groaning / from throats unseen below our feet". The men return, and the poem ends in a characteristic negative: "No end in time was near, or in space possible" (Morgan 1991: 32).

What is possible, however, is to praise the quest. The same collection ends with "Lamps", a science fiction poem that harks back in its vocabulary ("duguth") to the *Beowulf* band of warriors, and perhaps also to that poem's fatalism. Morgan stresses the need to live with uncertainty, prospecting deep below the dogmas:

No, we have seen what we have seen, but often
there is a blank you must not fill with monsters.
It is all for what is to come after.
It is for the duguth of firm intent, the voyage [...] (Morgan 1991: 81)

In Morgan's view, as we have seen, a blank is not nothing. Yet the question remains: if it is "all for what is to come after", what *is* to come after? Often the years bring round a kind of answer. In *The Second Life* (1968) "The Domes of Saint Sophia" was written in response or rebuttal to a postcard of this "church, mosque, and now museum", sent by a nun (a former student) visiting Istanbul. "Its perfection of form" she had written "would delight the eye eternally". Morgan firstly denies that eternal possibility, and then counters her perfection with great ruins, "dark, stoic, defaced / that cry out to be contemplated" (CP: 149) and that might even speak, in contrast to the silent dome.

Almost thirty five years later, in "Pieces of Me", a revealing sequence of memories that closes Colin Nicholson's critical volume *Edwin Morgan: Inventions of Modernity* (2002: 201), we find in "Istanbul" that the poet has slowed his step "as if the ground was sacred / and perhaps it was". Then minarets, domes, waterways and bridges suddenly "crowded the very / emptiest spaces / of the heart" and the poet "could not, / could not stop tears". Tears are useless, of course, and involuntary, and yet they are not nothing either. Perhaps the ground was sacred, as he says, or perhaps he had suddenly glimpsed the depths of the gulf between the voluntarist codes he had determinedly worked within all his life and this earthly though ideal and intellectualist sense of the numinous, caught in the sacred architecture of a faith.

John Burnside's Guarded Intellectualism

Give me a little less
with every dawn:
colour, a breath of wind,
the perfection of shadows,
till what I find, I find
because it's there,
gold in the seams of my hands
and the desk lamp burning. (Burnside "Prayer" 2005)

The idea of sacred ground, or at any rate of a mysterious re-
sanctification of the ordinary suburban British scene may account for
the early impact of John Burnside's poetry. It began to appear in book
form from the late 1980s onwards and seemed almost immediately
attuned to a radical hunger for alternatives to the politicised
transnational capitalism of those years, and the reticence or caution of
traditional religious structures in response to it. Burnside's prophetic
voice was not that of a Ted Hughes-like heath-dweller calling from
the wild margins. Rather, he finds the elemental already at work
within our familiar domestic defences of hedge and lawn, window-
ledge and stairwell. And his work is all the more resonant for that,
mixing the civilised with the savage, the spiritual with the material,
and Christian with gnostic or pagan imagery in unsettling ways.

His early reception was as a religious poet with Green credentials
(these were decades of growth for political ecology, Celtic spirituality
and New Age publishing) but he now finds himself irked by such a
designation:

I've never been interested in religious poetry. I was classified as a religious poet but I
find religion appalling, and I find it deeply saddening. [...] I used Catholic
iconography in my early poems trying to re-make it. [...] This description that I'm
interested in religious things and not in politics – I think it's the other way round.
(Dósa 2003: 15)

In the same interview, he emphasises the philosophical and in
particular the gnostic influences on his thinking and his poetry. His
early employment was as a "knowledge engineer" with an ecological
project. It is difficult, all the same, to ignore the label "religious" for

ideas which he continues to explore: "soul" and "spirit" are returned to early and late, albeit defined increasingly in ecological terms. Taking an intellectualist perspective on his work may help clarify some of these contradictions of poetic intentions and reception, by leading us to consider the extent to which he commits himself to practical reasoning as having a primary place in determining how we might act in the world and the kinds of worthwhile and ethically important aims that we might pursue.

Nor does Burnside much like the adjectives "nature" or "Scottish" that are also often applied to his work: "These are not useful labels for me" (Dósa 2003: 18). Although Scottish by birth, Burnside first wrote out of the landscapes of Surrey, Cambridge, Gloucestershire and Northamptonshire, to which county he had been displaced at the age of ten when his father moved the family from semi-rural Fife to the steel-working town of Corby. It was these southern landscapes and townscapes that created the recognisable elements in his early poetry of estrangement. Burnside has spoken with passion about this early sense of fracture and his "very strong nostalgia for that time" (Herbert 1992: 75). Alienated, he became disengaged and uncommunicative.

In this he may remind us somewhat of Edwin Muir, uprooted from his Orkney island to a brutally industrialised Glasgow, driven inward by this encounter with an alien culture, and finding only in the personalised landscape of dream and mythological journey a poetic means of combining the lucent visions of childhood with a simultaneous sense of menace or loss. There is a characteristically somnambulistic iambic pulse to the verse of both Burnside and Muir. Burnside talks about poems emerging from a passivity: "mostly, in the twilight times, in the early morning and late at night, when I'm on my own" (Herbert 1992: 81). Such passivity contrasts with the technologically driven and positivist vision of MacDiarmid and Morgan. Burnside's receptivity aligns itself more, perhaps, with one of the effects a Catholic childhood as identified by Seamus Heaney, which was

to give special value and even beauty to the concept of passive suffering. The religious vision [...] was shot through with the idea of sacrifice and self-denial. [...] I was sensitised to the reality of dumb sorrow, helpless endurance. (Brown 2002: 82)

Allowing for differences between Ireland of the 1940s and 1950s and Scotland/England of the 1950s and 1960s, there are resonances here with the tone of Burnside's imagery nevertheless. To that we can now add a more angry sense of "dumb sorrow, helpless endurance" in his recent revelation in an interview for the *Sunday Herald* (19 January 2003) of the abusive beating of his sister and himself by his father, himself a victim of childhood abuse.

This hinterland of violence clearly marks the poetry and, more obviously, Burnside's novels and short stories. In terms of his treatment of religious imagery from his childhood, or such Christian doctrines as sacrifice or forgiveness, there may also be an aggressive edge to his later testing of them almost to destruction. This could be a modern intellectualist revisiting the troubling question of whether moral or spiritual attitudes really exist out in the world: perhaps all those half-glimpsed, half-intuited presences or visions of children and animals in his early poetry are manifestations of that philosophical uncertainty.

Time and again the dead and damaged become familiar: "moleskin/figures amongst the lupins/nodding and waving" (Burnside 1988: 15) who combine love and menace in intimate fashion "with their blue smiles and mottled bodies/shuffling, pressing closer, making room." Part of the power of Burnside's early poetry might derive, in such in a speculative biographical reading, from the hiddenness of child abuse; the need to signal distress yet not to make domestic matters public; the guilt of the boy who could not do more to protect his sister; and the disassociation, perhaps, of mind and spirit from the bruised body.

Moving beyond the personal, however, we can also see ways in which disturbing elements in Burnside's early work resonate with a supernatural and fantasy tradition that is, as Colin Manlove has argued, central to the Scottish literary canon, and which indeed "represents a whole ignored area of the Scottish creative mind" (Manlove 1996: 7). Manlove's reference to dream analysis, other worlds, Christian mysteries and postmodernist visions, angels, demons, mirrors, doppelgängers and islands of holiness does begin to read like a cataloguing of Burnside's characteristic imagery and themes.

This is linked in turn to Scottish fascination with the supernatural, the fairy and folk tale tradition, and "a continuously mystic strain in the Scots' psyche, the sense of a deeper living world beyond or within this one" that is often combined with "a revelling in the grotesque and in the unreasonable that casts aside all restrictions, which is not merely to be seen as a reaction against repression, whether English, bourgeois or religious" (Manlove 1996: 10). Manlove sees the Scottish use of doubles and dream visions as being only to a certain extent explicable as a reaction to Calvinist repression and divisions between Scottish and Gaelic cultures, since it predates the Reformation and continues into the present day in its characteristic shape of the supernatural converging upon or bursting into the house of the lone dreamer or visionary outsider.

Examples of such convergence or dislocation of reality are everywhere apparent in Burnside's early work:

> Here is the wolf. The wind, the sound of rain,
> the kitchen light that falls across the lawn –
> these things are his. This house is his domain. (Burnside 1988: 29)

There appears to be in Burnside's poetry, however, a blending of the Scottish/continental tendency towards analysis of arcane experience or supernatural glimpses with the more English tendency (in Manlove's terms) towards pastoral escape and contemplation of detail. We see this blending in the opening poem of his second collection *Common Knowledge*:

> Something is in the wood but nothing
> visible. Continuance; a filmy, brackish
> misting of oak and moss [...]
>   And morning changes –
> sometimes to the angel we expect
> watching the tomb in a garden of blood and lilies,
> sometimes to the notion of a Christ
> we half-invent: the vinegar and thorns, the vacant shroud [...] (Burnside 1991: 3)

The analysis continues in the alternating prose and verse sections of this collection. The multiplicities of knowledge in a postmodern world are indicated through his radio's "delicate golden psalter filtered through immaculate receivers" (4), and souls appear to travel on suburban timetables through "stations emptied in the fog / where souls we almost are almost emerge / glittering from a wave of ice and stars" (Burnside 1991: 13).

The sequence "Annunciations" brings an intensity of inspection to religious paintings of this iconic Christian moment of incarnation, with the intellectualist quest for the existence of the spiritual in the world leading to heterodox contemplation of angelic gender and the possible forms of the soul:

> Or rather
> not the soul, but souls. I am even capable of believing all things
> have souls, not one each, but many, according to the time of
> day, or the light, or the season. (Burnside 1991: 18)

We can catch a glimpse of the origins of this searching in "Aphasia in Childhood", from his third collection, *Feast Days*:

> The questions I asked all the time, but never aloud: where
> is the soul? What does it most resemble? I had an image of
> something transparent, a fine yet indestructible tissue of
> buttermilk or chitin. (Burnside 1992: 3)

This early philosophical cast of mind was perhaps fostered by the overtly theological discourse that continued to inform Catholic schooling long after a phenomenological and "non-denominational" (albeit still largely protestant Christian) approach began to replace religious instruction in other state schools. Characteristically it leads Burnside into a use of negation that is different from Morgan's, one that is frequently channelled within a "religious" framework of imagery or an intellectual aspiration to know the real, as in "The Noli Me Tangere Incident", focused on Easter Morning:

> There was nothing to touch. The smell of daybreak
> tinted with frankincense; the feel of an empty sheet and
> something slipped away [...] a hint perhaps, or only a supposition;
> nothing you could mistake for resurrection. (Burnside 1992: 14)

Like a bright child helplessly schooled in these mysteries, he continues to puzzle over, analyse or quantify whatever might be sensed of spiritual presence and absence.

With *The Myth of the Twin* (1994), Burnside enters a slightly different territory and encounters there a sense of the other, the double, the twin (there are even two title poems) and the faint possibility of dialogue, or even community. The "someone" in the first "The Myth of the Twin" shares his insomnia and his dream; the "it" in the second poem "moved when you moved" and is "meshed with the birdsong and light/the way things are real." Its seemingly negative emptiness, stillness and silence are finally defined as "the common soul".

This communal turn is partly northwards – towards the Scottish traditions of "Halloween" (1), the several poems on his Scottish grandparents, as well as "Learning Gaelic" (9), and "Love Poem" with Gaelic words now heard as "remnants of healing and song":

or simply, when we come in from the dark,
to name things for the beauty of the sounds:
uisge; aran; oidche; gealach; teine. (Burnside 1994: 13)

The journey northwards points us again towards Gothic elements in Burnside's work, and the cultural interlacing in Scottish and English literature of Gothic, Catholic and "the Gaelic Other". Luke Gibbons traces a line from Protestant English identification of the Gaels as wild and cannibalistic to their metamorphosis soon after the failed Jacobite rebellion of 1745 into such Gothic tropes as the continuing insidious threat of Catholic "illuminati", arcane secrecy, and corruption of lineage (Gibbons 2002). It is as if progressive notions of Britishness and the purging of Northern barbarism, in which such Scottish Enlightenment figures as Adam Smith and Lord Kames had played influential roles, were unable quite to erase by force of argument deep fears of a Catholic Pretender's presence. The Gothic novel appears soon after 1745, often dealing with usurpation, illegitimacy and stain upon family honour. The contemporary cult of Ossian also pointed to persistent fascination with the melancholic and violent Gael.

The pity and terror that Luke Gibbon finds in this construction of the Celtic identity as Other is also evident in Burnside's uneasy approach to his own Scottish inheritance in *A Normal Skin* (1997). Returning to the Fife landscape of his childhood, he feels "the dead against my skin,/the standstill of accomplished memory" and sees again his father climbing to free an owl entangled in the netting round a cherry tree, his face "awkward and well-intentioned, self-betrayed" (Burnside 1997: 6). Later we find the poetic persona longing for transformation from his sense of "containing, like a cyst, my father's soul, / his cryptic love, his taste for carrion" (Burnside 1997: 9). Later again, the poem aims at overcoming "the art of erasure, my father's craft: [...] recovering the forms he painted out".

But this involves Burnside in closer encounters with "Gothic" elements of his own flawed masculine inheritance of violence, darkness, guilt and an inchoate internal wildness that finds its authenticity in the giving and receiving of pain, or in unsettling memories of road-kills and carrion, enacted in the verse. Male and females ghosts still haunt the childhood roads, and Scottish role models seem to induct him in the ways of blood:

I've watched him skin a carcass in the yard:
skilful and unrepentant, drenched in blood,
he scattered the wet remains across the earth
and entered them, becoming what he killed. (Burnside 1997: 13)

The William Carlos Williams epigraph to "A Process of Separation" (Burnside 1997: 6) perhaps reveals another dimension of cultural return – the influence of a voluntarist view that may be enmeshed in the Scottish approach to relationships:

The business of love is
        cruelty which,
by our wills,
    we transform
        to live together.

To Burnside's earlier intellectualist categorisation of the lineaments of a spiritual world impinging on our own, and putting its materiality under question, is added the force of the human will in facing out what is shameful or painful in the past, or in the present. In the title poem, "A Normal Skin", a female neighbour who suffers from eczema "lies in the healing darkness, half-awake, / achieving a normal skin by an effort of will" (Burnside 1997: 1–2). Trapped by memories rising in the pathways of self-knowledge, Burnside's intellectual framework begins to reveal a heightened gnostic tension of darkness and light, and a quasi-alchemical quest for transmutation:

and here, in the lane, behind the Catholic church,
a litter of small, gold apples, newly-fallen,
wet with thawglass [...]
We'll spend a lifetime
finding useless gold
and learning how to read it as a sign. (Burnside 1997: 52–3)

That this poem "Alchemy," is one section of an eight-part sequence entitled "Epithalamium" emphasises, however, an attempt to move beyond a gnostic distrust of the body into a deepened sense of human dependence and interdependence. The husband haunted by dreams of violence discovers in the final poem "Penitence" a desire to be forgiven by the animal he has accidentally killed while driving, and hears the echo of his "own flesh in the body of the deer" (Burnside 1997: 61).

The killing seems, from lexical evidence, to have taken place in a North American setting, and this points towards a thematic change in Burnside's post-millennium collections, *The Asylum Dance* (2000) and *The Light Trap* (2002). In both, more open forms and longer sequences reflect a tension between home and foreign landscapes, and the desire to travel between. The first of these volumes opens with "Ports" and ends with "Roads". It is unclear whether such travel is freely chosen or whether the poetic persona is driven by a deeper restlessness to undertake his agnostic pilgrimage into alien territory. The direction is east and north, across the North Sea that rims his new found heartland of Fife and the Firth of Tay. Epigraphs from Luther ("God answers our prayers by refusing them") and Edward Munch ("From my rotting body, flowers shall grow and I am in them and that is eternity") point the uncertain way. Overarching his journey, the homing instinct of geese is celebrated (unlike Edwin Morgan's earlier vision of their voluntarist drive in "Flypast") as "this vast delight / this useless motion":

I couldn't imagine
        the pull and sway of home
unless it was play they intended:
        that no good reason
of purposed joy. (Burnside 2000: 10)

Although "purposed" seems to signal intention here, the poem ends by countering voluntarism in a recognition that the homing instinct's "purer urgency [...] is nothing like the mind's / intended space / but how the flesh belongs" (Burnside 2000: 11).

The intellectual underpinnings of Burnside's journeys across the created world and home again are made evident in the titles and epigraphs of *The Light Trap* (2002): "Taxonomy", "Being and Time", "Animals", "History" (two poems), "Of gravity and light", "A Duck Island Flora", and "A theory of everything". James Clerk Maxwell and Walter Benjamin join Heraclitus and Lucretius in this extended poetic analysis of the nature of habitat – a word that is read richly in the epigraph to the opening poem as "an organised relationship between the environment and the unconscious, the visible space and the conscious, the ideas and the creatures".

In a sense, John Burnside may be bringing his later work into closer alignment with his undergraduate studies in philosophy and his early career as a "knowledge engineer" or systems designer. Yet aesthetic difficulties can attend such abstract ambitions. For one recent reviewer, "The great theme of what can or cannot be redeemed is scouted by this gestural verse, but neither inhabited nor inflectedly addressed" (Robinson 2003: 11). Another critic considers that there is a danger of sermonizing: "a tendency to move towards a dying fall, (a 'resolution' in musical terms) that creates its own equation: poiesis equals wistful equals enervate" (Lucas 2003: 77).

It would be ironic if a return to Fife had unearthed in Burnside a peculiarly Scottish version of preachiness. Such criticisms seem close to those that could be made of any religious framework that has allowed dogma to disguise spirit, and I suppose that the ecological ideology towards which Burnside has moved (as expressed in Dósa

2003) and a gradual coming to terms with his own personal history, and possibly also a transference of the edgy, disturbing, gothic qualities typical of his early verse into the different rhythms of his prose – all may have combined to alter the impact of the poetry over time.

What has not changed is his engagement with the spiritual life. In his prose reflection "Iona: A Quest for the Pagan" he considers his own religious development: "Raised as a Catholic, I lived for years as a composite of all those elements of lingering attachment, revulsion, doubt and compromise which make up the psychology of almost any 'lapsed' person" (Burnside 2000b: 21). The dominant note in his response to Christianity now "is a good-humoured puzzlement", yet he does insist that "what is usually called 'spirituality' [...] is central to my life (and I am mystified by anyone who says that it is marginal to, or non-existent in, theirs)". Edwin Morgan (in conversation, 8 January 2004) admitted to being equally mystified by Burnside's poetry: admiring it, yet unable fully to understand its central concerns.

Burnside is aware of sharing "many concerns with religious people: like them, I believe in a soul; like them, I have a sense of some underlying pattern that informs the universe around me." Yet he finds it misleading to call that pattern "God", and for him "the soul" is "neither personal nor immortal (which, for many Christians, ought to be its essential features)". Rather it is a "fundamental self", discerned at isolated moments of absorption by "those who have transcended the contingent person [of their social conditioning] and experienced this authentic ground of being by some process of self-forgetting" (Burnside 2000b: 22).

He again reveals an intellectualist cast of mind here in that he thinks we can find a route to identify which goals are truer to our "fundamental self", and so are morally better ends. The epistemology of these better goals is discovered through an extinguishing of self, however, an approach that not so much Christian as Gnostic and pre-Christian. It is perhaps some such intuited experience of "underlying order, the fundamental connectedness, the soul energy that runs through everything" (Burnside 2000b: 23) that leads him on Iona to connect not with the abbey or carved Celtic crosses but with "the paganism that dwelt here before the Christians came – with the spirals, as it were, of those knots and crosses on the holy stones" created by a sensibility "which believed that everything – humans, animals, trees, stones – is connected in an almost sensual way to everything else" (Burnside 2000b: 23–24).

Quoting from Seamus Heaney's "A Sandstone Keepsake", Burnside finds himself not isolated on a Scottish island at the edge of the Atlantic, but as someone "woven into the continuum of human history", with an ultimately intellectualist sense of what is not achievable by the human will alone: "and not about to set times wrong or right, / stooping along, one of the venerators".

For Scottish poets of both the traditions proposed at the start of this chapter, then, it is only through such positive uses of negation that the spiritual can be translated for our time and place. Leaving behind the early negativities of rejection of the Calvinism or Catholicism of childhood, both Morgan and Burnside are engaged in a quest that will lead their readers through difficult imagined ways to a mysteriously variegated unknown, whether beyond the next ridge or within the next room. One can find it sometimes by striving, and sometimes by waiting in the dark.

Approaching whatever sublime and mysterious elements touch human lives, both poets choose a way of negation that is far removed from the "Thou Shalt Nots" of an organised religion used to underpin moral precepts or a judgmental society. Their message is hardly moral or orthodox, and advances no cause at all except the basic and poignantly human one of our responsiveness to life's suffering and beauty. Ethics and identity can meet, however, in the uncertainties that words explore and the meanings that they express in measured speech.

As commitment to Christianity declines in Scotland, both in its Protestant and Catholic forms, and as new religions or no religion become more visible, a gap is left in a culture that has for centuries defined itself in large measure through a radical religious outlook and through the moral force of democratic aspirations in education and politics that can accrue from such radicalism (or, some would argue, from its mythologizing). Gaps can, however, too easily become "a blank you must not fill with monsters", as Edwin Morgan warns us. It is here that poets become vital to our changing culture, in their professional attention to fidelity of language and in their honest placing of new writing within the whole complexity of traditions, pagan and Christian, voluntarist or intellectualist, through which that culture has defined itself across the centuries. In a "post-religious" age, or one at least in which religion is being redefined, their efforts of spiritual or moral translation take on a more than personal stamp. And like the negative theologians of medieval and modern times, they find that they can only talk of the divine in terms of what God's not.

Bibliography

Bateman, Meg, Robert Crawford and James McGonigal (eds). 2000. *Scottish Religious Poetry: from the Sixth Century to the Present*. Edinburgh: Saint Andrew Press.

Braine, David. 2000. "Negative Theology" in *Concise Routledge Encyclopedia of Philosophy*. London: Routledge. 621.

Broadie, Alexander. 1990. *The Tradition of Scottish Philosophy: A New Perspective on the Enlightenment*. Edinburgh: Polygon.

—. 1995. *The Shadow of Scotus: Philosophy and Faith in pre-Reformation Scotland*. Edinburgh: T Clark.

Brown, Callum. 1997. *Religion and Society in Scotland since 1707*. Edinburgh: Edinburgh University Press.

Brown, John. 2002. *In the Chair: Interviews with Poets from the North of Ireland*. Cliffs of Moher: Salmon Press.

Burnside, John. 1988. *The Hoop*. Manchester: Carcanet Press.

—. 1991. *Common Knowledge*. London: Martin Secker and Warburg.

—. 1992. *Feast Days*. London: Martin Secker and Warburg.

—. 1994. *The Myth of the Twin*. London: Jonathan Cape.

—. 1997. *A Normal Skin*. London: Jonathan Cape.

—. 2000a. *The Asylum Dance*. London: Jonathan Cape.

—. 2000b. "Iona: a Quest for the Pagan" in *Southfields* 6.2: 21–25.

—. 2002. *The Light Trap*. London: Jonathan Cape.

—. 2005. "Prayer". *The Times Literary Supplement* 27. (15 July 2005).

Craig, Cairns. 1999. *The Modern Scottish Novel: Narrative and the National Imagination*. Edinburgh: Edinburgh University Press.

Crawford, Robert and Hamish Whyte (eds). 1990. *About Edwin Morgan*. Edinburgh: Edinburgh University Press.

Crawford, Robert. 1988. "Edwin Morgan" in *Verse* 5.1: 27–42.

Daiches, David. 1984. *God and the Poets*. Oxford: Clarendon Press.

Davie, Donald. 1981. *The Oxford Book of Christian Verse*. Oxford: Oxford University Press.

Dósa, Attila. 2003. "Poets and Other Animals: An Interview with John Burnside" in *Scottish Studies Review* 4.1: 9–23.

Gibbons, Luke. 2002. "Gothic and the Gaelic Other". Seminar held at the A.H.R.B. Centre for Scottish and Irish Studies, University of Aberdeen, 25 November 2002.

Hadfield, Andrew. 2003. "Erasmus's errata slips" in *The Times Literary Supplement*. (14 March 2003).

Herbert, W.N. 1990. "Morgan's Words" in Crawford, Robert and Hamish Whyte (eds). *About Edwin Morgan*. 65–74.

—. 1992. "John Burnside" in *Verse* 9.2: 74–82.

Kirwan, Christopher. 2000. "Pelagianism" in *Concise Routledge Encyclopedia of Philosophy*. London: Routledge. 664.

Levi, Peter. 1984. *The Penguin Book of English Christian Verse*. Harmondsworth:

Penguin.

Lucas, John. 2003. "A Larger Assembly" in *The Dark Horse* 15: 74–81.

Manlove, Colin. 1996. *An Anthology of Scottish Fantasy Literature*. Edinburgh: Polygon.

McCarra, Kevin. 1990. "Edwin Morgan: Lives and Work" in Crawford, Robert and Whyte, Hamish (eds). *About Edwin Morgan*. 1–9.

McGonigal, James. 2000. "Millennial Days: Religion as Consolation and Desolation in Contemporary Scottish Poetry" in *Revista Canaria de Estudios Ingleses* 41: 55–76.

Nicholson, Colin. 2002. *Edwin Morgan: Inventions of Modernity*. Manchester: Manchester University Press.

Robinson, Peter. 2003. "Painters of the Forth Bridge" in *The Times Literary Supplement* (13 June 2003).

Sedgefield, W.J. (ed.) 1935. *Beowulf*. Third edition. Manchester: University Press.

Thomas, R.S. 1963. *The Penguin Book of Religious Verse*. Harmondsworth: Penguin.

Westphal, Merold. 2000. "Postmodern Theology" in *Concise Routledge Encyclopedia of Philosophy*. London: Routledge. 69.

Index